BAMBO

BAMBO

WHITETAIL DEER HUNTING 101

— A Complete Guide —

GARY LAWTON HARGIS

Wilderness Adventure Books
320 Garden Lane
Box 968
Fowlerville, Michigan 48836

Library of Congress Catalog Card Number: 90−050349

ISBN: 0−923568−10−7

Artwork by the author

Typesetting by
LaserText Typesetting
3886 Sheldrake Avenue ■ Okemos, Michigan 48864

PUBLISHED BY

Wilderness Adventure Books
320 Garden Lane
Box 968
Fowlerville, Michigan 48836

Manufactured in the United States of America

Dedication

To my wife, Marie, who backed my efforts to field research and write, by supporting our family while I sat in the woods.

To my dad, Lawton Hargis, who got me into the woods in the first place.

To my Mother and Sister who helped make it possible.

To everyone who let me hunt or study on their land.

To the Department of Fish and Wildlife.

CONTENTS

CHAPTER 1: *Why* Do You Want To Hunt? 1

CHAPTER 2: *What* Do You Want To Hunt?..7

Does ▪ Determining Sex ▪ Trophy Hunting ▪ Points ▪ Rack Estimation ▪ Tine Shine ▪ Antlers ▪ Estimating Body Size ▪ Mutant Deer

CHAPTER 3: *Where* Do You Want To Hunt?..................................35

Public Areas ▪ Soybeans ▪ Corn ▪ Thickets ▪ Backyard Bucks ▪ Waterholes ▪ Boats ▪ Camps ▪ Vehicles ▪ Guides ▪ Physical Limitations

CHAPTER 4: *When* Do You Want To Hunt? 64

Dawn to Dark ▪ Barometric Pressure ▪ Rut ▪ Rain and Sleet

CHAPTER 5: Accessories & Necessities 78

Plastic Bags ▪ Drop Cloths and Tarps ▪ Lights ▪ Axe, Machete, Saws, Shovels ▪ Watch ▪ Pack ▪ Underwear ▪ Hats ▪ Neck Cover ▪ Gloves ▪ Boots ▪ Keys, Wallets, Glasses and Valuables ▪ First-Aid Kit ▪ Knives ▪ Ropes ▪ Slings

CONTENTS

CHAPTER 6: *How* **To Hunt**...92

Scouting ▪ The String Method ▪ Trails ▪ Patience, Discipline, Endurance ▪ Scrapes ▪ Rubs ▪ Beds ▪ Droppings ▪ Feeding Habits ▪ Observing Cattle Movements ▪ Getting Permission ▪ Cattle, Goats, Horses ▪ Bugs ▪ Dogs in Hunting ▪ Wild Dogs ▪ Where to Aim ▪ Rifles ▪ Practice ▪ Flinching ▪ B.R.A.S.S. ▪ Scopes ▪ Range ▪ Muzzleloading ▪ Bows ▪ Spears ▪ Crossbows ▪ Handguns ▪ Talking, Coughing, Sneezing ▪ Noise Attractions ▪ Deer Bellying, Sneaking ▪ Baiting ▪ Deer Calls ▪ Stomping and Tooth Chattering ▪ Flagging ▪ Rattling ▪ Camo ▪ Comfort ▪ Energy Foods ▪ Water ▪ Peejug ▪ Your Scent ▪ Scents ▪ Meat Abstinence ▪ Smoking ▪ Mock Scrapes ▪ Decoys ▪ Deer Drives ▪ Still Deer ▪ Tracks ▪ Stalking ▪ Still-Hunting ▪ Sounds of Approach ▪ Tree Stands ▪ In-Stand Movement ▪ Predator Vibes ▪ Wind Currents ▪ Birds ▪ Sleeping in the Woods ▪ Wisdom ▪ Greed ▪ Fear ▪ Luck / Skill ▪ Wives / Husbands

CHAPTER 7: *After* **The Shot**...256

Leash Dog Retrieval ▪ Blood Trails ▪ Field Dressing ▪ Toting Deer ▪ Hanging Meat and Skinning ▪ Judging Deer Age ▪ A Guide to the Age of the Whitetail Deer Collected in the Fall

CHAPTER 8: *After* **The Hunt**...286

Trophies ▪ Rituals ▪ Litter ▪ Fence Respect ▪ Tree Respect ▪ Gratitude ▪ Utilizing the Entire Deer ▪ Processing Meat ▪ Drying Meat ▪ Sharing Meat ▪ Salvaging Urine and Musk Glands ▪ Road Kills ▪ Venison Recipes

CONTENTS

CHAPTER 9: Safety And The Law...311

Buck Fever ▪ Poaching ▪ The Law ▪ Alcohol, Pot, Drugs ▪ Dead Limbs ▪ Eye Safety ▪ Hunter Safety Courses ▪ Diseases You Can Get From Deer ▪ Snakebite ▪ Hypothermia ▪ Frostbite ▪ Buddy System ▪ Poison Ivy, Poison Oak, Poison Sumac ▪ Fires ▪ Getting Lost ▪ Hunter Orange ▪ Dangerous Deer ▪ Hunting Accidents ▪ Wounds ▪ Burns ▪ Poisoning ▪ Artificial Respiration ▪ Choking ▪ Broken Bones ▪ Shock ▪ Nosebleeds ▪ Moving Injured Hunters ▪ Other Dangers

A Last Word..359

What to Expect in the 1990s ▪ Happy Trails!

Introduction

HAVING COME TO DEER HUNTING by various paths the prospective hunter sets out to try his or her luck. Some do get lucky. Some have disastrous experiences. Most discover the challenge of the big game animal to be more than they expected.

The purpose of this book is to prepare the beginning deer hunter for a successful and enjoyable experience by providing basic information collected through many years' hunting.

The deer hunter who sets out on his own to collect knowledge from experience can expect to spend a minimum of three seasons learning through trial and error what this book has to teach. The veteran deer hunter may also benefit from these tips derived from experiences in the woods.

For each person, however, experience is undeniably the best hunting teacher, in that it gives each lesson a deep personal reality. Only through the hunting experience can the natural instincts of man the hunter begin to surface and make him a good hunter with inborn skills to employ instinctively as he becomes a natural part of his outdoor environment.

Several million hunting licenses are issued each year in the United States and Canada. Nevertheless, the whitetail deer population has increased more than 25-fold since the turn of the century. In most areas our present deer populations equal or exceed historical numbers. These adaptable deer have taken to the suburban and rural areas of the United States with few natural predators other than man, thus providing a great opportunity for recreation.

Deer hunting has become a national sport of ever-increasing popularity. The economic aspects of the deer hunt bring needed revenues to the city, county, state and federal governments. Each year manufacturers spring up with new gadgetry to make millions. Deer hunting has become big business for many. Game ranches flourish providing luxury accommodations for their guests. Individuals find grand relief from their city lives and a chance to vent their stress in the natural world.

Venison has become a popular food as exposure to it increases the demand. The tough but supple manageability of deer skin is regaining recognition. Mounted deer trophies have become fashionable centerpieces for homes, restaurants and businesses. Utilization of the entire deer can be a creative enterprise which completes the satisfaction of success.

While animal rights activists cry brutality and seek greater restrictions on hunters, motorists and farmers seek legislation to reduce deer numbers. Biologists confirm the need to control the herd through increasing hunter quotas and extending hunting seasons in areas where overpopulation has led to habitat depletion and starvation for the deer as well as a genetic decline in quality. Continual monitoring of state deer herds by competent wildlife experts effectively sets the limits of harvest to keep this renewable resource at an optimum productivity level to provide food, sport and enjoyment to many.

The whitetail deer at maturity is a big game animal. With its acute senses and mental capacities, it is a challenge to outwit. True, with rare exceptions, deer are not vicious to humans; nevertheless the deer hunt is quite challenging and involves more than effortlessly firing a rifle from a Land Rover. The hunt usually requires sharpened skills and stamina. The patience and discipline needed in most hunt situations are valuable fruit from the hunt.

The rewards may include a spiritual discovery or renewal. The time spent hunting may give the hunter rare time for thought and introspection. Contrarily it may take his mind off things, giving a respite from his problems that enables him to return to them refreshed.

Encounters with other wildlife while deer hunting are an open door to adventure. Interaction among hunters provides cultural

Apparently the inventor of the "Velcro" fastening technique made his discovery in the woods. The inventor noticed the stick-tights that clung to his garments so successfully and questioned why. Under a home microscope he observed the equipment nature had installed on the clinging seeds that enabled them to attach to clothing . . . thence Velcro, and wealth and fame. Indeed, more than one deer hunter has discovered gold while following hoofprints. Deer hunters have found the bodies of missing persons in the thickets, thus solving crimes. Many discoveries can be made by the sportsman who ventures into the woods, adding unexpected facets to the pleasure of the hunt itself.

Deer hunting, in short, can be, should be, and usually is a good deal more than the casual observer thinks it is.

Only the individual hunter can truly appreciate the experience he has had. Attempts to adequately relate the exciting reality are often futile.

So, if your husband, friend or neighbor seems obsessed with hunting deer, please understand that there may be more going on than meets the eye. Even the unsuccessful hunts have their rewards. There may be more "meat on the table" than one at first suspects.

IN THE BEGINNING GOD CREATED
THE HEAVENS AND THE EARTH
AND DEER HUNTING

1

Why Do You Want To Hunt?

SO, YOU WANT TO HUNT DEER? Are you sure? This chapter is not devised to talk you out of hunting, but rather to help the would-be hunter to make clear decisions from the outset.

Many people are just not hunters. They are not inclined to hunt, nor do they need to. Perhaps their ancestors were nut-gatherers and not meat-eaters. Vegetarians, who avoid meat primarily for conscience's sake, usually shun hunting altogether; their minds are firm on the matter of taking the life of an animal. Many such people are influenced, sometimes unknowingly, by Eastern philosophy and religions wherein the lives of all animals are revered. Most are just very kind-hearted people.

People who do eat meat processed and purchased through the food markets feel little if any contact with the slaughtered animal. They choose to not think about the animal as having been a live creature. Many of these individuals are revolted at the thought of eating deer, yet do not bat an eye at consuming cattle or other "domestic" animals.

The response the deer hunter receives from the general public is, "I don't see how you could shoot such a beautiful animal, for I could never do it."

Many non-hunters use the term "reverence for life." They do not comprehend, and do not wish to know, how someone would find it "fun" to kill deer. Such individuals seem to indeed have a respect for life but also a misunderstanding about that part of life called "death."

Some non-hunters have no trouble taking the life of a fish or that of a snake, relating their kill to the temperature of the blood, with higher regard for the deer as a warm-blooded animal.

There are those who make take the life of a rat with ease but balk at the taking of a similar animal, the squirrel, thus representing the type who separately categorize "good" and "bad" animals.

I once encountered a mercenary who had little conscience concerning the taking of human life however, as a non-hunter, had near-violent disdain for those who took the life of "innocent" deer.

One of the most wonderful animated films ever made is the favorite *Bambi*. This film, with its emotional plea to the conscience, has left many with what is termed the "Bambi complex." *Bambi* has been reintroduced every few years to the public. Deer hunters should see the movie if they have not. It is, after all, a deer movie, and it will increase overall hunter understanding as well as provide adult enjoyment.

Some anti-hunters have joined the bandwagon with the "animal lib" movie stars to develop groups which have money as well as prestige.

Many non-hunters are wildlife enthusiasts from way back who hunt and study deer and other creatures non-consumptively, such as through photography.

Some hunters convert to non-hunters after having a bad experience with wounded or suffering deer. To witness the victim of a misplaced shot, paunch shot animal fleeing from capture is a disheartening experience indeed. The screams of the animal are haunting and not easily forgotten. A fleeing deer stumbling over its own entrails is a very sad situation. Enduring the cries of pain is a torture which the faint-hearted cannot endure. Finding a fawn licking its lifeless mother is heartbreak.

Some anti-hunters are gun control advocates who do not believe in the possession or use of firearms by the general public. This controversy over our constitutional rights and their regulation became a heated subject with the slayings of John F. Kennedy and Martin Luther King with "deer rifles."

Another type of non-hunter enjoys having deer about but only for the enjoyment of seeing. The family who watch deer through their picture window at breakfast falls in this group. Likewise, resort owners, dude ranchers and park owners want a good many deer around for the sake of tourists.

The hunter should examine himself thoroughly prior to the hunt to determine his mental and emotional status with respect to these volatile, emotional matters. Some people make good hunters, hunters who can do it right.

In modern times we have a balance of nature in our civilization harmonious with the balance of nature in the wild. If hunting were for everyone, there would be no wild game. If it were not for the fear or distaste for spiders, snakes, poisonous plants, and so on, there would probably be no untrampled woodlands remaining as wildlife habitat.

Seasoned hunters appreciate non-hunters from this standpoint. When the proud hunter displaying his kill is greeted with scorn and ridicule by an anti-hunter, he should remember that each of them has a place in the world today.

The hunter who decides he will attempt to take a deer should realize he is in a position to be judged and that his actions and reactions will influence the overall opinion of society towards the sport of deer hunting. The age-old saying "It only takes one rotten apple to spoil the whole barrel" is true.

Having settled the issue of whether or not to kill a deer and made the decision to hunt, one should conduct his life in a fashion that will bring no reproach to himself or the general hunting population.

The majority of deer hunters cannot respond clearly and appropriately when asked why they hunt. This is because their desire to hunt is rooted too deeply within to be dug up and examined. The standard hunter cites the need to get outdoors, the challenge and excitement, meat for the freezer, and the companionship of friends as his reason—but all these are possible without hunting and killing deer. An exciting excursion into nature can be made without the burden of weaponry, and the road-kill deer is an underutilized meat source which is a great loss if left to waste.

Since all animals die either from disease, starvation, thirst, predation, accidental injury, or old age, the issue is not really whether the animal dies, but *when* it dies. How it does is not a good argument against hunting since in reality all the ways the animal might die naturally can be more cruel than the proper gunshot or bowkill.

Commonly, deer herds suffer malnutrition and eventual starvation before the public shifts its awareness to the need for number reduction. People who stroll through the woods and fields see lots of greenery apparently available for the deer and find it hard to imagine deer lacking food.

Anyone who does not think that deer can overbrowse should witness the experiment used to illustrate browse depletion. Here a portion of consistent habitat is enclosed for a few years with a deer-proof fence to demonstrate the striking contrast. Malnutrition leads to disease.

Automobiles and trains cause the greatest number of deer fatalities. Next to hunting, winter losses, loss due to crippling, poaching, being caught in forest fires, getting trapped in tree crotches and vines, running headlong into fence, falling through ice and drowning, disease, and predation all take their toll on deer.

Only 10% of the deer herd is killed by hunters in the fall, while a harvest of 20% is what it takes to maintain a proper herd balance in terms of available browse, agriculture, and forestry.

Everyone loves a provider. Deer meat has no preservatives. There are no growth stimulants, hormones, antibiotics, or other artificial additives to the meat. As our society becomes more scientifically oriented in its productive farming methods, research on the effects of such farming and marketing practices stays a step behind the production of the animals. In many cases the products hit the market and are consumed before the consequences are thoroughly examined. There are farmers who, for their own table use, raise cattle which have not been subjected to additives and are relatively organic, just as there are grape growers who don't spray a few vines intended for their own use. Thus, many people prefer the meat of wild game to that of domestic animals because they know what is in it.

The hunter should:

a. work toward making clean kills that limit animal suffering
    through sufficient practice with his bow or firearm,
b. at all times abide by every applicable law,
c. be respectful to Mother Nature and leave her the way she was
    before he became her guest,
d. be safe, and
e. search for and find any animal he shoots and utilize the entire
    creature.

In short, the deer hunter should be a model conservationist.
"Conservation" is defined as "the wise use of natural resources."

The deer hunter should be settled in his understandings and
courteous to those whose thoughts differ.

Let us not add to the "too many fools in the woods."

Mother Nature is a lady. She entertains many gentlemen
guests and she sends intruders away.

Chapter

2

What Do You Want To Hunt?

HAVING DECIDED TO HUNT, you must determine what it is that you wish to accomplish.

Some initiates begin their hunt with chief emphasis on the deer's food value. Indeed the majority of new hunters just go after a deer, period. The primary motivation may be recreation, fellowship, a soul search, or a trophy. Reasons for the hunt may overlap one another and are vastly susceptible to spontaneous change. For example, a hunter simply intent upon bringing a deer home by shooting the first one seen may catch a glimpse of a monster trophy buck and subsequently spend the rest of the season pursuing that animal and desiring to accept nothing else.

Although just about anything can happen, the hunter should begin with a clear goal to pursue. In this fashion confusion can be minimized, as careful planning and detailed organization pay off.

What are you seeking in the deer hunt? Providing yourself with this answer will surely help you to reach your goals.

Often "What you see is what you get." Use your wonderful, inborn creative imagination to envision your quarry from the beginning. There is something magically positive about this thought process in the hunt. Not only will this skill assist the hunter in developing hunter strategy by eliminating unnecessary steps, it may be the key to success. Knowing exactly what you are after may help you to more readily identify it when it actually appears before you.

What happens inside the head is something difficult to talk about, but any hunter who has been at it a while will tell you that there is something going on there. The continually successful hunters just have it together to be winners, and this is a total mind set and not just blind luck or the ingenious employment of techniques.

Are you after meat? If so, minimization of time and cost may be in order. A legal doe or smaller buck may be your tender quarry. You may choose an area to hunt where doe populations are relatively high and fill your freezer with comparative ease. Leave the big antlers to grow larger for the trophy seekers. These genetically superior bucks make the best breeders in the herd. Take a spike antlered deer or a puny racked deer. These are the ones that usually don't achieve big, wide antlers anyway. You don't eat antlers.

The well-balanced deer herd requires some culling by meat-hunting outdoorsmen—the hunters who should be honored, rather than belittled by their peers. Given the choice of shooting two, side-by-side deer, one with puny, bent spikes and the other with well-shaped forks, the conscientious hunter should choose the lesser animal and allow the better formed one to go on to maturity.

In these 1990s we can expect to see a major improvement in wise game management. Hunter awareness and participation will increase.

The hunter who enters the woods with a defeated attitude usually leaves the wilds that way. If the voice of truth inside you tells you you are not going to get a deer that day, you may as well stay home and do some needed chores. Save your deer-hunting energy for another day. This is positive. Separate and heed your intuitions. The positive, confident hunter has a much higher productivity level than the one who really doesn't believe he will score. If you think you are unlucky, then you will be unlucky. Have confidence, have faith, and listen to your inner self.

DOES

When deer were a threatened species due to vast market-hunting and poor laws to govern the hunt, many hunters revered the female deer as the source of fawns and future populations. People who took the lives of does were mocked, jeered, and even persecuted by those who hoped to see the deer herd reach the point that it has in 1990. The superior value of the life of the doe was imprinted in the minds of sportsmen. Fathers passed this idea down, and it is still prevailing attitude. The sanctity of does as management policy contributed to the most successful wildlife restoration in history.

Now there are upwards of 15 million whitetail deer, where there was scarcely a track 30 years ago. An older friend of mine can remember spotting a deer track while squirrel hunting in his youth in my home area of Kentucky. When he told the elders at the country store about it they did not believe him. Now there are tracks in their gardens.

In many areas more does need harvesting and hunters are encouraged, rather than forbidden, to take them. Buck hunter pressure with doe protection in established herds produces eventual buck-doe ratios of poor proportions.

In areas where the deer population needs increasing, doe kills are forbidden by law. Here shooting one reproducing doe is like shooting several deer, since the hunter is eliminating the future offspring of the animal as well as the doe itself. In such an area (one in which biologists forbid doe-shooting), the hunter should be very careful when he shoots that he has indeed seen antlers and that the buck is sufficiently separated from the does to prevent a poor shot or a shot in which the bullet or arrow goes through the buck to the doe. The accidental kill of an illegal doe can be a bad experience. If the hunter happens to accidentally shoot an illegal doe, it is recommended that he leave it in place and go to a telephone to call a local conservation officer. The chance that the officer will allow him to salvage the animal upon honest explanation is worth the call. If the hunter was to load up the animal before the call, the conservation officer would have reason to expect a purposeful game violation. Don't try to pull one on a game warden. They have been around and heard it all. There is nothing they appreciate less than someone trying to put one over on them. Trust the warden to be your friend when you are tempted to hide a doe under the leaves and brush. The wasted animal might be buried, but you can't bury the memory.

Some doe protectionists have a notion akin to "send the men

to fight but leave the women at home." The same attitude is reflected in the idea that it is all right to strike a man but never, ever, to strike a woman. This attitude is giving way to "doe lib." The doe is liberated game in the 1990s.

We no longer fire biologists who recommend doe seasons but have become educated along with them. We have learned the ills of overpopulation. We have to give up the idea of large, unmanaged herds of deer in favor of smaller, well-balanced and healthy herds.

Long, cold winters are the great deer killers in the north, but we realize that it is not the cold itself that kills, but rather the lack of food in the winter months.

People who see does caring graciously for their fawns think they will share food with them when it is scarce. Contrarily, does chase their fawns from food sources when it is sparse, just as dogs do. Larger does eat the low browse first then turn to the higher limb tips which the fawns and younger deer cannot reach.

Even in the south, where food is generally abundant, deer dieoffs occur where they overpopulate. A viral infection called "epizootic hemorrhagic" disease, which kills deer in very high populations, often develops. This disease is carried by flies and gnats, insects which spread rapidly where larger numbers of hosts occupy a home range densely. Internal parasites spread more quickly where larger numbers of deer are concentrated. Cattle stomach and lung worms are parasites found in the south where too many deer are located together. These one-inch worms find their way to the organs of deer and suck blood.

Almost all deer diseases are aggravated by malnutrition, which is brought about by overpopulation. Disease can wipe out 80%—90% of a herd in one year. There is always the possibility that a large scale natural disaster could alter the trend toward deer abundance and health we are now experiencing. It would only take one widespread disease to make the whitetail a rare animal again since the deer have overlapping ranges from coast to coast.

The deer, being elusive and wild, could not be inoculated as a mass. Successful immunization is impossible in 97% of the herd. Unlike cattle, which develop the same diseases from overcrowding, deer cannot be supplementally fed and medicated.

If we do not hunt and kill does, nature will find a way to perform the same function. The wolf and the panther, the deer's natural predators, are all but extinct. Efforts to replace these predators are limited to rather small locations in relation to the extent of the whitetail deer ranges. Coyotes are not efficient enough predators since they kill only fawns or crippled deer. That leaves man alone for efficient herd management.

If we allow nature to control deer populations, we wind up with big numbers of deer one season and a big dieoff the next. Nature's way is not compatible with our desires for good hunting seasons yearly and long-lived bucks producing mature antlers.

After the success of methods to increase deer populations, instituting hunting controls and regulations, refuges, and stocking, what remains for the management of herd quality is to promote doe hunting to prevent devastating overcrowding.

While some areas have much higher or lower deer populations, the carrying capacity of the land on a national average is one deer to 32 acres of habitat. The ratio of does to bucks should not exceed six does to one buck, or 6:1. On game ranches, which are managed for sport buck-hunting, does are maintained at 3:1 or 2:1.

Does which have outlived their own fertility at eight years or so consume forage yet no longer give birth to fawns. In areas where does are not hunted, some of these animals are as old as sixteen. This means that for eight years those does consumed food, produced no offspring, and were never utilized by man. Having a doe season in these locations would actually increase the deer numbers by making way for younger does, more fertile ones, to give birth to more fawns, since most hunters shoot larger does in preference to smaller ones for their freezers. Proponents of the "more is better" philosophy should realize that for this reason doe seasons do not necessarily reduce herd size or their chances of obtaining deer.

The most serious threats to deer herds are:

a. habitat destruction such as bush and bogging, land clearing, grass pasture improvements, rural subdivisions, new lake impoundments, expanding cities, surface mining, and sloppy timbering.
b. poor range or inadequate food supplies due to overpopulation of deer or overgrazing by domestic livestock, resulting in large scale deer dieoffs.
c. disease and parasitism.
d. illegal hunting.

The methods to eliminate these threats are:

a. supplement feeding (preferably with deer pellets).
b. augmenting natural browse with food plots.
c. maintaining the herd within carrying capacity, the least expensive method.

It is best for hunters and best for deer as well to selectively take does from the herd where deer are plentiful. Does provide both good food and attractive trophies. Yes, a doe makes a very nice wall mount next to a buck.

Hunters intent upon the preservation of their sport to assure good hunting for future generations should become a part of the solution. It is a generalization yet a truth that the majority of out-doorsmen would rather hunt and fish than work. Paper work, communications, research, and other such endeavors are what they hunt and fish to escape from. This results in hunters having a reduced voice in legislation. A large number of hunters are un-able to read or write. Even though they may have viable plans for game management, they are unable to share them with those who could turn them into reality. It seems that the animal lib people are by and large well educated, and since they spend most of their time indoors, they have plenty of time to write to their Congressmen. If we want to ensure the future of deer hunting, then we must do our share.

Conscientious outdoorsmen can make a difference by doing the following:

1. Contact your state's Fish and Game Department to offer your assistance in volunteer work during deer surveys and habitat improvement labors.
2. Discourage poachers.
3. Write your Congressmen.
4. Become personally involved in encouraging stripmine owners and timer industry personnel to preserve or restore habitat.
5. Contribute money to conservation organizations.
6. Join hunt clubs and lease land which will be left in thickets and kept forageable.
7. Encourage ranchers and farmers to provide adequate deer habitat and forage.

DETERMINING SEX

Antlered does are a phenomenon most hunters would like to see increase. It would really be great if does sported racks everywhere like bucks. If you do shoot an antlered deer that turns out to be a doe when the genitals are examined, it is a good idea to inform your district biologist so that the expert may examine it for research purposes. A few such animals turn up every year.

Sex determination becomes important especially when bucks are the only legal quarry. When population levels are not up to par, hunters are allowed to take antlered deer only. Quite often the hunter shoots a deer thinking it is a buck and finds it was actually a doe. Many of these animals are purposely left to decay. This is a situation which is usually preventable. The hunter who has made this mistake has usually done so through neglect. In most cases he has simply not paid enough attention, while in others he has gotten impatient and trigger-happy.

On the other hand, sometimes looking for antlers can cost you a trophy because it is only at the last moment that the rack of a deer becomes visible.

The hunter should understand that he is not expected to kill every deer he sees and that missing a chance at a shot because he was cautious is never a failure. The deer will be there next time.

Antlers are not always conspicuous. Deer horns often blend in with the brush so well that they cannot be easily seen. It is sometimes necessary to make a rather swift scan over a group of approaching deer to determine which deer are of which gender. In such scans the shape of the body is the first consideration. Bucks and does are shaped differently. The doe is elegantly shaped as a rule. Normally she is shorter in height and in length than her male counterpart. She is smaller in comparison. Her head is more streamlined and not designed to support heavy antlers. A big physique, swollen neck, squared-off body, and of course, a pair of antlers obviously spells b.u.c.k.

The neck of a buck, especially during the rut, is greatly enlarged. The neck of a buck increases in diameter as much as ten inches immediately before the breeding cycle and stays that way until it ends. Glandular changes in hormones produce the swelling. The swelling is designed to make the buck's neck stronger as he uses his antlers in fighting other bucks for does to breed in the natural selection of the fittest breeding animals to produce future generations.

The difference in the general outline and shape of bucks and does will become more obvious the more experience one has in the field. The comparison is easily made when the two are spotted side-by-side.

Occasionally there are mature antlerless bucks. Bucks without antlers are generally either very young or very old. Castration produces antlerless bucks. Hormonal imbalances produce the antlered does.

A SUREFIRE WAY TO GET A BIG TROPHY ANIMAL THE NEXT YEAR IS TO SPEND ALL YOUR MONEY MOUNTING THE PUNY ONE YOU TOOK THIS YEAR.

TROPHY HUNTING

I once knew a successful hunter who had a garage shelf lined with eight-point antlers from deer he had killed. He took them all in the same place, at nearly the same time of day, year after year. He was admired as a hunter by all his peers as he inevitably returned from his hunt with a nice deer. He had developed a pattern which provided venison and modest trophies which he eventually found hard to break. When he went after a larger trophy deer by switching locations and methods, his first efforts were unfruitful as they most often are. He could not bear his family and friends asking the inevitable question: "Did you get a deer?" Having received so much admiration for his previous successes he could not bear having to tell them "no." It was only after the local limit was switched to two deer per hunter that he renewed his interest in taking a true trophy. He took the first deer (another eight-point) "for success" and kept his remaining tag open for more impressive possibilities.

The true trophy hunter, the hunter seeking an exceptional animal of possible record class, lets a lot of deer go free in his search for the superior animal. The question "Did you get a deer?" is an ongoing challenge for many people simply do not understand the goals of a significant trophy or possibly record deer. Frankly, they don't believe that you are much of a hunter if you return home empty-handed, and they can hardly swallow that you're turning down six and eight-point bucks.

There is nothing that equals the thrill and excitement of bagging the first deer. This and the adventure of the chase are what it is all about. As you progress in your skills and become successful at normal deer hunting, as you have plenty of venison in the deep freeze, chances are that you will not become bored with the sport, but will begin to strive for bigger and more impressive game. "As we grow older the drink must become stronger to produce the same effect."

When you are beginning deer hunting, it hurts not to get a deer. But as the hunter gets older and more seasoned, the mere fact of bringing home a deer becomes less important.

The major breakthrough comes when the hunter turns down his first eight-point deer. Since there are some outstanding eight-pointers out there that might be the trophy of a lifetime, I should perhaps rephrase and say when the hunter turns down his first large-racked animal. I have been trying to outwit a big eight-point with antler bases which appear larger than beer cans for several years.

Trophy bucks are seldom careless. They got to be what they are by playing it smart. Hunting them requires more work. The hunter has to learn to think as they do.

The trophy hunter has conditioned himself to glance at does only briefly. If the hunter looks at them too long them seem to grow horns—the ears begin to look like antlers. The trophy hunter looks for the buck, spending as little time as possible assessing the does. The trophy hunter watches the does for signals as to where to look for the buck. The oldest doe in the group is the one to watch. She is the one chosen by the buck to check out the area. If you have not spotted the buck, then focus your attention on her. If a buck is around she will betray its presence. She will stare in the direction of the buck and work for you like a bird dog.

Smart old bucks often put younger deer out in front of them for safety purposes. If you go ahead and take a quick shot at the beautiful ten-pointer that just walked into the clearing, you may have just blown it on a chance at a record-smashing deer which was behind it. Big bucks stick together more than most hunters think. The dominant buck will be to the rear, after using, whether intentionally or not, the lesser buck as a decoy for you, the hunter. If it is truly big antlers you are after, then these are what you set your mind's eye on. Give does and anything less of a buck only a momentary glance, and look for the larger rack in the shadows.

In this book, and in deer hunting itself, there are contradictions to general truths and exceptions to the rules. These "contradictions" are actually separate truths to be rightly divided in accordance with the particular circumstances.

For example, take these two statements:

"To find a trophy deer, it is a good idea to check records and hunt the area that indicated such deer are present."

"Most trophy deer are found where they are not expected to be."

In this case the area that produced the outstanding deer may have drawn hunter pressure when it was publicized. Thus the area, although proven capable of producing superior animals, may no longer have any bucks living long enough to reach maturity. The wise hunter would blend the second statement with the first and look for an area in the same general location which seems to be overlooked and to have less hunter pressure.

Passing up a lot of deer in search of a trophy, the hunter becomes calloused and too unexcited about seeing deer. Such a hunter does not react swiftly enough and misses his chance at a trophy. When passing up deer becomes routine, it can hinder performance. Stay alert and train yourself to size up a rack swiftly and accurately.

When you have disciplined yourself to be patient, long-suffering, have kept with a workable plan, and have found the trophy deer you plan to take, there comes a moment when the whole enterprise can collapse. When you do, finally, get that shot at the deer you sought, you may be mesmerized by the massive antlers and fall prey to "buck fever" and freeze stiff, just locking up, shake violently, or shoot loosely as your eyes roll around in their sockets. Read the chapter on buck fever in the safety section.

Some older bucks choose to be loners. Very old bucks which have lost their zeal for cohabitation would rather take their chances alone and keep the risk factor to themselves. During hunting season they will usually just select a good spot and sit the daylight hours out until hunters have left the woods. Perhaps such deer prefer to remain alone since they know that more deer mean more tracks, more scent, more movement, and subsequently, more danger. These deer will run other deer off unsociably. Some are real hermits year-round.

Very old deer, and some of the best trophies, leave no sign of their presence such as territorial rubs and scrapes. They have advanced to the point of survival where they realize that leaving these telltale signs for hunters is not in their best interest. They will avoid leaving their tracks in barren places and will actually leap over such spots to avoid leaving visible hoof prints. Big, old bucks are often found where there are fewer deer and less sign. Hunting these animals has given me reason to assert that the whitetail deer is definitely a reasoning animal.

A world record deer is worth millions of dollars to the hunter who tags him.

POINTS

The usual questions asked of the successful hunter is "How many points did it have?" This is usually a reference to how many antler projections one and a half inches or longer were on the rack and seldom refers to the Boone and Crocket or Pope and Young scoring methods. Selective states have their own methods of determining official point scores which differ also.

What is defined as a point in hunting lingo also varies widely. What is a point down one hollow may not be a point over the ridge. In many locations a point is considered anything that you can put a ring on.

The best definition may be that in order to be called a point the projection just be at least one inch long and longer than the length of its own base. Anything smaller is ignored.

There are lots of puny deer out there with very small-beamed antlers, close together and with very little symmetry or tine length. Some of these may be ten-pointers or so. The problem with associating the number of points with the determination of quality is that a four-pointer may actually be a superior animal to a ten-pointer, because the four-point deer has a larger and better formed rack. There are some tremendous six and eight-pointers out there of superior size and shape, and there are some ten and twelve-pointers that look like your two outstretched hands attached at the wrists.

By the old method one-point deer could be a spike with one antler 32 inches long, a great rarity and an exceptional trophy, which would be considered a "one-pointer" instead of being recognized as a superior find.

The point being made here is that the number of points does not necessarily denote the quality of the deer. A 200-pound deer with large-girthed spikes may be a catch of higher value than a puny eight-pointer of lesser nutritional and genetic quality.

Record book point-scoring is best provided by an authoritative individual who has been trained and approved to score antlers officially and serve as an acceptable witness.

RACK ESTIMATION

If it is a trophy mount you are seeking, or perhaps a record-class deer, then you need to become thoroughly familiar with its appearance. The beginner has many channels available through which to learn about the type of deer he is going to seek. Magazine racks abound with photographs of prize deer. Some magazines have deer centerfolds like girly magazines. Other sources of information are calendars, television, videos, game farms, zoos, books, and personal sightings in the wild through stand-sitting, glassing with binoculars, and spotlighting in the night.

Seriously, a lot of subconscious input can be obtained through exposure, visual exposure, which will help significantly in developing hunting skills. Look at the antlers you see in restaurants, lodges, and other places, visit taxidermy shops and sporting goods stores. Study the deer specimens. Put your hands on them if possible. The hunter needs a broad spectrum of understanding here.

The hunter must learn to make quick and accurate judgments on the trophy potential of wild game. True, there are times when hunters get good long looks at their deer with plenty of opportunity to size it up, but more often than not the hunter has only seconds to judge the animal and shoot.

After the hunter intent on taking a trophy has learned to tell that a deer is a doe and quickly move his eyes away to look for a buck, he comes into the more difficult area of determining what kind of buck it is once the body outline and the shape of the antlers have been spotted.

Counting points can cost you a trophy. There are times when a rack first appears to be rather small and the hunter makes the decision to pass the buck up, but when the buck is making his exit with his rear end facing the hunter he sees that the antlers are much larger and wider spread than he was able to observe from the side. In fact the hunter could have estimated the size of the deer rack sooner by looking at the ears of the buck. Ears are about six inches long from the white at the bottom of the ear. This white is nearly always visible when antlers are visible. Judgement of tine length and thickness can be made by using the ear as a gauge.

While looking at a buck from the front or rear angles the hunter can also use the ears as a good spread gauge. The distance from one ear tip to the other is about fourteen inches as the ears rest alongside and in front of the antlers. A big boy needs to be at least a few inches wider in the antlers than in the spread of the ear tips.

The term "greatest spread" is the measurement taken across the widest part of a rack, including any points that project outward from the main beams to the antlers.

From head-on the deer can also be judged by looking at the chest size. If the height of the antlers equals or exceeds the distance from the lower chest to the neck, it is a large rack.

If a whitetail spotted from the rear has antlers that appear to exceed its body width, it is probably a trophy.

Learn to size up the trophy potential quickly. It is much better to be able to do this before the actual spotting in the wild of the animal you wish to harvest. Development of the ability of the beginning hunter to accurately size up an animal is very good preparation for serious hunters. If the beginning hunter learns to turn down smaller antlered deer which he has judged to lack trophy potential, he may be leaving a deer in the woods that will be his trophy the next year.

The most frequently encountered rack has 7 or 8 points. Next to this on either side of the frequency scale are the 5-and 6-point on the one side and the 9- and 10-point on the other side. A rack with 11 or more points is found on one buck in 20 to 70. One buck in 300 to 400 has 13 or more points. One buck in 1,000 to 1,300 has 15 or more points, and one buck in 4,500 to 5,000 has 17 or more points.

The chance of obtaining a state record buck is about one in one hundred thousand. Depending upon your geographics, upon the subspecies of whitetail dominant in the area you hunt, your chances of obtaining a world-record buck is about one in twenty million nationwide. It can happen at any time to anyone.

TINE SHINE

The sun shining on a deer antler can make the rack appear much larger than it really is. The well-polished antler of a rutting buck can give off an illusory glare. The hunter intent on taking a trophy-class deer as his allotment should be aware of antler glare in making his shooting decision. The disappointing deer that is shot today may have been the deer of a following season you would be happy with. A hunter who takes a shining-antlered buck is in for an unfortunate surprise when he walks up to the downed animal. He will look all around for the deer he shot at, finding it hard to believe that the downed deer was the one he saw.

Tine shine can be the factor that betrays the presence of a hidden buck in a thicket.

The hunter who still-hunts with the sun at his back will encounter antler shine often.

ANTLERS

The size of antlers depends upon the age of the individual deer, the quality and quantity of forage available to it, and its hereditary background.

Deer need forage from regions rich in limestone deposits if their antlers are to reach exceptional size. The minerals found in limestone, calcium, and phosphate are essential to prodigious antler growth.

Winter malnutrition can stunt antler growth.

Drought can decrease antler size.

Damage to antlers in the velvet stage can stunt their growth.

The color of antlers ranges from polished white to deep brown. The coloration has been attributed to staining by juices from rubs, but this is not so. In fact, the color reflects the amount of dried blood in the antler when it hardens.

By definition:

Tines: The antler projections of longer length which flow from the main beams.

Mass: The volume, the thickness of the beams and tines.

Spread: The distance between the main beams of the antler set.

Brow points: The normal first point (eye guards) in an antlered trophy.

A.

B.

C.

Beauty points: The profusion of tiny points between the burrs of the antlers and the brow tines at the flare of the antler base where it attaches to the skin of the skull.

Eastern count: The points of both sides of an antlered trophy area counted together.

Western count: The points of only one side are counted. If the number of tines on each side of the antlers differ then the animal is termed a four-by-five or an eight-by-six, and so on.

As mentioned previously, bigger bucks often run smaller bucks out in front of them to run point for them, clearing the way of danger. A ten-point deer may have an eight-point deer out 50 yards in front of him. The author is convinced that smart old bucks know most hunters will shoot the lesser trophy upon sight, allowing the dominant buck to escape. There are those who might disagree and insist that the larger antlered deer is holding up the rear to guard it from rear predators, or that the reverse situation occurs in nature more frequently with larger, more experienced deer usually out in front and the lesser deer pulling up the rear because he knows that the older deer can provide him safety. Whatever the appropriate explanation, both situations occur.

Often, too, a hunter shoots great non-typicals which make impressive and unusual trophies. Some of these have many points and irregularities which make the deer look as if it has driftwood tree roots on its head.

The three drawings on the preceding page relate the normal stages of development of a buck deer considered to be a trophy. The deer illustrated here is a "typical" buck.

A.

The first fall season after the birth of a buck, the fawn has two nubs projecting one to three inches from the skull. He is classified as a "button buck." The next fall season the buck is classified as a "yearling." A healthy yearling which has enjoyed good food supplies and has a good genetic background will sport a thin rack with two or three point projections on each side. Deer at this stage with forked antlers, or "forkhorns," generally have more potential than yearlings with "spikes," which are antlers without forks. A spike deer at this stage which has large, nicely shaped spikes which form a "halo" may yet go on to grow full antlers in later growths. Deer at this stage of life are "culled" when their antlers are very small and irregular. Yearling deer are easy to identify by their young bodies.

B.

During the second and third year of life, the same deer will begin to form a larger antler growth and to reveal the trophy possibilities of the animal. Deer in this stage usually have six to eight pointed tines with smaller brow tines. Brow tines may not appear at this stage since the buck is not ready for any serious mating and subsequent natural-selection fighting and thus does not need them for eye protection. It is at this stage of development that the vast majority of bucks are killed. The average hunter seldom sees deer past this stage. Deer at this medium age are very tempting to harvest. Spikes and spindly antlered deer of this age should be culled from the herd to reduce food competition and keep the superior animals as the breeding stock. Very nice horn growth with thick beams, nice spreads, long tines, and balanced symmetry should be left to become even better.

C.

The fourth, fifth, and sixth years are the years in which a buck will develop antler maturity. The rack of a trophy animal has spread out well beyond the width of the body. This deer is ready for harvest. He has bred does and his good quality will be handed down to continue in other deer generations. Most deer keep a

1. Piebald (Calico or Pinto)
   Melano (Melanism or Black phase)
   Albino (Albinism or White phase)

2. A typical deer with one non-typical forked antler tine

3. White part is typical antler growth
   Blackened parts are non-typical
   "D" indicates drop tines

4. Similarity to world record non-typical

5. Excessive hormonal excretions caused this buck to grow antlers in velvet which were too heavy for the deer to support resulting in death of the animal.

6. Palmated antlers

large rack of antlers from their sixth year till death, which generally occurs at eight to ten years of age. Some deer experience a decline in antler growth in old age due to tooth wear and ensuing nutritional deficiencies and hormonal changes corresponding with lack of sexual desire. It is unfortunate that most deer are not allowed to reach this size. The deer that support such fine antlers are indeed trophies. Few deer of this caliber are harvested not only because they are less numerous but also because they have learned how to survive and will likely die of old age rather than by a bullet.

ESTIMATING BODY SIZE

Learning to determine the body size of a deer in the field comes through actual sighting comparisons. Deer sizes range from that of a medium-sized dog to a full-grown mule. Truly big deer, does or bucks, are worthy game and in themselves trophies. In many states doe records are wide open for new entries. A doe exceeding 140 pounds is big anywhere. Bucks exceeding 200 pounds are considered big on the national average. Many such bucks are taken each year in most localities. Does exceeding 150 pounds are rarely recorded. Bigger does are prevalent with some becoming quite large. You may have a record doe if it exceeds 150 pounds field-dressed weight so be sure to check with officials. The current officially recorded largest whitetail buck was taken in Minnesota in 1926. It field-dressed at 402 pounds with a live weight approximated at 511 pounds.

Deer grouped together are easy to size up. The hunter can spot outsized animals through comparison. Single or widely separated deer are more difficult to gauge in size.

Most hunters who take deer to check stations and have them weighed are surprised that they do not weigh more than they actually do. They seem to shrink the longer you look at them. Hang around a check station where scales are available and you will learn a lot about deer size and weight.

What appears to be a large buck may turn out to be a small doe due to the effects of sunlight, shadowing, and cover. On the other hand, what appears to be a small doe may be a large buck. If the size of the animal is important to the hunter, then he should hold off for a better view before taking it.

In Maine, trophy status is popularly established by body weight.

Generally speaking, the farther north one goes the larger the deer are. Northern sub-species are just normally bigger deer. One would think that longer periods of forage abundance in the warmer climates of the southern regions would produce greater numbers of larger deer than the north, with colder winters and reduced food supplies. This idea holds true, for example, for bass fish. The reason that this is not the case with the whitetail deer is genetic. All the same, there are large deer to be found in the south too, and the rule that larger deer are found in the north has exceptions. Northern deer have been introduced into southern localities. Body size does not necessarily correspond with antler size, so record trophies can come from any part of the continental United States and Canada.

Texas deer rarely exceed 160 pounds in body weight but sport large racks. Texas has the largest population of deer in North America and some of the finest game and land management experts in the world.

During an "acorn year," when mast production is at a premium, deer gain weight. "Mast" is a term used to describe the forage which is found in sufficient quantities, has high caloric and nutritional qualities for wintering, and is preferred by the deer to fatten up on before the cold weather. The season following an acorn year is generally found to produce better antler growth in subsequent deer.

As a rule a fawn at birth will weigh approximately 7 pounds, 7 ounces as a male, and 5 pounds, 11 ounces as a female. As an adult the average doe will weigh 50 to 120 pounds, and the buck from 57 to 231 pounds.

The same locality can produce 30-pound deer and 300-pound deer, but most often the majority of deer in a given area are nearly the same size.

MUTANT DEER

The variety of deer encountered can add excitement to the deer hunt. You just don't know what you will see. In addition to the prized, perfectly shaped antler growth of the typical deer are the many and varied forms of non-typical antler growths.

A "typical" is a deer with regular antler configuration on both sides of the skull. Typical antlers need not be exactly alike or absolutely perfect to be classified as typical.

A "non-typical" is a deer with irregular or unusual antler growth. Deformities fall into this wide category. Non-typicals may range from fist-sized globs of antler with mushroom shapes to massive tangles which look as if the deer got some driftwood stuck on his head.

Mushrooming on antlers is produced by the deer in velvet butting bluntly and deforming the soft antlers in the early stage.

Palmation is an often desirable trait of some non-typical deer. This flattening and widening of the antlers produces racks similar to the shape of those of moose. Palmation is prevalent in the fallow deer imported to various areas of the country. Fallow deer which have escaped from preserves or have been released in this country have helped to bring more palmation into the whitetail populations everywhere through interbreeding. Palmated antlers are also called "cactus."

Other than injury to the antlers in the tender velvet stage, the greatest reason for racks significantly altered from the norm is hormonal imbalances. Calcium metabolism problems and bone tumors alter too.

Antlered does are actually hermaphrodites. Antlers on the female are produced in some animals by non-functional ovaries and in others by a malfunction of the adrenal cortex which results in a hormonal imbalance.

Antlerless bucks usually result from very early castration or from malfunction of the pituitary gland. A hunter's arrow or bullet or a predator attack can castrate a buck.

There are over 30 sub-species of *Odocioleus Virginianus*, or the Eastern whitetail deer, from Central America to the tundra of the North Country in Canada, with all sorts of crossings and variations in between. Differentiations between sub-species of the whitetail are an interesting subject to explore. The more popular subjects are the "Coes" deer of the Southwestern states and the "Keys" deer of the Florida Everglades.

The principal deer of the United States is called the "Virginia whitetail deer" because the first specimen described scientifically was killed in Virginia in 1784.

Some say that albino deer should be culled from the herd. It is said that this mutation results from in-breeding. True albinism is an inherited trait, but partial albinism may occasionally result from improper diet, an accident to the tissues involved, or even psychological shock.

In terms of overall population levels, albino deer are rare, appearing more frequently in certain regions than in others. Many hunters insist that they have spared the lives of white deer they could have shot. Someone who does shoot an albino deer usually receives scorn from the hunters who claim to have let it go. Some hunters are quite superstitious about these animals as were some Native Americans who traditionally revered the white phases of various animals. It is your right as a licensed hunter to harvest an albino during deer season; this is not illegal. I suggest that you let it go, however, as I have determined through interviews with those who have shot them that they would have been more pleased with themselves in the long run if they had allowed the animal to remain in the wild and breed. I was once faced with the decision of shooting an albino or not while bowhunting a thicket. It was tough to decide. The white animal turned out to be a cat—thank goodness.

True albinism is a genetic trait that is passed down the line. However, it takes an albino of both sexes to produce a guaranteed albino fawn, and the chances of an albino doe and an albino buck managing to find each other during this brief period are minimal. If the deer is a really exceptional trophy, it is easily understandable that the hunter may be tempted beyond his limits of resistance to take it. Let's hope he receives a minimal amount of scorn for doing so. The taking of white does is considered to be in poor judgement, but they, also, are tempting. It is at times such as these when the handy pocket camera would serve the need to record such encounters and provide you with something to show to friends. The photo of a live albino left in the field to continue the show is of greater value than the photo of a dead one.

The black phase of the deer is no less common than the white one. Sightings of black deer are less frequently reported because they are not so outstandingly visible. Since most deer sightings are in the darker hours, the black deer is camouflaged very well. The black deer is solid black, black as an Angus cow, with the usual white underneath, on the tail, and around the nose, eyes, and ears. These colors make a striking contrast. The black phase is called "melanism."

One late muzzle-loading season I spotted a melano doe walking point for a very large group of deer. Since she led the herd (and the big buck pulling up the rear) away from my position I tended to believe that she was exceptionally smart as a mutant and that she was chosen to lead the group due to her superiority. The only way I could explain how she knew I was there was by sixth sense. When I explained the encounter to an older and more experienced hunter he said that the reason that the black deer was in front was because she was inferior.

Some areas have "calico" or "pinto" deer, terms used to refer to deer with blotches of white, black, red, or brown in unusual places. Biologists call these deer "piebald." Sometimes whole local deer families are blotched in coloration.

Hunters who observe adult whitetail deer with fawn spots in the fall deer season are probably seeing the results of a fallow deer, which is spotted at maturity, having been crossbred at some point of time. Whitetail fawns lose their fawn spots in about August of their first year.

Mixing deer breeds is going to turn up more and more mutants. Sitkas, fallows, red deer (axis deer), and other animals imported from one area to another are going to create many phenomena over the next years as mixed breeding results in odd racks and colors. A tree can fall on a game-proof fence at a zoo or exotic game ranch and start a whole new breed of deer. The result of such interbreeding will not be dramatic, however, since the foreign genes introduced will be absorbed into the local gene pool and made less conspicuous as time goes on.

Chapter

3

Where Do You Want To Hunt?

IT IS NOT NECESSARY to venture far from most areas to find deer. They are almost everywhere. They occasionally even wind up in downtown metropolitan areas. Some of the most overlooked places are the small woodlots, swamps, and fallow fields adjacent to our cities. It may be necessary simply to walk out the back door of your home. Some may choose an exotic deer hunt far from home. The choices are virtually limitless, bounded only by the amount of time and money you have to invest in the hunt. These are not truly limitations, however, since you could possibly shoot the world-record deer in the first few minutes of hunting with a borrowed rifle and a license obtained by salvaging aluminum cans.

If you can decide to hunt in a particular area, choose an alternate place to go in case a bridge washes out, there is a fire, the area swarms with hunters, or other unexpected things go wrong. Always have a minimum of two places to go. It can be a sad situation to plan a vacation around deer season and miss out through improperly planning alternatives. Think it all out. Have a place to hunt in the rain, such as the loft of a barn, the protection of a ridge cavern, an old car body, or a covered tree stand. Take an umbrella which you bought camouflaged or camoed yourself. If you can't get that together at hunt time and all you have is a bright yellow umbrella, then smear some mud on it to break the glare and outline. As the Boy Scouts say, "Be prepared." Even if you prepare yourself for anything you think may happen, surprises will always enter the picture through doors you forgot to lock. Then you will improvise, cope, adapt! This is when that piece of plastic, those zip-lock baggies, or that piece of string become valuable.

A terrific way to find the place to hunt is to seek the advice of your local game warden. He is busy enough to avoid the extra duties of hunt director and tired enough not to want to be bothered at home. It is unlikely that he would be enthusiastic about directing you to quality deer hunting and providing inside information when he has been awakened from his sleep after having been out all night following up on poacher reports. It is best to politely ask for his help when you see him at a restaurant or somewhere else in public. In these situations you will find game wardens most eager to help. They are usually quite cordial over the phone, but they will more readily give you the answers you need in person.

People who hunt deer regularly are usually the best sources for hunting directions. Most deer hunters know several good places to hunt in their area and will be happy to share some of this information. Most hunters will share locations they themselves do not plan to utilize immediately, for they want others to harvest deer and enjoy other people's successes. Also, hunters will often tell you where the big one they have seen is hiding simply because they would like to see it up close if you should manage to take it as they have not. They will tell you to be sure and let them see it if you get it.

You can benefit greatly by choosing to go with an experienced deer hunter to an area he is familiar with on your first hunt.

You may choose to apply for a limited hunt at a local state park or national forest. Information concerning such hunts can be obtained by writing your state Fish and Wildlife Department at the state capitol.

Sightings from roadways are a way to discover good deer-hunting areas. At dawn and at dusk sightings are frequent for commuters to and from the work place or on other trips. Even road kills can be good evidence of game abundance. There are signs in many areas where deer crossings exist. These are scout-worthy areas although deer may cross just about anywhere. Since deer are creatures of habit and display patterned behavior 40% of the time, they do cross preferred places regularly. Signs are usually posted after several motorists have collided with deer in a particular spot. Note black skid marks on roads on long stretches of woodlands or other deer habitat as these are telltale signs of motorists braking for deer. If there are no big chunks of black rubber, you can bet there was no blowout. Get out and check for deer tracks or other deer sign.

Farmers can tell you a lot about deer. Some farmers see few deer or none at all, but others can put you right on top of old mossy horns. Since these people spend their lives in the same areas as the deer and are essentially feeding them with their crops, they are very informative sources.

Oil men who frequent rural areas to tend their pumps are also good sources. Coon hunters can fill you in on a particularly good ridge side where they have had trouble with deer. Timber industry field men such as forestry agents and timber cutters can give you a good steer. Such people work in the woods and are knowledgeable about the wildlife there.

You may choose to hunt an area just because you like the scenery and suspect deer habitation.

A canoe or boat trip down a creek, river, or stream can be a way to scout for deer. Likewise, spotlighting, where legal, can be a good way. At any rate, you need to know where you are going to hunt so that you can obtain permission and gain some familiarity with the area prior to the hunt.

Beginning deer hunters have three main options in choosing

a location to hunt deer. The first choice is private land. The second is leased land. The third is public land.

Private land where permission to hunt is granted is generally hard to find. You usually "have to know somebody." Often permission to hunt on these lands involves some sort of reciprocal arrangement also.

Leases, hunt clubs, and commercial preserves offer higher than usual quality sport but are too expensive for most hunters. Leases can cost anything you are willing to pay.

*LOOK FOR DEER IN THE DEEPEST WILDERNESS
AREAS, FAR FROM HUMAN HABITATION.*

PUBLIC AREAS

Public areas include national forests, state and national wildlife refuges, federal reservoir lands, national park properties, state wildlife management areas, state forests, public utility lands, military reservations, and other federal, state, and local holdings which fall under the public domain.

To obtain information about public lands available for hunting write:

The U. S. Forest Service
The U. S. Army Corps of Engineers
The U. S. Fish and Wildlife Service
Military reservations
Public utilities companies
State-owned and operated wildlife management areas

Timber companies, mining companies and other commercial interests with large land holdings are usually very cooperative.

SOYBEANS

Game management has been given proper credit for reestablishing the deer herds, but it is actually the deer themselves that should be credited for changing their habits to adapt to our civilization. Soybeans are not exactly the native forest environment of deer.

Deer love soybeans. Soybeans are a particularly good food source for nursing does because they enhance rich milk production. The excellent protein of the soybean produces fat little bucks. Deer can be spotted at night in soybean fields in prolific numbers in areas of successful repopulation. Soybean fields are a great place to scout in order to estimate deer numbers or to select a particular specimen. Simply shop for deer from the convenience of your automobile by using a spotlight. This is generally legal providing the spotlighters do not shoot the deer, an action which is illegal everywhere. Some states allow no spotlighting at all. The individual law may state that it is legal only if no firearms or other devices for taking game are in or on the vehicle. In some instances, local laws do not even allow a scouter to shine his headlights over a field and will prosecute for "harassing wildlife." Check with officials before attempting to spotlight a bean field. Never use your vehicle to chase or harass deer.

Red lights are less alarming to deer. The kind that plug into a cigarette lighter are the most popular. White lights will do quite well, however, and will show up antlers instead of just eyes.

Soybean foraging by deer is a growing concern for farmers. Small numbers of deer cause no major crop damage, as the deer selectively nibble a little here and there. But in areas of high population density, deer congregate to socialize as well as to dine and become a nuisance. Often bean farmers welcome hunters with outstretched arms until the hunters destroy more beans than the deer do. Hunters often show little or no consideration for crops by driving through crops or dragging deer through them.

The fallow fields are primarily hunted during early season, which is generally bow season. Mid-October is the usual harvest time in most areas. After the beans are harvested, the deer will move into other areas in search of other food supplies. It is usually true that acorns become the new primary food. Sometimes beans are harvested early enough that a good number of soybeans which fell away from the harvester root and sprout. This new growth is prime deer forage and suitable hunting ground for later hunters.

In shooting deer in the soybean fields, the hunter must take care not to damage the beans. Deer must be carefully carried out and not dragged.

Deer are most destructive to soybeans when they are first sprouting from the soil in the spring. This is the only time that deer will consume the whole plant. This is not often a problem, however, since the woods and fallow fields are also producing new growth at this time.

I dressed a doe that was road-killed exiting a bean field. This nursing mother had a stomach full of mature soybeans that was larger than a basketball. She had plenty of milk but was destructive.

Later in the season deer merely eat small parts of a plant here and there. They do not uproot plants or take them to the ground. Groundhogs (woodchucks) do a lot of the damage to soybean fields that is attributed to the track-leaving deer.

Farmers sometimes get upset when they spot a couple of deer out in their beans. Such farmers can have their crops inspected by conservation officers and biologists upon request. Farmers are issued special hunting permits which allow for some departures from the regular laws of the harvest. These permits are often handed out by the farmer to hunters who might assist him in reducing the number of deer in his area. These permits are usually for does only, since does do the reproducing. Bucks are to be left for regular hunters.

Sometimes the farmer may be allowed to sell these permits to recoup some of his income. For foodfare these animals are of the finest quality. Those who complain of "wild-tasting" venison (providing that the wild taste is not the result of poor cleaning methods) should consider hunting beanfield raised deer.

To find out just who has these special permits allowing hunters to take more than the regular number of deer, the hunter might check with the game warden, the feed and seed store, or the local agricultural office, co-op, or other farmer-related places.

For beanfield hunting during gun season, a flat-shooting, long-range rifle with a scope is recommended. A field that is barren of deer upon first observation might at any time have deer all over it suddenly appearing which had been bedded down out of sight in the shallow cover of the bean plants. Scope out the field for antlers.

*NOAH SPENT 120 YEARS PREPARING THE ARK,
SEVERAL OF WHICH WERE SPENT ROUNDING UP A
PAIR OF WILY WHITETAILS.*

CORN

Big bucks like corn fields. When the hunting pressure hits unpicked corn often harbors incredible numbers of whitetails. Corn left standing during deer season is excellent hiding for deer. Here they have shelter from the overhead-stand hunters shooting at them since there are seldom any trees in the fields. They have plenty of corn to eat. They can usually find water in a nearby drainage ditch without exposing themselves excessively. They can hear most advancing hunters as they rustle through the stalks. Indeed, few hunters will venture into the scratchy stalks. Here the deer nose can work well, their ears can work well, and their sight, the least developed sense, is adequate. Escape routes are uncluttered and available in all directions.

Deer are becoming more agricultural every year in their living habits.

Hunters who choose corn fields should hunt them on windy days when the corn is noisy already. Stalk into the wind or across wind for shots at unsuspecting animals while peering through the rows. Hunt cross-row slowly, carefully peering down the lanes. When you really feel you may be getting near a deer you might get down on your knees to slowly scan the distance for deer where the foliage is sparse.

Deer can be quite destructive to a sweet corn patch. With their sweet tooth, in sweet corn, deer are a true problem. In early bow season sweet corn plots might be good hunting locations. In field corn, they are not generally considered nuisances. Raccoons, squirrels, and woodchucks do more corn harvesting than the deer. It is not unusual for a stand hunter positioned next to a corn field to see a fox squirrel hauling an ear of corn as big as he is from the field.

The greatest reason for deer inhabiting corn fields is the cover the corn stalks provide. The corn itself just makes the patch more inhabitable. Deer come out of the corn fields at night to do most of their feeding on natural browse in the woodlands.

Deer munch hard-kerneled field corn kernel by kernel like a snack food. They gluttonously scarf down sweet corn like we do corn on the cob. Deer will travel considerable distance to visit a sweet-corn planting.

Circle the perimeter of standing corn in search of deer sign. Hoofprints should be clearly visible in the cultivated earth. If rubs and scrapes are found you have located a good spot.

Cornfield-hunting with bow and arrow is safest. Various methods of stalking or still-hunting deer in standing corn rows are employed. Driving deer from such areas to waiting hunters is the most logical. Some hunters work out systems whereby two or more hunters work a corn field in search of deer. These are close and quick shots. The situation is very dangerous when more than one hunter is involved.

The best guns for standing-corn hunts are shotguns with

buckshot or slugs, 30/30 lever actions, or even 458 magnums, or any other gun with quick sighting and shorter range capabilities. I use a .41 magnum handgun.

The hunter can get turned around easily in large corn fields. It is suggested that anyone planning to enter a big field with corn higher than their heads devise a system of row walking by counting rows and use a compass or a high landmark which is always going to be visible. It can get very frustrating to be lost in a cornfield.

Corn is usually used by game management biologists who are live-trapping deer as a lure into the cage.

Plowing under corn stalks to clean fields and compost the stalks is detrimental to the wildlife that feed on the missed ears of corn over winter. This modern farming technique is good for the earth and makes the farmer's job easier but is injurious to wildlife.

Farmers should compromise by leaving some of the crops around the edges of their fields standing for wildlife. Some states offer farmers incentives for such practices.

Farmers agree to leave a percentage of their crops for wildlife in exchange for being allowed to grow their crop on government lands.

THICKETS

It is hard to believe that an animal as large as a big buck deer with the equivalent of a chair on its head could move about as easily as they do in a dense thicket. This is the choice place for them. One would think that they would choose easier walking paths, but they are seeking security and want to hang on to those trophy racks. At night they choose easier paths, and in fact they do most of their meandering at that time. But since you are a daytime hunter, the thickets are your best chance for a good deer. A stand near a thicket is a great bet for tempting a buck out into view by various means. A big buck can go through brambles like a rabbit. They have this uncanny ability to "get small" and sneak. There are rare recordings of antlered deer having been caught up in vines and dying as a result, but these are indeed uncommon. These situations probably occur when antlered bucks attempt to fight off predators in vine entanglements.

In the daytime, deer go where people are not expected to travel and where, if they decide to do so, their intrusion would be noticed.

Pressured deer go in search of such places. Big bucks head there as soon as they see early headlights on the roads and hear car doors slam. Any unusual activity sends smart deer hiding.

Deer in thickets stick tight in the relative safety of the underbrush. Scanning the edges just inside by careful glassing is a good bet. Rattling, or racking, or calling by various mouth calls are good methods to get them out to investigate.

If you build a stand overlooking a thicket, don't give up looking for deer there. Deer bedded down stand up to stretch their legs just as we do. Keep looking for movement or some part of a deer. If you have chosen a likely thicket and have found good deer sign there, then you may catch them getting there when they seek it out. On a normal day most anywhere the time of day for such an encounter is generally around 9:00 A.M.

I have had the experience several times of getting within a yard or so distance from deer in thickets before they bolted. On each occasion I had not noticed the deer until the deer took off.

Since it was always when I paused or switched directions that the deer arose so close to me, I am certain that I have passed by many deer which were laying low and expecting me to pass them by. Jump-hunting deer in thickets is a lot like hunting rabbits in the same habitat. One hunter can walk through a high field and not see a single rabbit. Another hunter can come through right after him and by zigzagging with frequent pauses cause the rabbits to panic and provide a shot. One time I had followed some fresh tracks to a thicket and while crawling on hands and knees noticed the legs and underside of a deer in the trail ahead. I slowly rose upright and shouldered my rifle to catch a look at the deer's head some twenty yards ahead when a humongous buck which was hidden in the honeysuckle thicket to my immediate left, bolted over the top of my head and scared the living daylights out of me. This big buck would have let me pass right by him had I not paused in that exact spot.

Good thickets are often found in "transition zones." Transition zones are the vegetation of midsize between, say, a field and a woods. Transition zones are located around the borders of clearings, fields, creeks, roads and other low-profile areas that are next to woodlands. These zones offer lots of branch-tip forage at forage height to the deer and also offer concealment. Since deer are considered "edge" animals such locations are natural choices for hunters to locate deer.

Abandoned cotton fields in the South which have fallowed into thickets are good deer locations.

Fallow fields which have overgrown with staghorn sumac make terrific choices for locating bedded bucks. The sumac offers high protein winter forage and deer antlers blend in perfectly with the branch structure.

For the stand hunter scoped rifles are useful for spotting animals in thickets and choosing shots which bypass obstructions. The stalker and still-hunter are better off using a brush gun.

Christmas tree plantations harbor deer herds.

BACKYARD BUCKS

While most hunters tend to think the biggest bucks are to be found in the farthest reaches of the wilderness areas, many are realizing that the deer they were after might have been right there at home all along.

Of course it is true that unhunted places harboring really big bucks do exist in some of the less accessible, out-country areas. These places become less and less of a haven each season as the motorized hunter enters the wilderness.

Many a buck has crouched low to watch the ATV go by and gone back to the normal routine after the noisy intrusion passed by.

A stand of pines, a blackberry thicket, or a honeysuckle thicket right behind a house which is cut off from the rest of the woodlands by a cow field or other fields is ideal for deer.

You might find big bucks next to urban areas in the most un-expected places. These bucks have chosen these places to hide from hunters. There are fewer natural predators here also. Here they feel safer. The sounds of farm activity intrigue them. They like to keep tabs on the enemy. Regular activity is unalarming. Some like music and will take up residence near a regularly-played radio. Although dogs can be a formidable enemy to deer, deer might feel more at ease bedded down near dogs they know won't bother them. These dogs will keep other dogs away.

Campfire stories at any deer camp will eventually include some story about a deer being encountered in an unsuspected, nearby place. An example is one I heard about a farmer who headed off in early morning to the wilderness in search of a buck. When he returned worn-out and empty-handed, his wife said, "You should have stayed at home; that old buck got his horns stuck in the cow feeder."

WATERHOLES

During periods of drought, watering places are choice places to hunt. They are not the best selection when water is plentiful. Wounded or sick deer will go to water often, but healthy deer can do without it awhile, finding needed moisture in vegetation or snow.

Deer have definite water preferences and are quite choosy about what they drink when they can be. A mineral spring is the choice type of water source. A valley spring is ideal for a stand. The minerals found in these sources make the antlers large and firm, a fact which the bucks seem to instinctively know. Big bucks will frequent such places just as body builders go for protein supplements to health-food stores. Deer prefer sulphurous water to clear water. Water can be quite dingy in appearance yet be delightful to deer.

Deer do not hang around ponds, lakes, streams, or waterholes long because of the steady animal traffic to these locations. Does searching for bucks or vice-versa may prove an exception to this rule, but if they do hang around they will be concealed and on the alert with choice escape routes handy. Generally they just drink and leave. All the predators frequent the water, so any deer here exhibit an unmistakable wariness. Their ears move endlessly, and they spend several minutes waiting, looking, and scenting the air before each drink. In groups, one will drink and then the other.

Swimming deer are easy prey for boaters. Harassing swimming deer is strictly forbidden by law. Taking a swimming deer is subject to a strict penalty. The hunter can, however, position himself on land and harvest a deer which has reached land fully. This method of hunting is productive at some larger lakes and on rivers of larger size. The hunter positions himself across river from prime deer habitat which is certain to be invaded with hunters on opening day. This prime deer habitat is usually the low-lying side of the river, the flood plain. The hunter takes a vantage point on the high bank opposite and glasses the water for deer. When spotting his prey he plots a possible landing point for the deer and while disguising his movement positions himself for a telescopic shot.

A 200-pound live-weight deer will drink two to three quarts of water daily at average weather temperatures.

DEER ARE EXCELLENT SWIMMERS
WITH HOLLOW HAIR

A deer which has drowned does not make good eating. Drowning can be avoided by allowing the deer to fully clear the bank before shooting.

A deer disease commonly called "blue tongue" dehydrates deer and sends them to water continuously. When deer are affected by this disease, it is usually publicized by state officials. The tongue of such a deer will be swollen and blue. These thirsty deer are discovered drowned as they died while attempting to quench their thirst. It is said that the meat of such an animal is still consumable, but I suggest that no diseased deer of any kind be eaten unless you are desperate.

Islands are good places to find deer, for they are isolated from dog packs and have fewer predators. Often island deer seem to have a generally happier attitude about things and roam more freely as a result. Islands with agricultural crops bordered by tree-lines or other cover on the banks are particularly productive. Willow thickets are great food in themselves. Farmers who take advantage of the fertile flood-plain silt soils carry their machinery by ferry to such places.

Deer are excellent swimmers. A big river or lake is no obstacle, but rather a pleasure for them to swim. Deer have been known to cross considerable distances in the water, such as the Great Lakes. The hollow hair makes them buoyant, as when a person swims with a life preserver strapped around his chest. Nature's equipment for the deer allows it to exert minimal effort to stay afloat and transfer its energy to movement. Deer can swim at a speed of 13 MPH.

When hunting pressure hits, large concentrations may flee to island retreats. Big bucks particularly favor islands for security. There are islands which are traditionally used for the rut that generations of deer instinctively head to for breeding.

Deer like to cut off their scent paths by crossing water and placing a barrier between themselves and their predators. Of course, islands are not fool-proof protection from coyotes and dogs since these animals can swim also, but they will swim reluctantly. For all these reasons, islands are good places to find deer which other hunters cannot reach. Predators do sometimes invade island herds and chase them away, but this is the exception and not generally true.

Islands in the Atlantic Ocean have sub-species of deer which are found nowhere else. These islands are generally fairly far from the mainland, making commuting by deer unlikely.

Remember that rifle bullets can travel long distances when glancing across the water in ricochet unobstructedly.

BOATS

Float-hunting for deer is an old Indian method. Camouflaged canoes flowing with the current allowed the hunter to get within stonehead-arrow range of unsuspecting deer which had gathered at the water's edge to cool, to drink and feed. Deer eat aquatic vegetation. In addition to the general succulence of browse to be found at the sunlit edge of waterways, such as the favored willows, vegetation draws deer into the water for food. Deer will bring up whole lily pad plants with their feet to consume them or actually plunge their heads underwater to forage for other aquatic vegetation. Almost all aquatic vegetation makes good salad-bar food for deer. They will separate the earth muck around cattails in swampy locations a foot deep to reach the tender and starchy roots. Cattail wallows actually made by deer look like the work of hogs.

Canoeing to scout for deer along creeks is one of the best ways to scout. Boating rivers and creeks while looking for bank trails and deer sign is also very productive. In shallow streams, look for disruptions in color in the stream bed as telltale signs of deer crossings, as well as the obvious paths and skids down banks. Remember that deer do not often go straight across waterways but attempt to confuse their backtrails by going upstream to exit the water. Enjoyment is likely another reason that deer take a long route crossing a stream.

A boat is at times the best method of reaching wilderness hunting areas, where the moving water naturally took the easiest route. This path of least resistance can be the most practical method of bringing deer out as well.

A houseboat makes a good base camp for a party of river or reservoir hunters. The entire camp can readily be moved.

Scouting or hunting waterways is the best method known to give you access to prime deer habitats. Some of the land you cover may be posted. You have a right to navigate the waterways but are considered a trespasser if you leave your boat to hunt land without permission in privately-owned areas. Upon locating a choice spot to hunt you might check with the local court clerks to find the owner of the land to obtain permission.

Use all the common sense you can muster in employing aquatic transportation. Safety should always be the first thought. Since you are entering areas by the "back door" instead of by the highway access "front door" you may not be able to accurately judge what is beyond the trees that border the creek You should take the time and exert the effort to obtain a map of the waterway to help you familiarize. A shot from a high-powered rifle can throw an unstable canoeist into the water. Attempting to stand in a wobbly canoe to fire an arrow can be very awkward. Find a stable canoe for hunting, one of the functional, rather than recreational types. There are canoes made for a variety of purposes. With a brief search, the hunter can locate the canoe exactly suited to his needs, considering portage, weight, purpose, and everything else in deciding the appropriate size and shape. There is great variety.

CAMPS

Deer camps are special places where story-swapping camaraderie plays a big role in the overall experience. Hunters learn a lot from one another. Members who have enjoyed success themselves often assist others who have as yet been less fortunate. Here seasoned hunters give newcomers advice and counsel. Deer camps can be ideal for beginning hunters providing that the members or guests, staff or elders, are serious hunters interested in the welfare of others. A deer camp guide can point the way to success through his various experiences and familiarity with the particular area. Small, family-style camps set up from a mobile camper, hunting cabins, or tents are necessary for some hunters who travel considerable distances to hunt, making the drive to and from the site too long. These camps can range from a handful of hunters with sheets of plastic for shelter and sleeping bags for beds around a campfire to lush extravaganzas with saunas, video presentations, casinos, and all the trimmings of the international playboy scene. Whatever the circumstances as far as comfort, cost, and conveniences, the fellowship can be great. The opportunity to interact with people you might not encounter in the ordinary circles of your life leave you with something tangible that trips by yourself do not.

Resort camps on private game preserves are wonderful retreats. The operators of such camps are familiar with the needs of the hunters and equip the camps to cater to them. They try to make the stay as comfortable as possible after a day of rugged experiences in the field. It can be a comfortable vacation. These facilities have bathing, laundering, hot meals, telephones, meat lockers, taxidermy services, and comfortable beds. They keep track of their guests and are ready to assist should an emergency arise.

Choose a camp on the basis of a good recommendation from a trusted friend, or write to camps which advertise in hunting magazines for information. Perhaps you will be asked to join a fellowship of hunters who have a lease and organize hunts. Leases and commercial acreages are swiftly becoming more common due to dwindling habitat, the need for herd regulation, and hunters' desires to have someplace to hunt they can count on. Some hunting preserves offer other types of hunting coupled with deer. Perhaps you would like to take home a boar, a turkey, a bear, quail, sheep, pheasant, fish or waterfowl. Exotic deer are available many places.

If you choose to hunt alone and have a place to do it, this is of course your prerogative. I have mentioned the commercial camps for their merit to those thus inclined. For those with a desire to rough it by primitive camping, I hope you enjoy it, for the opportunities for the rugged enthusiast are unending, as are the adventures.

VEHICLES

What vehicle to use to scout or hunt is a decision largely based upon availability. Some hunters use elaborately set up rigs with big recreational vehicles sporting a canoe on top trailing an all-terrain two, three, four, or more wheeler to the rear. In some instances a bicycle may be just the thing to take you to the outskirts of town and stow away noiselessly where there are no places to park anything else. Of course packing your deer out may be another consideration! Most any automobile in good running condition will carry you to good deer hunting. The most popular mode for getting into the woods and getting the deer out is the four-wheel drive truck.

Maintenance and repairs should be performed on all vehicles well in advance of the hunt. An old fan belt or hose could be just the thing to foil your plans. A low battery can absolutely ruin your day. Make sure there is a good jack and spare tire. Gas and oil should be put in a day or so in advance to avoid the smell on your clothing and hunting boots. There are the rare instances of hunters having automobile trouble and having good luck hunting where their car broke down, but we choose to avoid these circumstances when possible. Remember Murphy's law. Murphy said: "If anything can go wrong, it will."

Only take your vehicle to the limits of its design. Although it is a display of determination and fortitude to gun your family car as far as you can down a muddy logging or farming road until you become stuck, so you can hunt and worry about getting out later, this is simply asking for trouble for yourself as well as for those who will have to help you. This is a situation all too often encountered by hunters who find their roads blocked by someone unequipped to be in there. Farmers who live near old, muddy, rutted roads to deer woods have many encounters with bogged hunters seeking their help. Use common sense and avoid unnecessary hardship. If you are going to travel one of these roads, get out of your vehicle and check out the pot holes and ruts before endeavoring to cross them. Don't go in over your head. Remember that going in means you must come out. If it looks as if you may become stuck, keep moving, as this greatly decreases your chances of getting bogged down. Keep up good speed over sand or gravel especially. You may let some air out of your tires to give yourself more traction in snow, sand, or mud. If you have extra air stored in a tank or a cigarette lighter operated air pump, you are well prepared, but if not you will just have to take it slowly to a gas station. If you get stuck and your tires are spinning, let your passenger get out and push right from the beginning instead of after the rut is deepened. Here a stitch in time saves nine. If you bury your vehicle you will have to use that shovel you thoughtfully placed in the car or jack it up to put something under the tires for traction. In these conditions you will need a good piece of wood for the jack to keep it from burying itself. When attempting to drive out, shift from drive to reverse in automatic transmissions or from second gear to reverse in manual and rock out. If you have a handy power winch attached to your vehicle which you can hook up to a tree you are in luck. A less expensive come-along tool can be very useful. Improvisations made with ingenious use of available materials have gotten many a wayfaring hunter out of a rut. In the Kootenay Mountains region of British Columbia my hunting partner and myself were caught in a predicament where we managed to remove our unequipped jeep from a ditch by using vines and our trouser belts to twist-winch our jeep out. We got out but if my friend at the twist end had slipped with the post he was using to twist with, the post would have beat him silly and I might have been smashed since it was my duty to push the jeep uphill at the rear. Awkward situations of this nature should be avoided by planning.

It is a good idea to carry alone some or all of these materials for getting stuck: winch or comealong, good bumper jack, block of wood, short-handled shovel, pair of grate tracks, pull chain or tug rope, tire inflation device.

If you should get stuck or have a breakdown, be patient and wait for another vehicle to assist. Don't panic. Carefully build a fire to keep warm if necessary. Even in the most remote area someone should come around eventually. If you consider it a better move to seek help, then leave a note stating your intended direction. To avoid misunderstanding you may wish to leave a note on the windshield explaining who you are and what you are doing.

Even if you are so far out in the wilderness that you would never expect anyone else to come there, and you are not stuck, you should leave space for others to park. Be sure to park your vehicle in a way that is considerate of others. It is courteous not to block roads or take up space other drivers may need to turn around. Avoid parking in fields and crops and leaving ruts in the fields to create poor farmer relations.

Park your vehicle in a location where it could be watched. Few thieves will be foolhardy enough to risk being shot at by an armed hunter who may be watching or may be appearing at any moment. Anti-hunter fanatics have been known to slit tires and otherwise vandalize hunters' cars. Likewise, greedy, land dominating hunters who are unwilling to share their hunting site may seek to run you off by damaging your vehicle. It is a good idea to cover any valuable temptations visible to thieves.

An effective auto heater may be a necessity in colder areas. To be without one may be life-threatening.

Deer are not usually afraid of moving vehicles and rush off only when the vehicle stops. A deer within hearing distance is well aware of a stopped car and knows what a car door sounds like. The squeak of a car door may put the local trophy on the defensive for the rest of the day. When launching your hunt, make as few noises with your vehicle as possible, and you will enjoy increased success.

With deer poaching being such a problem in many regions, deer are wary of automobiles. Cut your headlights as you enter an area to hunt and use your parking lights to creep along the remainder of the way if this can safely be done.

Carry a basic repair kit that includes at least a crescent wrench, pliers, and a screwdriver along with standard tire changing tools. Having a screwdriver handy more than once has made the difference between a good hunt and a bad one.

We can only hope that three- and four-wheelers won't be recreational slobs during the deer season when hunters are trying to be the least disturbing as possible.

A Citizens Band radio is good equipment to have in wilderness areas. If you plan on never being without one of these in your hunting vehicle, you will always be able to call for help. The use of radios is also common in regions where large drives or the dog is used to push deer. Hunters coordinate with radios.

A working horn is useful for calling other hunters and signaling for help.

Be careful when operating winches. Always be mindful of the possibility of cable break or release under stress. Stay protected from cable whiplash. The floor mat from your vehicle or your hunting jacket are handy to be placed on the tightened cable to foil the backlash.

GUIDES

A qualified professional hunting guide may be the choice option for the urban hunter with little time to scout and investigate hunting prospects. When attempting to hunt unfamiliar territory, a guide can make the difference between a good and a bad hunt. Unless you have thorough knowledge of the land you wish to hunt, you might spend unfruitful days in the bush without the help of a guide. Another name for a guide might be a "scout."

A guide can keep you out of trouble. He can limit frustrations and save you time. A guide can help with retrieving, gutting, and caping trophies. The guide can accurately predict the packing and preparation needs of the hunter, thereby eliminating the need to purchase or pack certain items. He will tell you what you should bring and what will be furnished, what is available locally and what is not.

Most hunters balk at the thought of "pay hunting" and feel no need for someone else to help them with a hunt. These hunters generally think that such setups are for "tin horns" or the corporate executive class. The price of a guide service may appear large at first, but after examining the whole spectrum of things you may find that a guide will even save you money in the long run. It is often the case that a hunter would have come out better if he had hired a guide.

One good source for finding a guide is the National Registry organization.

Personal recommendations from other hunters who have used the guide or guide service are the most often used leads.

It is a good idea to do a thorough job of investigating a game ranch or guide service located through a magazine ad before making the leap of employing them. Ask for references, preferably from your area. Get several of them and check each one. The time spent here is worthwhile. In writing to request references, include a self-addressed, stamped envelope and be courteous. If telephoning for a reference, then do so at an appropriate time of day. References should be current. They should be references to hunts the year before and not several years ago. The clients which you locate might pass on pertinent information to you concerning your guide such as that you should pack a can opener because the excellent guide always forgets his.

Any guide worth his oats will guarantee a shot. Other guide services and game ranches charge a set fee to hunt and extra for a kill.

A few phone calls or letters prior to the hunting scheduled with a guide could get you in with a hunting partner, not just a guide. It helps to break the ice and form a friendship before the hunt.

If contracting the services of a professional guide service or game ranch is not in the cards for you yet you need the help such an outfit would provide, then you have other options.

Ask a successful hunter of your acquaintance for his assistance in guiding you. Most hunters will enthusiastically help you get your first deer. They remember their first deer and really want to enjoy the experience again through you. Offer to pay for the hunt if they are willing to take you along, and at the very least, split the cost of the gasoline.

Some backwoods types would consider it the opportunity of a lifetime to receive a hundred dollars for leading you to a deer they are familiar with. Paying someone to help locate a nice deer for you does not mean that they will bring it to you on a leash. There will still be plenty of sport involved matching wits with the wily whitetail.

PHYSICAL LIMITATIONS

Deer hunting is a sport open to the young, the old, and the handicapped. There is a way for almost every person who desires to hunt deer to do so. Deer hunting is one of the most widely accessible sports.

The blind can participate to a remarkable degree by going with a companion to a hunt and experiencing all but the actual shooting. Many blind people become adept shooters by learning to compensate for their sight loss by increasing their hearing perception. Their marksmanship is usually limited to gun ranges where little bells are attached to targets and pulled by strings. Some blind hunters, with the aid of an assistant with eyesight for obvious safety reasons, may actually take deer.

The wheelchair-bound hunter has an advantage over most hunters in that he will not be able to yield to the itch to get up and walk around when his patience runs thin. Although wheelchairs are not practical for the roughest terrains, the majority of hunting areas are to some degree accessible to them. One of my acquaintances who is without the use of his legs manages to take his deer each season from an adapted ATV.

Determined individuals often overcome physical limitations through improvisation. Their hunting techniques may be creative and grandly satisfying responses to their handicaps. Such hunters are granted special privileges by law-enforcement agencies to allow for their differences and encourage their participation in the sport. Physical limitations might suggest that a person should hunt close to a roadway and not attempt to track or retrieve a deer without assistance. Taking part in drives and risking becoming lost by walking deep into the woods should be avoided.

Hunting with an able-bodied companion may be a must. The companion should be aware of specific physical limitations and of any first aid he might be required to administer.

It is important to consider physical limitations in planning the hunt. Access to the hunting area, the type of stand, the selection of a companion, weapon type, and other matters should be scrutinized in advance.

There are far too many instances of heart attacks in the deer woods.

If you are under medical supervision and using a prescription medicine, be sure not to forget it in the excitement. Not only could forgetting it cause medical problems, but having to go home to get it could foil your hunt.

Where there is a will there is a way for the handicapped who wish to hunt whitetail deer. Disadvantaged hunters derive greater satisfaction from their efforts.

4

When Do You Want To Hunt?

FOR MOST PEOPLE the answer to this question is when they *can*. It is dependent primarily upon the legal hunting dates. When you can get off from your job may be relevant too. There are hunters who work around deer-hunting seasons and there are hunters who hunt around their work schedules. Some people hunt year-round and others hunt only an hour or two. There are those who travel across states and around the world hunting deer at all times of the year, taking advantage of different climates and seasons; there are those who scout and observe deer year-round even though they may actually hunt only one day or a couple of weeks each year. Most people must *take* time to hunt. They are not likely to allow anything to interfere with their hunting time.

I asked my wife to include in our marriage vows that she would not interfere with my hunting and I make it a practice to forewarn employers that I am an avid hunter who needs more than average vacation time during deer season.

Hunts in all states are organized to allow the deer ample time off from hunter pressure to bear their young and nurse them. Hunting from February through August is virtually non-existent for this reason. Full-blooded Native Americans have the right to take deer anytime regardless of the season as part of their ancestral rights.

Deer seasons are scheduled in the fall throughout America. There are several reasons for this. The rut is well advanced, which makes the bucks less cautious and creates an advantage for the hunter. Also, it is only during the fall and early winter months that deer sport antlers, which most hunters prefer. In old times it was when most of the farm work was done that deer-hunting took place. The hunt season was also governed by when meat would not spoil and could be laid in to provide food for the winter months. Fall hunts were usually when there was a good tracking snow, making it easier to hunt and also to locate wounded deer. Animals were fat in the fall, having feasted on acorns, crops, and other mature mast food. Roads are frozen over, making them more accessible. Fawns are well developed and most does are bred. In the autumn there is a sharp increase in deer activity which peaks in late fall with the breeding cycle and maximum acorn availability. All these conditions helped to establish the tradition of fall deer hunting.

Quite apart from the biological reasons, the convenience of the hunter and the traditions of hunters are the chief factors in the establishment of the hunting season. The legislature is out to please the public, which is the voting public, of course, and they are the elected "public servants."

Some farmers and entire communities keep Saturday or Sunday Sabbaths on which they do not hunt and allow no hunting on their lands. It is always best to respect these local traditions. In some locations, Sunday hunting is not only shunned but forbidden by local law in the form of ordinances. It doesn't make for good hunter relations with the public when a Sunday morning church service is interrupted by gunfire on the ridge behind the churchhouse.

DAWN TO DARK

The majority of hunters like to be in position to hunt deer before daylight. Some anxious hunters are so intent upon early light hunting that they enter the woods at midnight and sit quietly until dawn in hopes that they will be undetected by the deer moving into the area and be able to see deer in the vicinity as soon as the sun comes up. This is, of course, going too far for most people, but getting there early might put you right on top of deer when daylight comes. I am the type that likes the woods more than my urban life. It is no problems for me to enter before dawn and exit after dark. There is seldom a rush to get back home. Daylight has found me perched in a tree with deer bedded beneath more than once.

The hunter who has prepared himself properly to enter the woods under cover of darkness to go to his hunting spot and wait for sunrise has the most intensely exciting hunt. Spotting the stately dream buck as he becomes visible through the fog and filtering light is dramatic. Arriving at a stand in darkness without alerting the deer in the area can indeed mean that deer are right under your nose. Quietly entering the woods with deer-like footsteps and with a flashlight held pointed to the ground and used minimally can really be the first step in the greatest of hunts.

Proper scouting allows hunters to enjoy the most success with the least effort in the least amount of time.

If you take your deer in early morning, you will have the whole day left to enjoy the after-hunt experiences, dress and preserve the deer, or hunt for another deer.

Remember not to shine your car lights into the area and not to slam your car doors.

It is important to carry a flashlight whenever you are in the woods in darkness, but keep it aimed at the ground so as not to arouse the deer but to notify other hunters of your presence. Never presume that there are no other hunters about! You can bump heads with another hunter in the most unexpected places at any time. Simply that there were no other vehicles about means little. If you could avoid the flashlight when entering the woods pre-dawn it would be to your hunting advantage. Safety must come first. Carry a flashlight. There is no deer worth dying for.

The transition from the darkest hour before the dawn into the slowly increasing light is one of the best experiences in deer hunting. It is majestic. It is a new dawn. The whole woods is resonant with the sounds of good morning.

During gun season, and especially on opening morning at sunrise, you will hear guns going off in the hills that excite the imagination and may stir up visions of the Civil War.

One drawback is that it is usually quite cold in early morning, and sunrise does not produce expected warmth. It is during this transition period that shivers can make you shake and spoil your steady shot. Take it easy in your early morning trek, being careful not to get heated up. Lighten up on the clothing for the trek in, and put more clothing on when you reach your waiting place in order to avoid the handicap of shivering.

As mentioned earlier, most states stipulate that the hunter may take deer no earlier than one half-hour before legal sunrise and no later than one half-hour after legal sunset. It is a good idea to find out just what time legal sunrise and sunset are for the given day of the hunt. This is particularly true for hunts on tightly regulated government lands. Terrain differences allow sunlight to filter in later or earlier in some locations than others. Deep valleys have later sunrises and earlier sunsets. The rising sun in the east may be delayed by an hour or more by some topographical obstruction such as a hill, and the same may be true of the sunset. Overcast days are slow lighting and quick darkening.

In some popular hunting locations such as the public hunting areas of state forests and military installations, especially those where hunters are monitored by check stations upon leaving for the hunt and departing, officials are equipped with a device which can determine almost the exact time that an animal was shot. The test is reputed to gauge the time of kill within 15 minutes with accuracy. When it is suspected that an animal was shot before legal hunting time, this test can be administered and used in court as evidence. All game wardens are capable of applying this test.

If a deer to your liking should appear before legal hunting time, then let it go by while carefully observing its habits. Perhaps you will be able to rattle or otherwise call it back to you once the sun has risen. Maybe you can track it down, or you might move your stand for better placement the next day. If the deer walked by in dry leaves then you stopped hearing the rustling leaves, you know it is near the spot where you last heard it and you still have a chance to take it.

Scopes offering light filtration greatly increase visibility and enhance shooting ability under poor light conditions.

Iron sights should be clearly visible in darker situations, particularly the sight at the distant barrel end. If these sights are not factory illuminated, then add a little fluorescent paint to them. The little bottles sold for model airplanes are good for these small-scale applications. White is not recommended due to the white parts on the deer's anatomy. Check your firearm under dark conditions before venturing afield.

Bows can be lighted by solar or battery-operated devices attached to the bow. These little lights illuminate the sight pins.

Bright light is blinding. A good pair of hunting glasses is helpful. If you are not ready for this investment, or lose them as I do, then use any sunglasses. A billed cap is also useful.

Infra-red scopes are illegal for deer-hunting at the present time, as are flashlights taped to bows or gun barrels to illuminate the deer.

Dawn is not necessarily the best time to hunt, though the favored time. Indeed, this depends upon many factors. When possible, the hunter intent upon a total woods experience should spend as much time in the woods as he can. A sit, still-hunt, or stalk from before dawn to after dark will be memorable and worthwhile in one way or another. If you cannot manage to do it this way, then take whatever time you can. If you can hunt only for a half-hour, you can still hunt. Some have their dreams fulfilled before going to work in the morning, some after getting off, some during their lunch hour.

It is generally considered that morning and evening are the best times to hunt. The author feels certain that any time is a good time to hunt.

Many hunters have the traditional camp lunch at noon, or they leave the woods and return to their truck for a noon break. Sometimes hunters have returned to their stand to find that the buck they were hunting walked by their stand while they were gone, leaving his sign as tracks, droppings, or a new scrape or rub nearby. Deer get restless just as we do. Although the noon feeding time is of the shortest duration, deer do go "out for lunch."

Deer which have bedded down all morning after feeding at night will get up to stretch their legs and have a midday snack before again reclining to wait for the onset of darkness and safety from hunters.

Rutting bucks will move all day and all night paying little attention to rest or food when there are does to be bred.

The vast majority of hunters believe that the only times suitable for deer-hunting are early morning and late afternoon. In most areas these are indeed the times that deer sightings are most frequent.

Hunters which I polled stated that they took their deer around 9 A.M. most frequently. This is due to the number of hunters and hunter movement in the woods at that time, as well as to the normal behavior of deer. Of the bigger bucks most were taken at midday.

Biologists state that there are three main times of increased deer activity in any given area. These times are early morning, noon, and night. Since deer-hunting is currently prohibited at night, this means that the three most likely times for the hunter to encounter deer are early morning; lunchtime, or midday; and late afternoon, or dusk.

Deer do sometimes feed heavily all day in colder weather and before a storm front. In the overall analysis, however, most deer feed just prior to nightfall, during the night, and at daybreak and then bed down all day.

Some hunters position themselves where deer are likely to be at specific times of day. A good example of a favorable hunting position is the forest edge where trails emerge as they feed and socialize at night. At such intersections the hunter may intercept deer anxious to return at dusk or exit at dawn. Here scouting for hoofprint directions should have revealed whether the trails were used primarily for entering or leaving the feeding area. The deer may use the trails for both access and departure, but more often, they have separate trails for these processes.

Proper deer scouting should reveal the right place for the hunter to be at the right time. This is not always a matter of the hunter using his reasoning power but is also a matter of instinct. A man's intuitive sixth sense is a far better guide for locating deer than pure reasoning ability. The hunter who learns to compatibly blend his hunches with reason and acquired knowledge is the most successful. The best hunters are the ones who tell tales such as, "I got a feeling that the buck might be in a little thicket in the middle of the field, so I circled downwind of the spot and sneaked up on it through a ditch so that the deer couldn't see me."

A good place for a twilight stand is near, but set back a little from, a feeding area. Deer often hide in logged-over areas with hard-to-hunt treetops everywhere overgrown with saplings and briars. As nighttime approaches they often move in closer to the agricultural crop, or to the standing timber. In areas of high visibility nearer human habitations or locations with high hunter pressure, the deer usually remain inside the thickets until the cover of darkness. Deeper into the woods, they may show more freedom of movement. When there is a full moon twilight is a very active time for deer, as they will most likely be moving all night. The very last moments of daylights are the only times when nocturnal bucks show their faces. You've really got to be in the right place at this time to get these animals.

When you have hunted all day without success the last few minutes of daylight are intense. The countdown brings heightened energy focused upon success in the last minutes. I have taken deer when the temptation to get up and head for the truck while there was still light was almost overwhelming.

Drawbacks to hunting late are mosquito attacks in early season, a more difficult walk back, and the possibility of having to follow a blood trail in the dark.

BAROMETRIC PRESSURE

The barometer is an instrument used to measure atmospheric pressure. Cold, dry air registers higher on the instrument than warm, wet air, which has less weight. Thus, larger air masses of cold, dry air are called "highs," and masses of warm, moist air are called "lows."

Understanding the barometric readings can alert deer hunters to times of increased activity in the woods. Deer movement increases greatly just prior to and after thunderstorms. A change in the atmospheric pressure which results in a low or falling barometer puts deer on the move. These changes in weather can be predicted by deer through their barometers, the ears, and other pressure-sensitive parts of their bodies. Over generations, deer have been conditioned to respond to the feelings their ears detect by preparing for impending foul weather and for the moves they may have to make to seek protective shelter. For example, they will instinctively turn to the getting of food while the "getting is good."

Moist, still, and warm atmospheres preceding a rain increase a deer's ability to collect scent molecules in its nostrils. Low barometric pressure puts scent lower to the ground, the area inhabited by deer, within their nosing height. With the increased ability to detect scents, deer will move.

It is clear and indisputable that deer hunting is better when the barometer is falling.

If you are at home, you can get a barometer reading from the television weather report or from a barometer of your own. If you are in a camp situation a good barometer is a camp fire. Fire smoke will rise higher during barometric highs and lower during lows. If the smoke filters through the woods instead of rising above the trees, you will have good hunting weather—if, of course, you didn't run off all the deer with the smoke.

RUT

"Rut" is a word used to describe the breeding season of the polygamous whitetail deer. It is the period when the doe is receptive to the buck for mating.

The period in which the doe is receptive is called the "estrus." This period lasts for a short 26 hours; the doe is in heat for only a short time. Different does in a given area come "in" at slightly varying times, but all within a period of a couple of months in the fall. The rut is as short as two weeks in cold climates and it is spread over greater time duration in the South.

During this period the libido of the buck may overcome his higher psyche. The buck may blow it over sex. He is carnal and "horny." This appropriate word may have originated as a description of buck behavior.

Bucks leave their territories in search of receptive does, running from one group of does to another fulfilling the powerful mating urge.

The area a buck travels in search of does is dependent upon their availability and may range from five to twenty miles square.

Each rut is divided into three periods:

1. Pre-rut
2. Peak-rut
3. Post-rut

Although the deer follow a biological time clock to rut, this clock is powered by the weather. The rut is based on timing in such a way that most fawns are born after cold weather is past. Shorter hours of daylight in the fall trigger the rut. The adrenals, the thyroid, and the testicles are the glands which start the sex drive, and they are activated by the amount of sunlight entering the eyes of the deer. As daylight shortens in the fall, those glands release hormones into the blood stream. This brings on the estrus cycle of the doe and causes the testicles of the buck to drop and fill with semen. In the pre-rut the thyroid causes the neck to swell to ten or more inches in diameter larger than normal, and the pituitary causes the antlers to stop growing and the velvet to dry up and harden.

The buck is ready to mate a month before the doe.

Biologists can forecast the rut with a measure of success. Unexpected weather conditions can alter their predictions. The strange things that have been happening with our weather over the last decade seem to become more unpredictable each year. A lot of dark and rainy weather in the fall prolongs the rut. Drought delays it. Sometimes there are even two rutting periods as a result of the weather conditions.

Although colder weather does not start rut behavior, lower temperatures do make deer more active in all respects, including sex.

RAIN AND SLEET

Under normal conditions, deer move less in inclement weather, preferring to nestle under cover. If the hunter does desire to hunt in this weather, he has a much greater chance of getting a deer than he would if he too were nestled at home under cover as the deer probably are for the most part.

Deer do not like to move and expose themselves to possible danger when the wind is high. Deer seen traveling are few and far between on very brisk days.

Although whitetails can handle exposure to some of the worst weather extremes imaginable, they prefer the soft life. On very windy days, expect deer to be behind windbreaks such as protective ledges, or look for them in lower places with good shelter.

On winter days deer favor coniferous cover on southeast slopes.

A great rainy-day place to hunt deer is from a barn loft. Deer sometimes even enter old, isolated barns for shelter. Some hunters build rain shelters for hunting in this weather, or they cover their tree stands with roofing material. When scouting make note of old blown down buildings. Inspection of these places usually reveals deer beds in the dry dust patches beneath the old barn tin. Look through the dust for white deer belly hairs.

An umbrella is a good tool for a rainy-day hunter. It can be a camouflaged umbrella with a little spray paint. Since the shape of an umbrella is foreign to the woods, environmental blending is necessary. There are camp umbrellas available which are made with a slot designed to fit around a tree for the portable tree stand hunter. There is also a stand umbrella which is rigged with an extension arm and tree band so that it protrudes farther from the tree trunk. That handy piece of polyethylene plastic that you brought along for a ground cloth may prove useful as a makeshift rain shelter.

Hunting during lightning storms requires caution. It is believed that lightening strikes the highest object in a general area. If you are in a tree stand hunting this may be your tree. If you are on the ground and touching a tree or are very near a tree which is hit, the electrical discharge can afflict you also. Don't think that you can climb a lower tree than those surrounding you and be free from lightning bolts. Lightening comes from the ground up and takes the most direct conduction route so it is not always the highest tree it chooses. If you choose to brave an electrical storm perched from an elevated tree stand then the beech is the best choice. For some reason beech are the least often struck by lightning. If you desire to take cover under a tree in the forest then select the beech.

Wool garments are good for hunting in such weather. They can be completely wet and yet continue to provide warmth, as they did for the sheep. Water-repellent, protective rain gear is available in hunter colors and a wide assortment of designs for all types of weather.

Rainy days are good days to stalk and still-hunt. Go to the deer instead of expecting the deer to come to you unless you have chosen a well-used dry bedding site.

The kind of place where one of us might go during a storm to keep dry is likely to be the kind of place a deer will go. I once sought shelter in an abandoned farm house which was overgrown in the deer woods. I entered the front door of the house and surprised a very large buck (and myself) which went out the back-door. These abandoned dwellings belong to the deer now, and are a part of their landscape. Hunt such places in the rain. A long, soaking rain will cause deer to hold up in whatever dry areas for a long time. A heavy downpour may be just the right opportunity to creep up on such a place. The pouring rain will diffuse your scent and knock it out of the air. The sound of the rain will mask the majority of your sounds. Deer will not be expectant of hunters since most people are trying not to be "too stupid to come in out of the rain."

Spells of hot weather which often invade deer seasons cut down on deer activity. Such weather is easy on hunters, but seasoned hunters far prefer the cooler temperatures. Warm weather prolongs the rut and slows down rutting behavior and subsequent buck movement. Deer will move to shady areas in hot weather. During these periods of unusual autumn weather, the deer will be located in cooler areas near stream bottoms.

In a moist, warm, and still atmosphere such as a stream bottom, the deer has a keen ability to detect smells. For the whitetail, there is nothing more comfortable than being able to use its nose at peak performance.

The ideal conditions for a deer's scenting ability are humidity levels at 40—50%, temperatures at 40—60 degrees Fahrenheit, with light breezes of 5—10 M.P.H. or less and the barometric pressure falling.

High temperatures produce thermal air currents which make scent rise. These convections carry scent molecules upward before the deer can pick them up.

High humidity, exceeding 50%, increases whitetail activity. Whitetails are able to detect smells over great distances with moisture in the air holding scent molecules at lower levels. Deer are more alert and aware during these conditions and subsequently harder to hunt.

Low humidity, below 30%, hinders deer activity. Low air moisture dries out the deer's nostrils and prevents its nose from working at full capacity.

Excessively low temperatures during cold spells push scent molecules to the ground, keeping the scent out of the air. Deer travel less under these conditions, when scents are not flowing through the woods. Deer encountered in adverse conditions of the extreme are nearly always spooked or driven. You are better off at home.

Deer are active in fog. The fog affords security from long distance rifle shots. Bow hunting in the fog is lucrative. Foggy conditions enhance scenting, hearing and require less visual strain for whitetails. Be sure to not draw your bow or point your firearm at a dark movement within the foggy veil until you are absolutely sure of your target being a deer.

Deer hunting is best during the darker lunar phases. Whitetails spend less time moving about at night with decreased light. A full moon hunting day will be best looking for deer in the middle of the day, when deer moving at night have bedded for the morning. Early morning and dusk are more productive during dark lunar phases.

Accessories & Necessities

PLASTIC BAGS

There are many uses for bags of different sizes and types on the hunt and especially in the camp.

Garbage or lawn sacks are handy. They are primarily used for trash, your own, the deer remains, or someone else's unsightly litter which you took it upon yourself to pick up. Lawn bags may be converted to makeshift ponchos by cutting arm and head holes. They can be torn open and put under a deer in a truck of the car or back of the truck. They can be used as boot liners to waterproof boots, as can bread sacks. They can be used as a manure bag to contain a scent pile for boot-scenting with little mess. They can be used to put clothes in to scent them with cedar, pine, or something else appropriate. They can keep a change of clothing scent-free and dry. A plastic bag can be a good ground cloth for sitting on the damp earth. Keep a supply under the seat of your vehicle.

There will be a use for them. Buy the large, heavy-duty kind and carry along some smaller ziplocks and bread sacks. Our Native American predecessors would have traded great wealth for a box of ziplocks.

DROP CLOTHS AND TARPS

A tarp or drop may be used to make a pull for retrieving the deer without tearing up the hide. It can line the trunk or bed or your vehicle to contain blood flow from the carcass. It can be used to crawl under the vehicle should it be necessary to tie up a muffler or pull out a stick in snow, gravel, or mud. It can be used for shelter as a makeshift tent. It can prove a useful wrapping for your deer to keep critters off of it while you get help fetching it from the woods. It can protect the meat from insects in warm spells. It could be used as a stretcher if you encounter someone injured. In short, a tarp or drop is just another good thing to have along.

LIGHTS

Lights with high candlepower will enable you to scout areas as night. For scouting fields with road access, the type that plugs into a cigarette lighter is handy. Permanent installations are availble which operate directly from the car battery. These lights have the added advantage of recharging the battery through the generation system of the automobile which means that you will not be likely to suffer from diminishing power at the crucial moment. High intensity lights are made for toting afield when there is no access for an automobile or it is thought an auto might be alertive. Car lights can be used in lieu of other lights but offer less flexibility. In any event, bright lights which cover a good distance should be used when spotlighting. When using a light, remember to avoid prolonged contact with deer. Whitetails do not seem to be bothered by lights in most instances, but overexposure to them or someone yelling "There's one!" will run them off. Deer which have not had encounters with poachers jacklighting them are mystified by "seeing the light."

Always use a flashlight when moving through the woods in darker hours to avoid being shot by trigger-happy hunters. If you are going in before dawn to hunt, then keep the light to the ground. If it is not an area of hunter activity, then use your flashlight less often, only when necessary. It is important that you turn the flashlight on occasionally, pointing it to the ground to alert any other hunters who may have come in before you from another direction. The luminescent rimmed flashlights are best for this. The red glow of the rim is clearly visible and recognizable to hunters.

A hunter walking over the hills to his stand from his vehicle with the aid of a flashlight before dawn is easily avoided by the intelligent deer, which has seen his car lights appear and cut off and observed the hunter making his trek to his hunting site. To avoid this situation be careful with your car lights. Cut them off before you turn in to face the woods. Let your eyes adjust to the darkness without them or use your parking lights while moving slowly. Carry a flashlight with you to the stand but do not use it except when you absolutely must. When using it, keep it down to the ground as well as you can. If you need to shine it up in the trees to look for your treestand, to judge a tree for a climbing stand, or to follow a trail, then you did not sufficiently familiarize yourself with the site prior to the hunt.

Flashlights should be non-noisy, non-leaky, compact, and unscented.

AXE, MACHETE, SAWS, SHOVELS

An axe is very handy to carry in your vehicle. An unexpected fallen log could block road access to your hunting spot or keep you from coming out. Chain saws are also good to have along when you are expecting to venture down small, less traveled woodland roads and pathways, but they can leak gas and oil smells which handicap your hunt.

A hatchet, machete, or handsaw, or perhaps a knife with a sawing side on the blade, can come in handy for the chores of cutting obstructive limbs from shooting lanes or around your stand, making carrying or "tote" poles, cutting fill material for mud bogs in the road, or various other uses. You may need one of these instruments for splitting the connecting bones between the pelvis of the deer in order to pack the animal out of some deep crevasse or canyon quartered. If you thought to bring a handful of #16 common nails along and you should happen upon a select place for a tree stand then you can use the saw to cut material for the stand and steps leading up to it. Incidentally, steps cut from tree limbs need not be placed horizontally onto the treetrunk like the steps of a ladder but are less conspicuous and less apt to loosen if placed vertically, allowing the hunter to place his foot on the end of the round of limb.

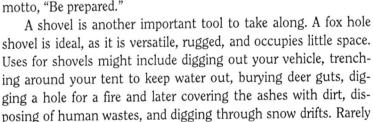

The automobile trunk usually has a little space where you can tuck in some of these tools just in case. Boy Scouts had it together when they coined the motto, "Be prepared."

A shovel is another important tool to take along. A fox hole shovel is ideal, as it is versatile, rugged, and occupies little space. Uses for shovels might include digging out your vehicle, trenching around your tent to keep water out, burying deer guts, digging a hole for a fire and later covering the ashes with dirt, disposing of human wastes, and digging through snow drifts. Rarely does anyone dig pits, or underground blinds to serve as hunting stations for whitetail, a practice reserved primarily for Great Plains animals.

A handy wire-type saw is available which will fit into a small pocket cannister. There are also fold-up gardeners saws.

WATCH

The tick of a watch can be audible to a deer in close proximity on a still day. The woods can become so still and silent that a pin dropping can actually be audible even to a hunter. Further, watches can shine and produce glare from the glass as well as the metal. They can also produce a sound by hitting your rifle stock or bow string at just the wrong time. If you need a watch to organize a hunt with other people, then carry it in a pocket and use a quiet watch. You can wrap it in paper to muffle the sound. The modern digital watches which are dull black plastic and do not tick are good choices.

 Some might be wise to leave watches, like neckties and briefcases, behind as they escape from this world to that of the whitetail.

PACK

A small backpack, shoulder bag, or gym bag is handy on the hunt. Backpacks and shoulder packs free the hands to do other chores.

Packs taken on the actual hunt might contain a peejug, a camera, some cord, food, water, extra clothing, or space for clothes you shed or any number of miscellaneous items you might choose to take along.

Blackpowder hunters traditionally carry a "possibles bag," a bag of supplies to allow for taking care of whatever might go wrong with the weapon. Regardless of weaponry every hunter should have the necessary tools available for quick repairs.

A good pack for an archer on a shorter hunt is the "fanny pack." This pack does not get in his way when firing. Packed right it will provide a comfortable cushion against trees when taking stand.

Packs or bags can be removed and kept handy at the stand site. All items in the bag can be kept scent-free by the use of zi-plock baggies.

A brown pack can also be sprayed with scent to attract deer and placed in the brush to function as a decoy to lure the deer's attention away from a hidden hunter.

A pack of some sort is a must for hunters who anticipate spending the entire day in the woods. It is a good move to have everything with you and to reduce the chance that you will need to leave the woods sooner than desired.

UNDERWEAR

Layering is the best way for hunters to seal in warmth, seal out wind and cold, and allow for flexibility and comfort.

Insulated underwear is best colored red or another bright color since the traditional white color might become exposed at the wrist, ankle, or neckline and alert deer or create a target for another hunter. In an emergency when the hunter has to empty his bowels, the white long-johns make a formidable target to white-seeking shooters. If you can't find colored underwear or, want to stick with your old white ones, then dye them.

Too many layers of clothing will make you sweat as you trek in, increasing your "odor" and your risk of hypothermia or a nasty cold. Stick with lighter layers until you reach your stand and then add the additonal clothing you need to stay warm when motion-less.

If you expect the temperature to become much warmer in the day, it is good to prepare for the long run and suffer a bit in the cool morning rather than have to remove every bit of your clothing to take off hot long-johns later on. Old moss horns could come shooting through at just that moment, and you would be a real sight hopping along naked after him. Layers should be arranged so that they can be quickly and simply added or removed.

Underclothing should be loose-fitting to allow for good air circulation, for an air space between the garment and your skin, and for comfort in awkward positions. Buy underclothes a size large for hunting.

Pantyhose are surprisingly effective for warmth and flexibility in deer hunting cooler weather. Football players use them, as do many construction workers. You can use some of your wife's old ones or pick up a pair at just about any grocery store.

Silk underwear may sound a little dainty to most of us hunters but silk is very comfortable and effective underclothing which will not overheat you and will retain warmth. Oriental cultures use silk in hot weather and cold. The investment in silk underclothes for hunting will prove worthwhile in the long run when the lasting properties of silk are discovered.

HATS

Hats are obviously necessary in cold weather or rain. Sun hats are also desirable. In the cold, a hat that can be pulled down over the ears is useful. Orange hats, or orange-camo reversibles, are a good idea. A billed hat will offer some eye protection from limbs and twigs in woods-walking. Billed hats have to be turned around and worn backwards when using a bow or some scopes on rifles. A sock cap or an extra sock cap are easily stored in a pack just in case. Heat rises and a great deal of body warmth escapes from the head.

NECK COVER

A good deal of heat escapes around your collar when you are sitting or standing. Take a scarf for your neck, one of the longer, woven types. This spot is often neglected.

A common mistake is to cover other parts of your body adequately but leave this vulnerable spot for heat loss and breeze infiltration uncovered and be miserable. You can tuck a scarf into your bag.

GLOVES

Rubber gloves are recommended for field-dressing deer. The longer the gloves extend up the arm the better. It is necessary to reach into the chest cavity to remove organ tissue which cleaves to the ribs, tissue which is very bloody and messy. These gloves can easily be kept in your knapsack and can prevent you from becoming a bloody mess and possibly coming in contact with parasites.

Hunting gloves in camp orange are ideal for cool-weather hunting, as are cotton jersey gloves with grip bumps. Whatever type of gloves you choose, be sure they have a good grip so they will not cause accidental slips or loss of your hunting weapon.

Shooter's gloves and archer's gloves are a good investment for the continual sportsman.

If your gloves are too clumsy to actually shoot with them, take them along anyway. It will be easier to get them off to shoot than it will be to get your cold, stiff fingers into action.

Pocket hand-warmers are good to have providing they are battery-operated, since fuel-operated warmers have a distinct odor and thus are not for deer hunters but for duck hunters and fishermen.

For those who just cannot be comfortable with any gloves when it comes down to firing a bow or a firewarm, a muff is a possibility. This tube into which hands are inserted will allow for warm hands to be removed speedily at the crucial moment.

BOOTS

Fortunately, many good-quality rubber boots are available to deer hunters. Rubber boots are the favorites of all but a few since they effectively reduce the odor the hunter leaves on the trail. This is of concern to the whitetail hunter since the whitetail is a back-tracking animal, an animal which is hunted at close ranges, and an animal that is most often hunted by ambush. Rubber boots can be easily washed free of scents.

Some of the new insulated boots can be relatively scentless and maintain a steady temperature hot or cold. Some boots have removable insoles to wash and air out. Clumpy galoshes that slip over your shoes are not the best idea nowadays. Buy quiet, comfortable, washable, waterproof boots with good strings.

New boots for hunting should be bought half a size larger than the appropriate dress shoe. This allows for foot swelling during hard walking as well as the wearing of heavy socks or the addition of felt innersoles.

Ask around, and check the boots out before you buy them. Some boots are not what the retail stores say they are. It is unlikely that you can "try them out." You can spend a lot of money trying to find the right boot for your particular hunting requirements if you just go in and buy whatever they have.

Cold feet can make you really miserable and send you back to the house. It is particularly easy to get numb feet when sitting still in an elevated tree stand on a cold fall morning.

Prepare your boots by putting them out in the cold weather rather than by placing near the stove before the hunt. This trick defies logic but it works.

Sprinkling baking soda into your boots helps to keep puffs of scent from escaping as you walk. Although white socks help to keep fungus from developing or spreading on your feet, they can be a hindrance if they are exposed while you are perched in a tree.

Boots should always be loose enough so as not to restrict blood flow, but not so loose as to invite blisters or other discomfort. If you are going to layer socks under your boots, then get them a full size rather than a half size larger. Extra socks in tight boots only complicate things by restricting blood flow.

Good quality boots which are well maintained and reserved for hunting only are the most satisfying.

Waterproofing compounds applied to leather boots should be allowed to air out for a few days before use when possible.

KEYS, WALLETS, GLASSES AND VALUABLES

Losing car keys, your wallet, your reading glasses or other important or costly valuables in the woods can be tiring. Hunt concentration may cause you to forget about them until you are ready to leave the woods, a prime way to lose them. On the other hand, keeping constant track of them will detract from your ability to focus on the hunt alone.

An alternative to carrying them with you is to hide them near your vehicle. Be sure to place them where a critter will not carry them off; some wild animals collect such things. Putting them under a rock that looks undisturbed is a good idea. Tucking them under a tire with grass or leaves is another possibility. If you do carry them with you, place them in a zipped pocket in such a way that they will not rattle.

Having extra keys sealed on the exterior of your vehicle is always a good idea. A magnetic box is used for this purpose. Locking your only set of keys inside your vehicle is an ordeal you don't want to go through when you're out in the woods.

You can carry your wallet sealed in a zipped pocket with no risk of losing it if it makes you more comfortable to have it. Keeping your hunting license on your person is required by law, and it may save you a trip to your car and a hunt disruption to have it with you. In any case, plan how you are going to handle these essentials and valuables before you find yourself in a bad situation.

A large rubber band wrapped around your wallet will help keep it from slipping out of your back pocket without detection.

FIRST-AID KIT

Every hunting vehicle should be equipped with a first-aid kit. Band-aids for knife nicks are great to have. A burn salve may prove useful for camp mishaps with fires and coffee. Hydrogen peroxide is handy for cleansing small cuts. A snake-bite kit should be carried along in seasons and locales where snakes might be in circulation. Extra matches should be included. Extra prescription medicine should be included. Eye wash is valuable to have for those occasional bugs, leaf irritants and foreign objects that get into your eye and irritate. Sterile bandages are a necessity. Syrup of ipecac, activated charcoal, and epsom salts are added for poisoning first aid.

KNIVES

Personal preference is the key in choosing a knife from the great variety available. Whatever knife you use should be very sharp. A dull knife is useless in field-dressing deer. Knives may be obtained with sharp hooks in the blade for field-dressing.

Many people collect knives and have a multitude of various types at their disposal.

Swiss army type knives are especially versatile gadgets.

For skinning the deer, the three-inch, rounded blade on a pocket knife is fine.

Some hunters think that a big, combat-type knife is necessary for cutting through ribs and splitting the deer's pelvic bone by pounding the heavy knife with a wooden limb. However, big hunting knives can be a nuisance. Climbing a tree with a long knife poking your middle is annoying. Big knives are not necessary for cutting deer throats. Trying to cut the throat of a live deer is a poor idea. The tough neckskin is the thickest part of the hide. A deer which you may want to have mounted is ruined by a throat cut. Deer do not need to be bled like a slaughtered hog. The deer will bleed sufficiently through the wound and the field-dressing cavity. Since the heart of the deer has quit beating, slitting the throat serves no useful function as it does in live animal slaughter. You can remove all the blood through soaking dinner-sized portions of venison in water.

If the beginning hunter does not wish to invest in a hunting knife or two, he can pick up an inexpensive common utility knife suitable for field-dressing and skinning his deer. These retractable knives have many uses around the house. Hook blades used for making roofing cuts can be stored in the handle cavity along with a couple of razor-edged blades. Pack the blades inside the handle with stuffing material to prevent a rattle.

ROPES

Ropes, cord, string, line, or wire are accessories that you won't want to be without. If you have a length of cord along, it seems that the law of supply and demand comes into effect and uses for the cord pop up everywhere.

Some possible uses for rope and cord are:

1. Hanging your harvest from a tree by the ankles, neck or antlers to keep it off the ground, air out, bleed, and to skin it.
2. Raising and lowering your rifle or bow from an elevated stand.
3. Devising a safety belt for use in a tree.
4. Making a tote pole or skid for transporting deer.
5. Replacing a broken belt or tightening the waist of trousers that loosened as you hunted.
6. Forming an impromptu sling.
7. Tying down the car trunk for deer hauling but leaving an opening to allow air flow.
8. Rigging a tent or shelter.
9. Tying up the muffler that broke loose on a logging road.
10. Pulling out another vehicle.
11. Crossing ice.

SLINGS

Slings for your rifle are handy. Leaving your rifle in the woods because it is too burdensome when you are pulling out your deer may mean losing it. On the other hand, carrying out your rifle and leaving the deer may mean the loss of the deer. A sling will allow you to accomplish both chores at once.

A sling should be unscented, camouflaged, noiseless, and adjustable. Metal sling swivels should be taped in order to muffle metallic sounds.

Practice using your sling as a shooting brace. The sling can tie the rifle to the shooter's body to effectively make the hunter and his rifle "one." The value of a sling for rifle hunting cannot be overemphasized. Many experts agree that a good sling is more important for accuracy than a scope. Wrap your arm into the sling or form a loop with the sling for steady shots. When recruits are "snapping in" for the Marine Corps training many long hours are spent indoctrinating the value of the sling.

6

How To Hunt

SCOUTING

After determining the general area or areas where you will hunt your deer, the next step is to scout the area to locate the choice place to find your quarry. Scouting for deer is an art in itself. The principal objective is to put yourself in the best possible vantage point from which to harvest your deer.

Topographic maps and aerial photographs can help you to understand the lay of the land. When you have narrowed the possibilities down to a few hundred acres of land, you can benefit from a small investment in a map showing the land contours.

East of the Mississippi River, write:

Washington Map Distribution Center
U. S. Geological Survey
1200 Eads Avenue
Arlington, Virginia 22202

West of the Mississippi, write:

U. S. Geological Survey
Federal Center Building 41
Denver, Colorado 80225

In Canada write:

Canada Map Office
615 Boot Street
Ottawa, Ontario, Canada K1A0E9

The available maps can tell you a lot about your hunting area by indicating hills, valleys, and waterways. They help you to pinpoint apparent funnels that serve as escape routes from hunter pressure, probable bedding areas between agricultural crops and hardwood stands. It is best to have some idea of what lies ahead before venturing far into unknown territory. Even though you may not intent to go far at all, a working knowledge of land topography will help you to determine logical deer routes.

On flat land topographic maps are of little value. Here U. S. Forest Service Maps prove beneficial. They are not contour maps but will locate roadways, water, and other landmarks for you. For these maps write:

U. S. Department of Agriculture
Forest Services
Washington, D. C. 20250

Ask for brochure No. FS-13, "Field Offices of Forest Service." There are ten regional offices from which forest service maps may be obtained. Choose the office nearest your area of interest and write that office to request a map. Pinpoint the area in which you are interested as precisely as possible by listing state, county, and other information you can provide such as proximity to communities, road numbers or creek names.

Usually maps are available for study or purchase at the conservation agency for your immediate area. If not, the agency will know where you can secure them and provide any needed assistance.

The local courthouse can be another source of maps. The land office can show you where the boundaries are for local landowners within its tax division. You can view aerial photographs at the local county seat. Ask the clerk for help; he can find the map you need with ease. Although you will not see any deer in the maps, you can see vegetation which indicates certain stages of field or forest growth.

In some areas where cover is thick over large expanses aerial photos are used to determine deer numbers by biologists. The amount of available forage is directly indicative of the amount of game available. Fortunately, the maps are dated. Don't pay much attention to very old maps, since ten years can completely remodel a woods.

Detailed maps may not be necessary for the average hunt of short duration. But when you are really out there to outwit an old buck, they are definitely part of the picture. After seeing or hearing of a notorious buck in a specific area, you will find these maps of terrific value in plotting his likely whereabouts come hunting season.

Maps can help you avoid getting lost or find your way out once you are lost. They are useful in planning drives and helping others who are lost to find their ways. They let you know what lies outside your familiar hunting area. They can help you to determine where an ill-placed bullet may wander. And they can be enormously useful in finding or removing an injured or wounded hunter.

Maps may not be for everyone, but they can save you a lot of footwork.

THE STRING METHOD

In scouting an area, you may want to use thread or very light fishing line to note the direction of deer travel. If the string is broken in the morning, it indicates the direction of the bedding area. If it is broken in late afternoon or before dawn, it indicates the way to a feeding area. Dispose of this material when you have finished scouting by the string method so that birds will not use it for nesting material. It could strangle their young.

TRAILS

Trails or "runways" may be merely occasional hoofprints found by the hunter brushing back leaves to expose them, or they may be trampled mud furrows similar to buffalo trails. A heavily worn trail is a great bet for apprehending a deer but is not a common sight in many localities. Overall, deer are creatures of habit only a quarter of the time.

Whitetails are both nocturnal and diurnal. They move about and feed both day and night. They are nocturnal for the largest part. So, deer runways must be investigated to see when they are used. It serves no purpose to hunt a night trail during the day.

In scouting a trail, the hunter does the opposite of a person who is stalking a deer to shoot it. The scouting hunter backtracks in order to determine what type of trail it is without alarming the deer. Unless the scouting hunter is intent upon harvesting a particular specimen, he wishes to avoid contact with the deer since he does not need to actually see the creature. If the trail started at a soybean field or a white oak grove or other area that contributes significantly to the deer menu, the scout knows it is a route from a feeding area to a bedding area. If the trail starts at a bedding area, then the scout knows it heads to a feeding area. By determining the use of a particular trail, the hunter can plot stand position and approximate time a deer may be expected to appear. It is a common mistake made by the novice hunter to simply locate a trail and decide that it is a select spot to hunt without more elaborate investigation.

The scout should try to stay off of a trail when following it by moving off to the side at least a few feet. When backtracking, it is best to be as scent-free as possible and to use a good masking scent. Deer can recognize human footprints, so try not to leave any on their trails. I know of no one who owns a pair of boots with tread similar to deer prints but such a design on boot soles would be a virtue. If it should become necessary to urinate, the hunter should move as far away from the trail as he can.

Some trails are seasonal. Deer do not use the same trails all year long. Be sure that any trail you plan to hunt is fresh.

For early morning hunting the hunter should hunt a trail that leads from a feeding area to a bedding area. During midday the hunter should position himself near the bedding areas to hunt the less directional trails indicating that deer stir and browse on them. In the evening the hunter should hunt the trail that leads from the bedding area on the feeding area.

Deer use cow trails too, so don't disqualify a trail because it is used by cattle or horses, but examine the trail for deer tracks mingled in.

When hunting a trail, match the areas to either side of the runway for approaching deer. Alerted deer will often avoid all trails, choosing to take a more difficult path which offers more concealment. It is quite surprising to observe a deer walking a few feet to the side of a trail to keep its scent off the path like hunters do.

The trail hunter might expect that a wide-racked buck deer would simply have to choose to take the easy trail to keep his antlers from getting in the way. The truth is that a monster buck can go through tangles with astonishing ease. The rare cases in which bucks get their antlers tangled up occur in fights with predators or other strife.

When backtracking a trail it is preferable to head downwind.

Trails may be located on foot, by horse, by driving rural roads and looking for crossings (especially at muddy embankments), or by boat. It is true that deer are not afraid of horses, but they are extremely reluctant to be around a hunter on a horse. Horses do eliminate the hunter ground-scent problem when scouting. Tied up and positioned well away from the hunter, horses also make good diversionary decoys. The sound of a horse approaching may not be alertive to deer and may actually be inviting to them, but the sight of a hunter riding on the horse is a terrific fright. Perhaps the deer think that the rider may try to ride them as well.

The approximate time when deer use a particular trail can be determined with the help of a trail timer. The timer measures the exact time but deer follow no time schedules. These devices are available by mail order or through sporting goods shops.

WHEN A GROUP OF DEER WITH DOES IN THE LEAD ENCOUNTER A PATH WITH UNUSUAL SCENT, THE DOES WILL SUMMON THE BUCK FROM GUARDING THE REAR TO MAKE THE DECISIONS. THE DOE IS THE LEAD ANIMAL UNTIL DANGER IS IMMINENT.

The string method (mentioned in the section on scouting above) is an older one that can be used to reveal the passing of a deer. Thread or ultra-light fishing line are good indicators of trail use for a hunter who has time to check up on them and who travels the trails without leaving too much scent. Observing spider webs is a more natural stringline scouting method. It doesn't take long for most spiders to reestablish a web so it might be ascertained that the web was broken in the last two hours if it is not refurbished.

In areas with pressure from hunters or from dogs and coyotes, escape routes are sometimes trails. The best escape routes connect two pieces of ground to help the deer complete a large circle. Escaping deer usually like to head to high ground to keep an eye on things below and to slow down attackers. I hunt one escape route which is on a hilltop with a four-foot chain link fence on top. The fence bottom is tight with no place for dogs to run or crawl underneath unless they go a couple of hundred yards down the fence. The deer hop the fence with ease and use the spot with such regularity, while avoiding the pesky farmer's dogs, that the spot is prime hunting.

PATIENCE, DISCIPLINE, ENDURANCE

The patience and discipline acquired through deer hunting are rewards in themselves. Serious deer hunters often maintain motionless, yoga-type positions with deep meditation for hours at a time. There are those who remain perched in a tree from before dawn until after dark, moving very little.

Of the two basic types of deer hunting—outwitting and out-waiting—outwaiting is the more successful.

Being still and in solitude builds up the hunter's endurance. Some hunters hunt for several seasons before they actually harvest the deer they want.

And it takes tremendous discipline. Most of those who do it

have to force themselves, for very few of us are naturally equipped with such patience.

The hunter who walks about the woods hunting deer also has to be very patient to do the job right.

Some situations in deer hunting are true challenges to overcome. For instance, a hunter intent upon taking a buck home in a given hunt might have some does come in and bed down right below his treestand. The hunter realizes that the slightest sound or movement will send them off. He knows they are the best of attractants for male deer. He also knows he must hold his urine until the buck comes. Many such situations arise for serious hunters.

Even the casual hunter gains mentally, physically, emotionally, and spiritually from a hunt.

SCRAPES

"Scrapes" are spots on the ground pawed out by deer seeking mates. These are usually situated on the forest floor but may occasionally be found in pastures, in sand, or on dirt roads. Deer use feet and antlers to create the clear patches of earth.

Does do make scrapes, though not commonly. Doe scrapes are most frequent when there is a clear-cut absence of male deer. A scrape is evidently a doe scrape if you observe the doe making it. Other hints may be the absences of a "licking branch," antler tine marks on the earth, or rubs nearby. Doe scrapes, however, are quite rare. As a rule, the hunter should consider all scrapes as an indication of buck presence.

In scouting during the rut, finding scrapes will help the hunter locate a buck. A scrape, or better yet, a series of scrapes, is a sure sign of a good hunting location. Position your stand, or stands, 40 yards or more away from such a place and downwind for gun-hunting and 25 to 40 yards away for bow-hunting. Deer will check on the scrapes they have made at least once every three days, usually every day. Bucks will check the scrape until they get a date with a hot doe, who left her calling card, then mate, and return to the scrape to seek a date with another receptive doe. At night deer will tend their scrapes when hunter pressure is obvious, keeping them in defensive cover all day.

The most common scrape is in leafy cover under a low-branched oak tree. Generally they are on the edges of forests where the deer are most frequent. Basically deer are "edge" animals. Edges provide more dense security, lower and newer forage, and transition spots from one terrain type to another. Scrapes are, however, often placed along ridges and hilltops or other natural runways for deer in the deep forest. Deer place the scrapes in the places most likely to be encountered by their kind.

Scrapes made by bucks are of three different types. These are:

1. *Territorial or boundary scrapes.* These scrapes are long and thin instead of oval or round. They are usually made at night soon after the velvet is shed from the antlers. These scrapes are mostly made by young bucks, mostly yearlings, feeling a first, confused stirring of their hormones. These scrapes are not usually revisited, so they will soon be covered with leaves in forested areas. Territorial scrapes are not the choice place to hunt. They do indicate the presence of a buck deer but that of a young one.

2. *Secondary scrapes.* These scrapes occur near the rut. They are rounded or oval, two or three feet across, and deepened. They are made at night. These scrapes are made by more mature bucks to inform does that they are available for courtship. After a rain a buck goes back and freshens all his scrapes. If it has rained all night, then an early morning stand at a secondary scrape is choice.

3. *Primary scrapes.* Primary scrapes are at least three feet across. These scrapes may reach seven feet long. They are dug out a few inches deep and really worked over. If the ground is

hard, of course, they will not be so deep. Primary scrapes appear year after year. This is because they are always located in a breeding area. The same buck will use the scrape year after year as long as he is dominant. When he is harvested or otherwise ousted from his position as dominant buck, another dominant buck will take over the scrape location. These scrapes are the best to hunt. When the hunter has not made his presence known, there will be good deer traffic here in the daytime.

Scrapes may be as small as one square foot to as large as twelve square feet. They smell musky and earthy. A hunter with an average nose can sometimes locate a primary scrape by the strong deer odor. Hunters will find more and larger scrapes as the season progresses.

Bucks making scrapes urinate on them. They rub their hind legs together and let the urine flow over the smelly tufts of hair on the hind legs called the "metatarsal glands" into the scrape. The bucks also leave a hoofprint signature. Sometimes this is one very neat and well-placed print right in the middle of the scrape made with the same type of deliberation with which famous actors and such place their names in concrete in front of the Chinese restaurant in Hollywood.

The bucks sometimes scrape their antler tines through the finished scrape to show off their fork spread. It is like filling out a data sheet for a matchmaker's dating club. Deer are able to sort out all the data to tell them the sex, breedability, age, size, diet, and general appearance of the animal making or visiting the scrape. Does leave their marks by urinating on the scrapes and over their tarsals and by hoofprinting. The "interdigital gland" between the toes of both sexes also has a distinct individual smell.

Bucks rub their antlers on overhanging branches when these are present, depositing scent from the "sudophorus" glands between their antlers on the skull and excreting scent from the "pre-orbital" glands above the eyes on these branches. They also lick them, leaving salivary "pheromones" to further emphasize individual scent distinctions. These "licking branches" will be four to seven feet above the scrape. The buck may stand on his rear legs to reach it. If a limb is raked and chewed by many deer, you are on a hot spot of overlapping ranges and dominance struggles.

The buck deer looking for a date or the doe in fervent heat may sneak up on the scrape bellying down if it detects predator vibes or scent, or if it has been spooked, taking a very cautious risk—providing that the deer has not located the hunter himself. The mating urge often overpowers the survival instinct of these highly reproductive-minded animals. These deer that come sneaking in to a scrape will be doing their best to be unnoticeable. They have an uncanny ability to "get small." From a tree stand, such a quiet deer may look more like a mouse than a deer at first.

Bucks in the rut which are really anxious to check their scrape which have seen a hunter take his stand will usually wait until the hunter leaves. The hunter can go to camp for a half-hour lunch and return to find the scrape worked over.

"LICKING
BRANCH"

"Mock scrapes" are a popular method of hunting deer. Mock scrapes are made by hunters. Their purpose is to lure the dominant buck to the scrape to challenge the intruding deer which dared to invade his domain. In the 1990s mock scrapes will be a rage. They are usually scented with strong sex scents. Some hunters go all out in making them, even transplanting parts of scrapes from other locations, such as some of the earth or the licking branches. Watch out for mock scrapes. Check out the scrape you are planning to hunt. It may not be real. When you go to hunt it you may find a portable-stand hunter above you.

If a scrape has not been tended in the last few days, it is probable that the individual buck has been harvested.

Licking branches are used by buck deer year-round. They need not be associated with scrapes except near or during the rut. Hunters who have observed several licking branches closely learn to recognize these disturbances in the woods when scouting before and after deer season.

RUBS

"Rubs" are trees, shrubs, and branches used by bucks to remove the velvet crust of their antlers to expose the hardened jewel headdress for sparring and show during mating. Rubs are also made to mark off territorial domain. It is the territorial rub which is of major concern to the hunter. Bucks rubbing velvet usually choose fallen tree limbs for this purpose. These "velvet rubs" are found in early scouting since they are made prior to the hunting season.

Territorial rubs can sometimes be spotted from interstate roadsides as they glisten in the sun. Their newly-exposed wood stands out like a sore thumb.

A lot can be surmised about a buck by examination of the rub. Some aggressive bucks demolish a whole thicket in an awesome display of power. These are usually the scenes of "mock battles." A buck which has managed to wipe out an automobile without severe personal injury to himself will sometimes make these massive and destructive rubs while he is in a state of shock and feeling macho, indeed, from his encounter with the vehicle.

Most rubs take place on tree saplings one to two inches in diameter. Some rubs are simply tine point scratches artistically etched into the bark and not dramatically obvious. Others are very bold. Staghorn sumacs and cedars are the trees most commonly used for this purpose. About any sapling or younger tree will be used by the buck as it is apparent that location plays a greater role in selection than does the plant variety. Evergreens and other spicy trees are often used by the buck to perfume himself while mating. The sap from pine is collected on the antlers for rosin. The rubbing of cedars also aids the deer by repelling pesky gnats and flies from the eye area. Some bucks so like to mark cedars that they will mark every one in their home territory, killing a few of them. Bucks prefer saplings with no lower limbs for rubbing.

THE "RUB"

The size of the tree can be, and is generally considered to be, an indicator of the size of the buck. This is, however, not a rule due to the hormonal changes of the rut and variability among individual personalities. The biggest rubs are normally found later in the season. They are made during the peak of the rut and into the post-rut. Fencepost-sized rubs do exist. When you can barely touch your thumb tips and middle finger tips together in measuring the girth of a rub you have good reason to be excited. The hunter can be fairly certain that a tree with a large diameter that has a rub on it about chest high is made by one large buck deer and not a small one. On the other hand, a small rub on a smaller tree that is only faintly scraped by the antlers does not necessarily indicate that it is only a small buck which has made the rub.

Examining the hoofprints under such rubs may further attest to the size of the deer. Rake the leaves around and feel the ground for print size. Rubs do definitely indicate a one-time present of a buck. Freshness should be easy to determine by coloration and feel. The only exceptions to rubs being a good sign of a buck territory are those made by the rare antlered does, which make velvet rubs but not territorial rubs, and the mischievous deceptions placed out there to lead hunters astray by human beings. Deer do not have to rub most of their velvet off since most of it just peels away and drops off. Although unnecessary for velvet removal, velvet rubs are very common since whitetail bucks are quite vain in their concern about their appearance. What self-respecting buck wants to walk around with trashy looking antlers anyway?

An individual buck has a fairly consistent rub style, the characteristics of his personal "signature." His rubs remain nearly the same everywhere he makes them in a given year. They may change from one year to the next as the buck matures. Fully mature bucks vary little in their rub characteristics annually. In searching out all the territorial rubs of a buck, the hunter can clearly determine his area of dominance and probable whereabouts.

Rubs usually mark the outer boundaries of a particular buck's territory. Occasionally a hunter will encounter a thicket where an obvious boundary dispute has occurred between two or more bucks, as when property owners squabbling over their property lines move each other's stakes. Such multiple rubs of different designs are sometimes an indication of a good buck population and make for good hunting. Most rubbing areas will have old rubs from the previous year nearby and those from years gone by less obviously present. These might not have been made by the same deer year after year, but in some instances this is so. Some very old bucks are located through old rubs alone by early scouting.

There are locations where buck populations are large but no rubs are to be found anywhere. This is usually the case of feeding grounds, which are usually neutral territory in the social circles of deer. For a buck to stake a claim here would be a violation of whitetail law. I have repeatedly observed one old buck that makes an enormous rub each year after the rut and hunting seasons have past. I cannot help but think that the buck makes this particular rub to let me know he is still there.

Rubs themselves are not preferred places to hunt by taking an overlooking stand. Bucks do return to territorial rubs to freshen the scent deposits from their sudophorus and preorbital glands and activate the boundary, but they are unpredictable in this maneuver. If the hunter is really enthused by the display left by the rub, has encountered a territorial dispute, finds rubs and scrapes together, or perhaps rubs, scrapes, and beds, then he will be readily inclined to hunt the area. Bucks do not normally hang around their rubs and use them to cover areas that they do not oversee by their presence.

It is probable that deer realize such sign stands out boldly to hunters, since very old and experienced bucks leave no rubs yet are still often dominant breeders. Bucks will be closer to rubs when the area they can claim is small as in the case of an island or a small woodlot in farm country.

Be aware that false rubs are sometimes made with knives or other human devices. Some consider it a good joke to make a massive rub and scrape to waste your time. You will most likely encounter prank rubs and scrapes complete with hoofprints, but careful inspection will reveal telltale knife marks instead of tine marks. Some hunters make rubs in hopes of aggravating a dominant buck into spending some time on the hoof and out of hiding to search for the intruder. This practice is not without merit completely. I once came upon a small thicket of sumac bushes that had been skinned, broken and trampled by horses whose riders had harnessed to the bushes while they went hunting. There were horse tracks and horse droppings all around. The next year I happened to revisit the spot and found that the bushes had been skinned and broken freshly again but this time there were only deer tracks and droppings on the ground. I am left to surmise that the dominant deer decided to take over what he thought was a rub made in his territory by the uncommon horse.

After carefully examining rubs in different areas over a period of time, the whitetail hunter will learn the language of deer sign. Don't forget to use your nose. Some rubs you encounter will turn you on so much that you will never forget them.

BEDS

Beds are normally situated so that predators can be detected by sound and scent upon approach. Such places are seldom by a stream or busy road where noise detection is more difficult. Deer do choose to be able to see predators as well but this is the least concern for a pack or herd of deer because they have designated does keeping watch by standing guard with eyes, ears, and nose aloft. Single deer bedded down alone will rely on sight to a greater degree. They will sleep with their ears and nostrils uncovered and will usually select a spot to bed where present wind currents will be blowing in their direction from suspected predator entrances.

Deer have many possible bedding places in their selected ranges. For this reason beds are generally unproductive spots to stake out for hunting. If a specific area has proven secure to them, they will be likely to return to that general area to bed but unlikely to go to the exact same spot until the scent buildup from their last stay has died down. Take stand on a trail leading to the bedding area instead of right on top of the beds. Deer are very clean and scent-conscious animals who prefer clean bedding in the wild. Of course, this habit helps reduce parasitism, disease, and predation. Although deer do not normally use the same bed again and again, wintering "deer yards" are an exception, as are locations with limited possibilities for bed sites.

Beds are marked by pressed down vegetation or leaves. They are crumpled and cleaned places, sometimes under smaller trees. Log jams, especially tree-tops from logging operations, make good bedding areas when deer are wary of human encroachment. Honeysuckle thickets are popular with deer since they offer good concealment, cover scent when in bloom, and food.

BEDDED BUCKS ARE DIFFICULT TO SPOT SINCE THEY TAKE FULL ADVANTAGE OF AVAILABLE COVER. ALL THE SAME, A TRULY ACCOMPLISHED STILL-HUNTER CAN SLIP UPON A DEER IN ITS BED AND TAP IT ON THE SHOULDER.

A buck will bed down with does and sleep soundly with his trusted girl friends keeping vigil. Single, loner bucks will bed down most warily and will select sites where they feel they may defend themselves from predator attacks with their antlers. Big bucks with antler growth often bed in staghorn sumac bushes to camouflage their antlers. They have plenty of food in these bushes, which provide good wintertime forage for them. In the winter, glass or carefully eyeball all sumac thickets when scouting, still-hunting, or stalking deer. Big loner bucks will choose hilltop sumacs on small summits consistently and blend in with the antler-shaped branches to perfection. These big bucks will sit tight in sumac thickets all day when under hunter pressure and stretch their legs while lying down. It is the younger bucks that will have to get up and roam around a little. It is also the younger bucks that will give up their concealment to hunt does.

Hunt bedding areas and not specific beds themselves. Ideally, after scouting properly, the hunter will select a stand about halfway between a feeding area and a bedding area to intercept moving deer.

When groups of deer are bedded down together and there is a guard doe on duty, she might offer herself as a decoy if there is a buck bedded down with her. Her intention might be to lure an intruder into a chase away from the favored and protected buck. If you sneak into a group of deer and notice a very obvious doe standing broadside in the trail with her tail down tight, you can fairly well surmise that very near there is a buck in cover. That buck may be very close to you, perhaps between you and the decoy doe. When the buck discovers he has been detected, he will run for it as will all the others with flag aloft.

A successful stalk to a bedding buck can be a little dangerous. A startled animal will react defensively. The chosen defensive move is most always to run for it but some deer will attack.

DROPPINGS

Fresh deer droppings are sure "sign" of nearby deer. Any location which holds a significant number of deer will be spotted with occasional droppings. Next to actual sighting, fresh and abundant droppings are the most revealing evidence of good hunting locations.

When stalking or still-hunting, examining droppings for freshness can be the key to success. Soft droppings are recent. New droppings are shiny, so by judging the luster and the brilliance you can determine the approximate time the pellets were dropped by the deer. If the pellets have developed a crust, drying has taken place over some time period. The droppings can be gauged for warmth also. The outside of the oval will still be warm to the touch at your wrist. A warm dropping steaming in the snow can really make the still-hunter happy (if you can imagine getting overjoyed at a piece of dung!) The temperature, the wind, the sun, and humidity have to all be considered when studying droppings on any particular day.

The stand-hunter can use deer droppings to facilitate placing his stand also.

Deer don't just dump anywhere. They are very selective about where and why they leave their pellets.

Deer which have been alerted to a predator stalking them and which are planning to take evasive action by running, defecate just before they run. Deer accustomed to predation, which includes most deer, seldom defecate in their beds but are careful to relieve themselves of fecal matter before approaching their beds, which they try to keep as free from scent and bacteria as possible. Droppings found in beds indicate the deer was alerted and vacated in a hurry with no intentions of using that bed for awhile.

Deer leave droppings to communicate with other deer. This communication will be better understood in the 1990s as researchers pay more attention to this understudied subject in the wild.

If there are several groupings of deer droppings in a small area such as a specific spot on a trail, which can be judged by relative freshness to have been dropped on successive days, then the stand-hunter may choose to position a tree stand or ground blind nearby on the likely chance that deer regularly pause there. Groups of droppings on a trail usually represent a "rest" stop, where the deer routinely pause momentarily to survey the valley they are going to enter or otherwise check out the view ahead. These places are usually vantage points for scenting, sighting, or hearing.

Generally a number of pellet piles and tracks spread over an area of rather open forest floor indicate a "loitering ground." This is where the deer, after having fed, procrastinated while chewing the cud, before venturing farther into the woods or brush to bed.

Whitetails will deposit piles of droppings within sight of, but not too close to their bed. The usual distance of a pile from a bed will be 30 to 50 yards. The deer drop these piles at points that can be seen from their beds so that predators which stop to examine them will expose themselves. This trick is employed by wary whitetails on the side where their scenting ability will be poorest and they have to rely more on sight for predator detection.

Since deer are "ruminants," which means that they have a three-phase digestive system with three stomachs, they chew and digest their food so well that casual field examination of their waste material produces little information. Laboratory analysis is the only genuine way to tell exactly what the deer are eating. Only a few indigestibles (such as persimmon seeds, the majority of which the deer spit out) show up in field examination. Of course, a finding such as persimmon seeds or some of the smaller seeds found in the pellets does give you insight into current preferred deer forage locations.

One interesting bit of information obtained through laboratory analysis is that actual grass-eating or grazing accounts for only a very small percentage of the deer diet—3% or less. The deer you observe feeding in grass pasture are usually selecting the preferred herbaceous weeds and other flora from among the grasses. Good stands of wheat or rye grasses may tempt the deer into more voluminous usage if other food is not sufficiently available. Fescue fields are of no value to deer for food whatsoever.

It appears that a single deer usually drops about 12 pellet groups a day. This knowledge may be useful in estimating the number of deer in a location or the amount of time they spend at a site.

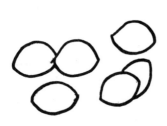   

1/2 — 5/8 INCHES   *1 1/2 — 2 1/2 INCHES*

DEER PELLETS — TELLTALE SIGN (ACTUAL SIZE)

Deer excrete very little waste material in comparison to the amount of food they ingest since they utilize their food so well. Most of what a growing deer eats is converted into deer meat.

Dropping size can be a good method for identifying deer size. Smaller ovals belong to smaller deer. Larger, matted chunks which resemble small horse droppings belong to larger deer, almost always bucks. A small oval pile next to a large oval pile with a matted layer pile grouped together and with the same freshness indicates that a doe, a fawn, and a buck are traveling together.

One thing deer communicate to other deer through their droppings is information about food locations. In their social structure deer look out for one another with a bond of brotherhood. The scent of a very healthy, sweet deer dropping will cause another deer to choose to join up with a particular group to share in their forage. Deer share their food well until it becomes scarce.

Collected droppings make a great masking odor for boots. Piles collected and placed in baggies can serve as first-quality cover scent. Nothing draws deer as well as other deer, so droppings make good attractant as well.

Deer, cow, horse, sheep, or goat manure all make good scent substitutes for masking human odor.

To utilize these scents, simply make a manure bag for stomping your boots into. Don't be concerned about getting the dung on the carpet at home or in your vehicle because it will wear off quickly while you are walking in the woods.

Fresh deer droppings (or droppings you have collected and frozen in a sealed container within the year) make useful deer-hunting tools. Fermented manure releases ammonia, which repels deer. So be sure that your collected manure does not ferment, and gather only fresh droppings.

For best results, spread the fresh wastes on the trail near mock scrapes, or place them near actual scrapes for hunting.

Although the wastes of a vegetarian animal are relatively clean, collect droppings with care to prevent possible health risks from bacteria or parasites. Never allow the droppings to come in contact with open cuts, abrasions, or, of course, your mouth.

FEEDING HABITS

Deer, like goats, are herbivorous. For this reason, in most of the East, deer do not compete with most livestock for food. In the more open range of the West, they do compete, especially with sheep.

Food preferences vary widely according to population levels, habitat, and availability of individual plant species.

*WHERE DEER HAVE ADAPTED TO THE
SUBURBANIZATION OF AMERICA,
THEY HAVE DEVELOPED A PREFERENCE FOR
DOMESTIC FOODS.*

There are different forage characteristics in the different regions of whitetail habitat, as plant species differ from North to South, East to West. Scouting the individual location should produce adequate information about what deer are eating in the specific area you are planning to hunt.

Many and varied are their foods, as deer are capable of dining on whatever is necessary for their survival. Deer, like all other animals, have food preferences and these tend to lean toward the best-tasting plants, shoots, twigs, barks, berries, nuts, and fruits. As a rule, whitetail deer will eat grass only when it is green and succulent.

Deer find many things to their liking that we, as humans, find distasteful or inedible. Such foods are almost always good for us in some way, and we would be more healthful if we did eat them. Deer ingest these wild plants and turn them into meat, an edible product in ideal form for human consumption. Deer eat foods that are free from chemicals, that are fresh and wholesome. When we eat venison we can be assured that we are consuming healthy food formed through a diet of natural herbs and other wild and healthy native flora.

I just feel truly sorry for those meat-eaters who balk at the idea of eating deer meat and especially for those who shun it through fear of what it may contain.

There are great regional differences in the normal feeding habits of whitetail deer. As populations reach high levels, in any given area, the most palatable foods disappear, followed in order by the ones less favored. Finally, as overpopulation reaches the critical stage, only foods of low nutritional value remain.

Deer eat 2 to 7 pounds of air-dry forage per hundredweight of live animal per day. Thus it can be said that a 150-pound deer will consume about 10 pounds of food a day.

The carrying capacity of the land on the national average is one deer to 32 acres of land.

Clear-cut forest areas produce the greatest amount of deer food per unit area in the form of undergrowth and new growth browse but produce less mast such as acorns, which only fall in more mature forest stands.

In some instances overpopulation and overbrowsing have caused the virtual disappearance of rabbits, hares, ruffed grouse, and wild turkeys. Almost any truck crop is eaten where deer are plentiful.

The following is a list of some of the more often utilized whitetail food sources, with preferred foods in italics.

Acorns, all varieties
alder
algae
andromeda
apple
arbutus
azalea
bearberry
beechnut
beggars lice
birch
black gum
blueberry
bog rosemary
brambles
buckeye
buckthorn
buffaloberry

cattail
cherry
chestnut
chokeberry
cinquefoil
clovers, especially red
club moss
coralberry
corn, especially sweet
lambs quarters

currants
dandelion
devils club
dock
dogwood
elderberry
ferns
fungi (mushrooms)
gladiolas
gooseberry
grape
green ash
greenbriar
hackberry
hawthorn
hazels
heaths
hemlock (trees, not plants)
hickory
holly berry
honey locust pods
honeysuckle
hops
horsetail
huckleberry
hydrilla
juniper
rose

larch	*rye*
laurel	sassafras
lespedeza	sedges
lichens	slippery elm
lobelias	sorrel
magnolia	sourwood
maple (sugar)	*soybean*
marijuana (hemp)	spicebush
mesquite	spruce
mosses	staghorn sumac
mulberry	sticktight
oats	St. John's wort
partridgeberry	*strawberry*
peaches	sweet pea
pecans	tobacco
persimmon	tulip
pine	viburnum
plantain	violet
plum	virginia creeper
poison ivy	walnut
pond lily	*watercress*
poplar	wheat
prickly pear	white cedar
raspberry	wild onion
rhododendron	woods grasses

The list goes on. It is about as possible to include all the foods which deer eat in this list as it would be to include all the foods that humans eat.

Many farms were abandoned because of deer depredations. Such old farms are ideal to hunt.

Deer movement is cut in half in an area that is being logged but increases by 300% later, the third year being the best for hunting.

Nutritive values of individual deer foods vary with the time of year and soil conditions. Protein content of deer food plants on recently burned forest areas is higher than in areas burned years before. Recent burns are good choices for locating large antlers.

At present, our knowledge of how to manage deer is far in advance of actual practice in most states. The only places where biologists are currently successful in developing workable programs are those game farms where they are hired to control the herd and manage for trophy bucks. The biggest problem is building up public awareness so that hunters will allow good deer management.

There is probably no other field of scientific study in which there are more self-professed experts than in game management. In far too many states, legislatures act under pressures from hunters, resort owners, and other lay groups rather than on the well-informed and considered recommendations of game biologists. The turnover of game management administrators, which is often the result of partisan politics, is one of the major obstacles to progress. It seems that as soon as someone gets the interesting job of running wildlife departments and learns to do his job well, someone else gets the job of governor and gives the wildlife management position to one of his supporters. Long-range planning based on sound biological principles and carried out by a wildlife department with the ability to sell the public on the program is the real solution to this problem in every state.

OBSERVING CATTLE MOVEMENTS

Watch cattle. If the cows are lying down, deer will probably be doing the same. Cattle have similar feeding cycles which are affected by the weather and the phases of the sun and moon. Cows, however, have no hunter pressure, so deer may be moving when cattle are not. Another difference is that ranchers often give cattle supplemental feed at regular times. Also, a doe in heat or a buck in rut will break these cycles. Generally, though, when the cattle are down, the deer are down also. When driving to your hunt, watch the cattle. If they are not up and about you can expect to see fewer deer. When this is the case, start out on a stand in the early morning, and use the rest of the day to stalk or still-hunt those bedding deer.

The brighter the moon phase, the more the deer are active at night. Around noon, deer which have been active all night and bedded down at dawn will move some. On nights when the moon is dark, deer may move more all day.

The height of the browse deer have been taking may be a good indication of deer size. After enough study of deer sign, you will be able to determine a lot about particular deer by examining the flora they have pruned. Deer do not maraud, with the exception of territorial bucks making rubs. Normally, deer are useful to the plants they choose to nibble from and do the plants service by trimming them. Some plants, such as the wild raspberry, rely on the deer to break their off-shooting canes to reproduce new plants as the deer forage on the leaves and berries. Thus deer prune bushes, trees, and plants instead of uprooting them or destroying them.

Deer are nature's gardeners. A good gardener knows that his raspberry canes will yield more and larger fruit if he cuts them back. This is exactly what the deer do. Except in areas overpopulated by deer, they do very little damage to agricultural crops. Much of the damage attributed to deer is done by groundhogs. Deer will eat a little bit of soybean leaf here and walk on down to eat a little bit of leaf or a pod or two there. A groundhog will unselectively consume entire plants. When the farmer sees deer tracks and doesn't spot the soft-footed tracks of the groundhog, the deer gets all the blame. In areas where deer are the actual culprits they should be harvested. I dressed a large doe which had just finished feeding in a soybean field. She had a pile of mature soybeans stomached that was larger than a basketball. If she repeated this behavior daily she would inflict significant damage. Few farmers can afford such luxurious feed for their livestock.

One plant that is making a comeback in the wild as a result of deer foraging is the ginseng plant. Hunters of this plant have caused the ginseng to all but disappear over most of its natural range. Deer have played a curious part in establishing this plant in new numbers, a phenomenon on which directly parallels the reemergence of the deer populations. Ginseng only produces one plant top from its prized, long-lived root in a year. In the spring and early summer, the deer like to eat the tasty leaves of the plant tops. This hides all traces of the root from ginseng hunters that year. It doesn't hurt the root. The hunter will not look for ginseng in that area again the next year since he found none the year before or since he harvested all there appeared to be in that area.

Deer which are about to raise their hands to look around while feeding will twitch their tails before doing so. If you are attempting to get within range of a feeding deer, watch for the tail twitch and stop motion when you see it. The deer will soon lower its head and resume feeding, and you can move again.

GETTING PERMISSION

In some states, it is the law that a hunter with a high-powered rifle must have written permission from the landowner on whose land he hunts. Although this requirement may seem bothersome, let us look at its virtues.

1. The landowner can limit the number of people on his land. This will make your hunting prospects better as well as safer. Rifles do fire projectiles that are capable of traveling considerable distances and ricochet.
2. He can direct hunters to specific areas and thereby limit hunter conflict.

3. By knowing when and where hunters are going to be on his property, the landowner can prepare domestic livestock for the hunt by placing them in protected areas, and he can keep his dog penned.
4. You need to know where you stand with the landowner. He could run you off or have you arrested for trespassing.
5. If you fail to secure the proper permission, the game warden could confiscate your deer or prosecute by various means.
6. If you placed a stand and went to it only to find another hunter perched there, written permission would be the principal determining factor in settling the issue of usage rights.
7. Permission can keep your vehicle from being towed away. Let the owner know what you will be driving so he will know just who has arrived. Many hunters have had their vehicles towed to the barn by a farmer who wants to be sure he has a chance to reprimand trespassers.
8. Some landowners have had bad experiences with trespassers. Some unscrupulous hunters have been trigger-happy and shot livestock for fun, for meat, or by accident. Some goats and donkeys have been shot in honest cases of mistaken identity but these are always a result of poor judgment or lack of communication with the landowners. Theft or vandalism during hunting season is always attributed to hunters.
9. In case of need, the landowner can offer you invaluable assistance.

If the private landowner does not reside on the tract you wish to hunt, you can find out who the owner is by visiting the court house. While there you can also take a gander at the aerial photos, topos, and boundary lines at the land office.

It is best to obtain written permission in person if possible. An impersonal letter or phone call may meet with less success, for most people prefer to meet those they allow to hunt on their domain. It is usually easier to get permission for no more than two people.

Approach the landowner with courtesy. Introduce yourself in a friendly and direct manner, and tell him or her what you are after, whether it is deer hunting in general, a deer for the freezer, or a trophy buck. Bowhunters find more acceptance overall since their arrows are short range, offering less hazard to others. If you are a bowhunter be sure to inform the landowner. If your intention is to hunt with firearms then conduct your conversation with safety, responsibility, and sportsmanship in mind.

If the property owner is a farmer who has had crop damage, he may be happy to see you. In fact, some farmers receive doe permits from the state government which allow the hunter to harvest an extra deer as a control measure. I have received permission from several rural residents who have had collisions or near-misses with deer on the local roadways.

If the landowner is an animal lover who enjoys watching deer from his dining-room window on snowy mornings, he may give you permission to cull the herd by taking an inferior buck for good game management.

Let the owner voice his opinion on the matter before you do. He may be negative about your hunt for some reason that you can easily dispel. He may also be encouraging and prove to be your best source for information about locating deer on his tract.

If he strictly forbids you to hunt on his property, he could be saving you from a bad experience. Hunters occasionally come upon illegal operations in remote and inconspicuous places. These situations can be dangerous. Marijuana plantings are commonly encountered by early-season bowhunters or gun-season scouters. During fall gun hunts, the marijuana is usually harvested, but the plantings are obvious due to the hidden locations and stalk stubs. If a landowner has given you permission to be on his land and you should happen to encounter such a planting, he would be happy to know that it is there and be left to do whatever he desires with the information. I am familiar with a situation in which a hunter was scouting land without permission who encountered a stolen car operation by accident. He was detected by an alarm system and was narrowly able to escape serious harm.

Give the landowner complete authority with respect to the use of his land.

For good measure, always ask if he would like some venison!

A good way to secure and maintain permission to hunt in a prime deer location is to offer labor help. The farmer may need some assistance mending fencing, filling potholes, pitching hay, cutting firewood, or something else of that nature during the year. Although few farmers actually take you up on it be prepared to do anything you mention.

Remember to send the landowner a card of thanks or an appropriate gift during the holidays.

If you shoot a deer on his property, he would probably like to see it. If you are unable to show it to him in person, send him a photo. Landowners like to know what comes off their land.

Ask him if it is all right to place a permanent tree stand or two in certain locations. If you plan to hunt by this method, let him know that you will not place a permanent stand in a harvestable tree. He may choose to guide you to a particular tree. Fence-row trees are usually good choices, for they are intended to stay for boundary markers and also have wire embedded in them which makes the trees unacceptable at the lumber mill. One nail in a tree is detectable at the mill. You may choose to use no nails.

He may prefer that you build your stands in trees of undesirable shape and species. These are usually the best trees for permanent stands anyway. He might also want the stand to be inconspicuous.

The landowner may want to avoid permanent stands altogether and only allow stand hunting from portables, taking no chances that you might injure trees and wishing no stands be left to invite other hunters to the location.

He may give you any number of rules and guidelines, which

you should indeed follow if you hunt there. Show him and his land all due respect.

Some landowners are reluctant to give written permission to hunt for fear of lawsuits. Many people are hesitant to do anything in writing. The landowner might know that an invited guest can sue if there is a dangerous item on the land that the landowner did not inform him of. The landowner is obligated to tell the hunter about any dangers on his land. Responsible landowners should, of course, take care of this situation by making their land safe, but this is not always the case.

The landowner may be unwilling to give written permission but still give oral permission to hunt. He may say something like, "I don't care about people hunting that woods, everyone does." Essentially he is telling you that you can hunt but that he does not want to be held responsible if you get hurt or hurt someone else.

Without a written permission slip, the hunter can be considered a trespasser. A trespasser is less likely to recover damages in a lawsuit. This situation is like a thief who breaks into a house and slips on a wet floor, breaks his leg, and sues unsuccessfully since he had the stolen goods in a bag. If he had innocently mistaken the door for his own and had slipped, however, he might recover damages since, technically, the door should have been locked. If he had been invited in and slipped he could easily sue. Landowners should make every effort to remove hazards from their property whether people are supposed to be on the land or not. Very dangerous situations like old wells covered with vines should never be allowed to exist unsecured.

"No Hunting" signs mean what they say. More often than not these signs are placed by the landowners to limit their own liability. They should always be respected. However, don't let "No Hunting" signs deter you from seeking permission. Often the owner will allow you to hunt when he meets you and sees that you are responsible.

Hunters have been known to put up such signs to stake a fraudulent claim to a hunt area although they are not the rightful owners of the land. In this case it is still better to find another place to hunt. To hunt near such a person is risky. It must be something else to find a "No Trespassing" sign posted by an unknown hunter on your own land!

Although you may be shot at while trespassing, landowners cannot legally shoot at hunters on their land. There is a famous court decision in which a landowner who was plagued with thieves breaking into a storage shed on his farm set a trap for trespassers by wiring a shotgun to the door. True to form, a young man broke into the shed, and he was severely wounded. Ultimately the trespasser, though guilty of breaking and entering, won a decision in his favor.

CATTLE, GOATS, HORSES

Deer are often located in transition thickets near cows or other domestic animals. Where the forest height gradually declines at the edge of a field, forage and cover are present, and the deer feel more security from predators due to the proximity of the farm animals. Deer know that the animals' scent masks their own odor and protects them from canine predation. In addition, they can keep an eye on man from these vantage points. Deer which have been subjected to no bullet fire probably feel security in assuming that if the livestock is unmolested then they might be likewise protected. Deer may also frequent the water, supplemental feeds, and salt and occasionally nibble the grasses. The barnyard animals may provide the deer with some comfort by attracting most of the pesky insects too. A cow field with accompanying agricultural crop next to a forest and water is an ideal spot to locate whitetails.

AS SOON AS TONY SAW ANTLERS, HE SHOT.
THE INSTRUCTIONS ON FIELD-DRESSING DIDN'T
TELL HIM WHAT TO DO WITH THE SADDLE!

In hunting these situations, be continuously mindful that you do not want to shoot a farm animal. These animals often escape their fence borders and wander the woods too. Always shoot away from livestock, and always be absolutely certain that what you are shooting is a deer. Some goats look quite a bit like spike deer or doe deer. You'll look pretty silly pulling into the check station with a prize milk goat. Moreover, a cow, horse, or goat might cost you more than you expected your hunt to cost.

FARMERS SELDOM TAKE SUCH DEFENSIVE MEASURES.

The killing of livestock is much more common than it should be. Those few unscrupulous hunters who purposely shoot livestock are a reproach to all and a true hindrance to good hunter-farmer relations. I once met a farmer whose land bordered a public hunting area who was bitterly opposed to hunters since the time he found a gunshot black Angus cow with a hind quarter removed. He had informed camping hunters that his farm was posted the preceding day and figured the lost animal to be a retaliatory gesture.

Ten percent of cow's diet is deer food. Goats and deer eat the same things, so they directly compete. Sheep have food preferences more like the cow. Hogs consume the mast crops that deer prefer.

AFTER PAYING HIS FINE AND MAKING RESTITUTION, THE COURT LET JIM HAVE HIS ANIMAL FOR MOUNTING.

A good way to approach deer which are foraging in a cow field is to act like a cow—like the Native Americans disguised themselves as buffalo. In the first rays of sunlight, in the moonlight of pre-dawn, or at twilight, the hunter who crosses a cow field should use the livestock to his advantage. This might include wearing black if among Angus cattle and walking on all fours. If you encounter the silhouette of deer in the darkness and they snort or paw or scamper at you before they hightail it, you can pacify them by resounding a bellowing *"Mooooo."*

Don't shoot over livestock because they can stampede at the sound.

*THE JUDGE WOULD HAVE DISMISSED THE CASE IF
JIM HADN'T FIELD DRESSED THE HUNTER HE
MISTOOK FOR A DEER.*

BUGS

What is the most dangerous member of the wild kingdom, the one that has killed the most people? It is not the crocodile, the lion or the cobra. It is the mosquito.

Cooler weather brings relief from the bugs. Deer love this, as do deer hunters. Most deer hunters do not have any worries about bugs. But during some warmer deer seasons, especially early bow seasons, insects can be a real problem.

Warmer weather hunting may require an insect repellent. Unfortunately, commercial repellents are very good at repelling deer as well. If the hunter is fortunate enough to find an odorless insect repellent he should buy it, although most repellents work by odor. Carry a repellent with you for those times that you absolutely have to have it. constant vexation by gnats and mosquitoes can ruin your hunt more readily than the smell of a commercial repellent. If you keep the repellent sealed in a baggie until it is needed you may be able to keep the scent down.

Commercial repellent for preventing chigger bites is best applied by putting a line of the chemical around the boot-tops, over the laces, and around the sock-tops. Run a line around the leg cuffs and up the seams of the trouser legs. Run a circle around the waistline and up the fly. Also treat the cuffs of your sleeves before setting off on those tempting berry-pickings.

A plentiful herb found in most deer locations which is useful for preventing chiggers is pennyroyal. This fragrant herb stuffed into boot tops is effective and won't alert deer excessively.

A string soaked in kerosene from your camp lantern can be wrapped around the pants and shirt cuffs for effective chigger protection.

Vitamin B-6 is useful for internally repelling mosquitoes. A swat at a mosquito is an alertive sound and movement, as those of us who have taken military basic training well know.

When hunting swampy and low-lying areas where mosquitoes are numerous, an effective natural repellent is calamus root. Break the root of the plant and rub the juice on the skin. The calamus is a swampy-smelling plant similar in appearance to a cattail. Although strong smelling, this plant will not repel deer but will likely attract them to cautiously investigate what is disturbing the calamus.

Ticks can cause serious problems to a hunter's health. Rocky mountain spotted fever is not as uncommon as most of us think it is and it is not restricted to the mountains of the West. And there are other infections and viruses which ticks transmit. Some tick bites can leave an itchy bump that lasts for a year. A repellent especially for ticks is valuable where they present a problem. "Deer ticks" are a common name for little ticks that can be encountered in large numbers. These are usually found in early scouting and can be a real nightmare. The baby ticks found near water in the spring and early summer can give you fits.

The common dog tick is not known to transmit Lyme disease. Lyme disease is spread by the deer tick. Deer pick up the parasite from another woods creature, the white-footed mouse. With the increase in deer numbers expected in the 1990s, we can forecast more instances of Lyme disease. Though seldom fatal, this disease can have dire consequences. The spirochetes that spread the disease can cause permanent brain injury as well as arthritic-type ailments.

Permanone is an effective insect repellent for ticks. It can be sprayed on clothing but not on the skin. Other insect repellents such as those containing DEET can be applied directly to the skin. Light-colored clothing is less attractive to ticks as well as mosquitoes.

It takes at least a few hours, and possibly as many as two days, for a tick to infect a human with Lyme disease. If you should find a tick on your body and attached, use a fine-tipped tweezer to pull it out, taking care to remove the head. Be careful not to squeeze the tick too tightly since this may cause it to inject the spirochetes into your bloodstream. Do not use alcohol or any other antiseptic on the tick before removing it. Place the removed tick in a container with a sprig of vegetation for future reference in case of complications.

The seriousness of the spread of both Rocky Mountain spotted fever and Lyme disease make the tick a threat to health which should not be underestimated. Hunters should check their bodies carefully after each day of hunting. Ask another person to check those areas of the back you cannot search!

Deer flies can be pesky. Some attacks by deer flies have been so bad that hunters have had to submerge in water to evade them.

Sweat bees can be an annoyance. Sometimes they are attracted to open sodas and fall in. Swallowing one can make a person's throat swell up so much that he will have to seek medical help.

Gnats and other small flying insects can release irritants into hunter's eyes and send them home.

Various caterpillars in the deer woods inflict surprisingly painful stings when disturbed.

Although they are not insects, spiders can be a problem. The two most dangerous spiders, the black widow and the brown recluse, are not very common to the woods itself but are often found around abandoned dwellings and woodpiles. There are many spiders which can cause aggravating sores from their slightly venomous bites. Shake out your boots. If your area is known to have scorpions you probably already know to do this.

As if these were not enough, there are also turkey lice, which spread and act like chiggers but worse. There are also ants. To break open a rotted log you are sitting on and expose a colony of ants can cause major problems. Fire anthills look inviting to sit on to those unfamiliar with their design.

During warmer weather, especially above 50 degrees, check your tree for bee traffic. Bees, hornets, or wasps could have built a nest in or underneath your tree stand. Look about the branches for hornet nests. Plug up hollow tubes of tree stands before placing them. Encounters with a hive of angry hornets could be tragic. Look out for hornet nests at head height when on the ground too.

Another problem connected with insects is that of flies attacking your harvested deer. Deer carcasses should be protected by material which allows air flow but keeps out flies. Wrappings for this purpose are sold commercially. A can of black pepper sprinkled liberally into the field-dressed cavity of the deer carcass will help also to repel flies.

One of the best solutions to the insect problem is to be properly clothed. The camo face mask is just the thing. These useful masks can be tucked into the shirt pocket and used to hide the face of the hunter as well as to keep pesky insects from running him out of the woods.

It is a curious thing that insects seem to be attracted to certain individuals more than others. The body chemistry, the scent, and the temperament of the individual seem to be the decisive factors. A calm hunter will attract fewer gnats than a sweaty and strife-filled hunter. It seems that insects play a role as guardians of the woods, fields, and swamps and notice things which are out of place.

DOGS IN HUNTING

Some states allow deer hunting with dogs. In some areas of the South it is completely acceptable to use dogs in "fair chase." In other locations, using canines is considered an unfair advantage and is illegal. Fair chase laws are instituted by the experts who are responsible for the regulation of the herd as well as for meeting the needs of the hunter population. When it is deemed necessary to keep deer populations in check at locations where thick scrub growth reaches for miles, a growth too dense to hunt on foot, then deer dogs become the logical hunting method.

Dog hunting is usually done with groups of hunters placed strategically on stands where deer are expected to flee from the hounds. Some hunts are over such large areas that radios are used by the hunters to coordinate their efforts.

Typically, dog-driven deer provide action shots at speeding targets. This is not always the case as many deer are reluctant to go blindly bounding off into other dangers when they are actually secure in their understanding of the whereabouts of the dogs trailing them. A deer is more likely to run completely out of the area when he is being followed by quieter, non-barking dogs and fast dogs then when he is being followed by barking and slower moving dogs. Deer hounds are usually bred for hunting deer.

There are many variations in types and preferences. Some hunters like dogs with long legs and others like short. The requirements for a good deer dog are mostly considered to be a good nose, a good voice, and the capacity for a short chase. Shorter-legged dogs make for shorter chases. Most hunters prefer their deer to remain within a reasonable distance and not run "plum out of the county." In hunting a very large tract of land longer-legged dogs might be chosen.

Deer use several evasive techniques to outwit dogs. The thrill of witnessing a good deer chase is unique to the sport.

1. Deer will *separate*, causing dogs or hunters to chase other members of the group.
2. Deer will *distance run*, by running a straight line completely out of the area. Big bucks do this most often, and it is the most successful evasive technique.
3. Whitetails will *zigzag or run circles*, exhausting the dogs, which will then pick up another trail.
4. Deer will *hold*. Here the deer wait until the dogs or the hunters driving them are very near, within a few yards, and then they break. This maneuver usually results in the dogs passing the deer and taking up a new trail while the deer doubles back.
5. Deer will use *habitat*. They may swim a river or otherwise use water to lose dogs. Jumping an irrigation ditch or ravine will throw dogs off the scent.

Often dog hunters release dogs from leashes when the hunters have jumped a deer of particular interest.

The hunter who frowns upon dog hunters altogether should take a visit to the South where these hunts take place and see what is going on. The dense thickets of young pine plantations, old clearcuts, hilly terrain, and swamps stretching for mile after mile will soon reveal the value of the hunting dog. Sporting hunt-clubs with true conservation-mindedness are the dog-hunt groups most often encountered. The hunt clubs that drive deer usually share the expenses and the harvest. The trophies go to the lodge wall or the individual who made the successful shot. The meat is divided among the hunters, with the person who took the deer in the group effort given first choice.

In some locations where dog hunting is permitted, some hunters, as a matter of personal taste, choose to stalk their game and employ skills which hound hunters do not need to use. There are as many traditional hunters in the South as anywhere else.

Dog hunting for deer is not limited to the South. Ontario is the biggest dog hunting section of North America. Here the dog hunt is desirable to properly manage the deer herd due to the few hunters and the need to successfully control populations. The near-absence of the wolf also contributes to the need for dogs.

California limits to "one dog" for deer hunts. Whitetails are quite scarce in California but other varieties abound. Check your state regulations before deciding to hunt by this exciting method.

WILD DOGS

The most serious predator to be found in most deer ranges is the domestic dog. The hot-scented deer is tempting to almost any dog. If a dog is free to roam about and has nothing better to do, he is apt to chase deer every day for the fun of it. Eventually some of his comrades join in, and then the time comes when the dogs find an advantage and make a kill.

Wild dogs are usually former household pets. Farmers and other rural residents are continually plagued with well-meaning city people dumping their dogs on their property with hopes that the dogs will have good country homes. These dumped dogs are usually big dogs which were found to be burdensome in tight city spaces. These dogs team up into packs to pursue deer. The pack will sometimes take shifts in running a deer, allowing some dogs to rest while others keep the circling deer running to exhaustion. Domestic dogs mate with coyotes, wolves, and other dogs to produce distinct breeds of animals whose primary food source is the deer. Most dog packs are mixed breeds with some members of a recognizable species but some other packs are composed of all members a particular type. These wild dogs have developed a strain through inter-breeding over a period of generations.

Does in the later stages of pregnancy are easy prey. Fawns are vulnerable. Even a big, healthy buck can fall to a dog pack. Wounded and unhealthy deer are not the only deer they kill. In deep snow with a light crust, dogs can tire deer easily.

In most areas, dogs seen chasing deer are shot on sight. It is considered the duty of the hunter to shoot feral dogs. It is sad to have to do it, and even the most hardened hunters feel some emotion in killing them, but there is satisfaction in knowing you have taken a step in the right direction. It is by no means suggested that hunters shoot all dogs they see, but only those that cannot be controlled by any other method that are clearly running deer.

Shooting wild dogs is beneficial not only to deer populations but to livestock as well. At some stages of their development, calves, sheep, goats, and virtually all livestock are vulnerable to wild dogs. Sheep are totally helpless.

Rabbit and bird dogs which run deer when they are not supposed to are often shot by their owners. Attempts to break such dogs from chasing after deer are popularly considered futile. However, there is a market for such dogs in the South, and the hunter wishing to dispose of a dog which has lost its value to him could sell it there. The gift of a good deer dog to an Alabama hound hunter will gain you admission to and favor with a hunt club.

Young dogs can often be trained not to chase deer. Methods of training are using "breaking scents" and shocking. Breaking scents are usually glandular odors which are placed on the dog until the dog simply gets sick of the smell. Shocking can be done with special collars or with the aid of an electric fence charger. A fresh deer hoof is wired to the electric fence wire. When the dog begins to chew on the leg, the hidden trainer gives it the juice. The trainer turns the fence off when the dog has gotten a good jolt. A couple of episodes of shocking and not more than three will break any dog from chasing after hoofs.

It is truly frightening to encounter a pack of wild dogs snarling as they form a semicircle around you. This is a remote possibility, but if it should happen to you (as it did my Dad) in your hunt, single out the leader for your first shot. If aiming directly at the leader doesn't cause the rest of them to back off as hopefully the leader does, then shoot the lead dog. The chances that the pack will retreat after their leader is dead are greater. With no tree to climb at hand and a limited number of bullets available to defend yourself, dogs can be a real threat. It is not a bad idea to carry a pistol when scouting, especially if rabies might be a threat.

If you find a lot of dog tracks in an area you plan to hunt, you may as well go somewhere else. Dogs can do an effective job of running deer from their home range for awhile. Most of the deer will return, uneasily, a day or two later. If the predation is acute the deer will abandon the area permanently.

WHERE TO AIM

The object of any hunting shot is to kill the animal as quickly as possible. The hunter should always try to make the first shot count. Hunters using semiautomatic weapons capable of rapid fire probably take less game than those using bolt-action or single-shot rifles. The tendency to take less time in shot placement is a real temptation with these entertaining semiautomatics.

The hunter should concentrate on one spot on the animal and not on the whole animal. He should reduce that spot to the smallest terms and look only at it. This seems terribly simple, I know, but it is the most important part of the whole hunt to pull off. After the often horrendous amount of time and work put into arriving at that one moment, it is a shame to make a mistake and blow it.

It is generally considered best to shoot for the vital area of a deer, which contains the heart and lungs. A hunter who aims for the heart and misses a little may still connect with the lungs, the spine, or the paunch.

The vital area is an area the size of a pie-pan just behind the front shoulder and midway through the chest of the deer. The target is the center of the pie-pan.

Hunters who are thoroughly familiar with their weaponry and have developed confident shooting skills often choose the spine shot. Hitting this target will drop a deer where it stands. The spine shot is usually directed toward the neck.

Broadside and quartering away shots at deer are considered the choice shots, but the deer does not always present itself to the hunter in these ways.

Avoid head shots except when they are absolutely necessary. Head shots are best when the head is down to allow for spinal contact. Another head-on shot to consider is directed toward the center of the chest area. Between the eyes is, of course, the brain shot, which will drop the deer quickly and also, with the wrong bullet, ruin a trophy quickly. Head shots are not recommended since the deer might be hit in the teeth and be condemned to an agonizing death.

The neck shot is gaining popularity as a choice shot. The spine, the throat, and two main arteries located here offer a good target. A neck mount might be blemished beyond repair for a perfect taxidermy job with this shot.

A rear-end shot can be very deadly at close range, dropping a deer in its tracks. At closer range the bullet may proceed entirely through the body to vital areas. At a distance the chance of hitting one of the femoral arteries which go down each leg from the butt are minimal. This is the poorest bow shot. A gunshot to the rear legs cripples the animal and facilitates another shot. A rear shot at a deer leaping a fence or log or a shot from an elevated view such as a tree stand at a fleeing deer can be made to the back of the head; this breaks the neck or connects with the brain. It is recommended that you try to avoid looking at the tantalizing white tail. I have taken deer with all of these shots at different times. I once jumped a buck and shot it through the anal opening as it got up like a rabbit. The 8 mm round traveled the bottom of the spine and cut the heart out before exiting the chest. I am very glad that the deer was not one of the cripples left to suffer.

For a deer running at 20 MPH, the hunter should "lead" his game. High velocity cartridges reduce the amount of distance ahead of the deer that the hunter must shoot. At 50 yards the lead with a 30/06 rifle is about 18 inches. The lead for a 30/30 is about 25 inches, or two feet. At a hundred yards this distance is doubled. You must learn what your bullet will do. A visit to a gun shop will yield this pertinent information.

If an animal is going straight away, or slightly quartering, the shooter is apt to aim at the big white tail target that the deer flashes above its back. This tail is usually all that the startled hunter sees, and he cracks a shot at the billowy plumage and overshoots the deer. Shots should be taken below the plume. Novice hunters often overshoot in these situations since they arise most commonly with jumping deer, and the excited hunter in an attempt to get off a quick shot forgets to pull down into the rear sight before firing. Likewise he might undershoot by not lining up the front sight. The inexperienced shooter must guard against the tendency to "shoot high" because the body of a deer is closer to the ground than most people think. We've all been exposed to more horses than deer. The vital area of a mature whitetail is only three and a half feet high, or lower when running, approximately the height of a table top.

When shooting uphill the point of aim should be low on the body, and when shooting downhill it should be high up on the chest area to put it in line with the heart and spine.

DONNIE SAID THAT HE HAD GOTTEN REAL GOOD AT HITTING A PIE-PAN, AND THAT IF HE EVER SAW A DEER WITH ONE IT WOULD BE HIS.

Try to get a stationary target. If a buck has been flushed by someone else and you believe it has not seen you, there is a good chance that it will slow down or even stop to look back. Deer don't look back while running at full speed. In this situation a little initial restraint might mean the hunter will get a better shot when the deer is just a little farther away.

If the tail of a deer is immediately lowered and kept in a tucked-down position, it is probably hit. However, deer will often throw up their tails when hit if the tail was lowered at first firing and will do it about every time they are hit in the back legs.

A wounded deer may either slow down or speed up rapidly. It is not true that a deer that has been hit will always slow down, stumble, roll, or make any other obvious gesture.

A deer that runs in a "humped up" position and takes short strides has usually been hit.

A hit on the front part of the deer torso may cause the deer to rear up on his hind legs. A wound in the rear will sometimes cause the deer to kick like a donkey in its panic.

If you should see a buck mount a doe for intercourse, let it mate *then* shoot it. It won't take long since after a couple of short thrusts and then one huge lunge the buck ejaculates and releases the doe. They do not lock together like dogs as many think.

A deer hit in the heart will sometimes give no indication of a hit at all. Deer have been know to continue at full stride for re-markable distances with their entire heart shot out.

A "gut-shot" deer is the dread of every hunter. We have been led to believe that animals hit in the paunch will always run off afar, will be very difficult if not impossible to find, and will always die from infection. A gut shot will haunt the hunter to the point of devastation.

The truth is that a lot more deer than we would ever believe survive the paunch shot (especially a clean arrow wound). The reason is that deer have a protective outer layer around the paunch that helps to fill small punctures that naturally occur in their intestines from the rough forage they at times eat, such as sawbriers and other thorny or splintered material. This lining is quite capable of plugging up holes made through the intestines by arrows, since arrows do not destroy quantities of flesh.

Deer have been found which survived some really unlikely wounds. Deer carcasses taken in one season often reveal wounds from previous seasons which have healed over. Deer are frequently harvested which have broadheads surrounded by calcium deposits surrounding them to heal them over. Since most firearms destroy significant tissue upon impact, deer are less likely to recover from their projectiles.

With a lung shot through both lungs, the deer will usually run no more than 80 yards. If only one lung was punctured, the deer can run 600 yards or more with the functioning lung. Deer wounded here leave lots of blood sign which is distinctively pink and frothy with air bubbles.

Deer hit in the heart usually run about 30 yards. They leave a light and spotty blood trail.

Liver shots allow deer to run 80 yards or so and take about five minutes to kill on the average.

Kidney shots usually send the deer 90 yards. They die within 10 to 15 minutes and leave a thin, dark blood trail.

When deer are hit in arteries they usually clamp their tails down and run to the nearest cover before continuing. This may be the only time a deer needs some pushing so that his blood doesn't have a chance to clot up.

Gut shots mean that the deer seldom dies sooner than 15 to 16 hours after hit. These deer, when not pushed, usually go no farther than 150 yards away. If pursued they may go on forever. It is best to leave the area and come back later to find the deer after giving it several hours to die. A gut-shot animal hit one day might best be sought the next day. The only times that a gut-shot animal should be pursued is when the hunter is fairly confident he will get another chance to place a better shot, when the hunter is certain that he cannot wait the long time necessary for the deer to die, be found, and utilized, and when there is heavy rain or snow to hide the trail. Gut-shot deer leave green and yellow in their blood trails.

RIFLES

The type of rifle you hunt with varies according to the type of hunting, the availability of the firearm, and personal preference. Local regulations also permit some and forbid others. Automatic weapons are forbidden everywhere for public deer hunting.

The 30/30 lever-action rifle and the shotgun have taken more deer than any other weaponry in this century. Don't hesitate to use rifled shotgun slugs for deer hunting. They are effective up to around 75 yards or more with adequate velocity and stopping power. Contrary to hearsay, they should not damage the choke of modified and full-choked barrels. The 30/30 caliber rifle with iron sights is perfectly suited to most deer hunting situations.

Anyone attempting to hunt deer should be thoroughly familiar with his or her firearm. What the hunter feels competent and comfortable with should be the chosen gun.

A small-caliber rifle such as the .22 will drop a deer with a precise shot to the brain or spine. Other shots with the .22 may leave no blood trail to follow since such small holes tend to close up and seal off external blood flow. These smaller-caliber weapons often lead to hunters losing animals which eventually die in the underbrush, utilized only by wild scavengers. Poachers usually use such rifles since the sound is not loud and may resemble a cracking tree limb more than gunfire. These smaller-caliber rifles are illegal in many states and, where they are legal, should only be used to place exact shots.

Buckshot is best suited for close shots in dense foliage or brush. Buckshot is just the thing for jump hunting and in situations where the hunter is engaged in deer drives as driver. Some hunters claim 100-yard kills with buckshot. This is the exception and not the rule. Often hunters simply roll the deer using this ammo then switch to other guns or loads.

Multiple-shot rifles tend to make the hunter less accurate on his first shot, which is usually his best shot and often his last. When the hunter knows he has several tries at a target, there is a tendency to try to use them. It is the law of supply and demand. When using semiautomatic rifles, the hunter should do his best to concentrate on placing his first shot well, forgetting about the other rounds available.

The hunter should carry plenty of shells—more than he deems necessary—for those rare occasions when he may miss many shots at a whitetail and still have a chance. Even the best of shots can have this experience. Some deer seem to have a coat of protective armor. Don't be so confident in your shooting ability or the infallibility of your weapon and load that you have too few shells readily available. Having a sufficient supply may also save you from the unfortunate experience of having no finishing round and needing to use a barbaric rock or club to end the deer's life.

The 30/06 with a scope is a superior deer rifle almost anywhere. The 30/06, though large in size, does not damage much meat. These rifles are a good choice for hunters who might hunt other big game as well as the whitetail. Shells can be purchased anywhere.

There is considerable controversy over which of the many rifles is best for deer hunting, what grain of powder, and what particular bullet size and weight are best. There is merit to these discussions, and they are an integral part of the shooter's sport. But for beginning deer hunters, we need not get into complex discussions of various loads or trajectories. Beginners would do well to seek the advice of a trusted deer hunter in making a rifle selection, to test the recommended rifle for personal compatibility, and to stick with factory ammunition.

The four basic types of actions in big-game rifles are the lever, the bolt, the slide or pump, and the autoloading. The choice of type is up to the individual. Many hunters have several models of each type at their disposal. Others make a single selection. My own personal preference for deer is the comparatively heavy military M1A (M-14) for rifle hunting, which I chose simply because it is the weapon I was trained with in the Marine Corps. I also hunt with a .41 magnum handgun, shotgun, muzzleloader, and bow. I don't get into optics, preferring good quality iron sights. These are the weapons that make me happy.

Purchasing guns is a lot like buying a car. Prices fluctuate greatly. Unless the buyer has paid too much to begin with, well-maintained firearms usually retain or gain value and are not bad investments.

Sights should allow high visibility for early morning or evening hunting or for hunting on overcast days. Remember that hollows become darker faster. Sights should be dull and shineless. Dulling can be accomplished by using flat paint, some of your face paint, soot from a candle flame, or other materials which are not detrimental to the metal parts or the finish of the rifle. Just a little glare from exposed metal on the sight tip can mean inaccuracy in sunlight. Gun shops carry gun blacking, as well as orange and fluorescent green.

The rear peep sight is used in conjunction with the front sight similar to that used with open sights. In use, the eye must focus on only two objects; the front sight and the target. A normal eye will "center" such an aperture naturally without actually seeing it.

Most peeps adjust for elevation and windage, an added advantage. These sights are particularly good for older hunters. The peep sight is an iron sight which can be little improved without replacement by a telescopic sight.

Firearms should be as scent-free as possible. Cleaning solvents are taboo near hunting time. Unless you are hunting near an oil rig, limit your gun oil also. The odor of burnt gun powder is quite strong, so to minimize the smell, brush out any loose powder with a wire bore brush before returning to hunt.

The firearm should be without rattles such as noisy sling swivels. Bolt actions and lever actions should be smooth. In extremely cold weather, very thin oiling is recommended to limit sluggishness in the actions of the weapons.

A sling is necessary for carrying the weapons when not in use. Climbing trees is easier with a sling. The rifle should be unloaded when climbing, of course. A sling can be used functionally as a superior steadying device for those long, steady shots by wrapping it around the arm or with the arm through a loop, as one learns in military training. Who knows? You may need a sling to hold up your pants if your belt buckle breaks!

Shotguns using slugs should have sights. Some shotguns are especially made for deer hunting, and these are the best. There are occasional 100-yard shots, but in reality the shot of 75 yards or less is more probable. Read the information on the back of the slug box concerning drop at different yardages.

Rifles are not allowed for deer hunting in seven states. These states are shotgun only with various exceptions for handguns, muzzleloaders, bows, and crossbows. These seven states are Delaware, Indiana, Illinois, Massachusetts, New Jersey, Ohio and Rhode Island.

PRACTICE

The hunter who expects to rely on luck is doomed to failure. Consistent success depends on practice and on confidence in your ability to connect with the deer. You must become skilled with your weapon. You will be happy that you spent the extra time and money. Missing deer, wounding deer, and the possibility of a hunting accident are all greatly minimized by practice. Practice is a discipline that can be exciting and a sport in itself.

If you are seriously interested in quality marksmanship a minimum of 100 rounds should be spent in qualifying yourself with your high-powered rifle. You should get groups of shots close together on the target and then get groups within groups at different ranges.

Practice in a situation similar to the planned hunt. If you intend to hunt from a tree stand, then practice shooting from the same angle if possible. Practice from the exact location or devise a facsimile.

Practice free-hand after truing your rifle from a bench rest or other stable position. Practice left-handed and right-handed for those shots which require a switch from the norm.

For practice with moving targets, roll old automobile tires with cardboard in the centers downhill. These unique targets bounce and gather momentum in ways quite similar to running deer.

Sharpen up your marksmanship skills by "varmint" hunting where rodents are over-abundant and need control. Most farmers will welcome you with open arms to engage in this off-season sport.

There are five shooting basics. They are aim, breath control, trigger control, hold, and follow-through. Breath control is the most important since it has a strong influence on the other fundamentals.

These fundamentals can be practiced at home by "dry firing." Contrary to popular belief, snapping the trigger without a round in the chamber will seldom cause a firing pin to break. Agreed, it is possible to break the pin if the pin is thin, as in a smaller-caliber rifle, or if the pin is of poor quality. Most deer rifles are equipped with larger firing pins made of high-quality steel which make your chances of breaking a firing pin insignificant. I recommend that you practice by dry firing well in advance of the proposed hunt, so that in the rare event that a firing pin needs replacement, you will have plenty of time to take care of this. Besides, the value of dry firing is much greater than the cost of replacing a firing pin. It will be hard to dry fire your rifle if you have been schooled that it is taboo.

Dry firing should be practiced in sessions of around 15 minutes. During this time the hunter should squeeze his trigger and simulate a shot approximately 100 times. If the hunter were using live ammunition, this process would be expensive, would require the use of an outdoor range, and would cause wear and tear on more than just the firing pin.

Dry firing should by no means replace live firing, just as bore sighting a new scope should not replace range-tuning one. You can dry fire in the luxury of your home on a rainy day.

FLINCHING

Flinching, which produces inaccuracy, is the action of the shooter as he jerks the trigger mechanism or otherwise moves the firearm when firing.

Flinching is usually caused by anticipation of the impending explosion.

To check whether you are flinching when it is not clearly apparent, have someone else load and hand your weapon to you when you are practicing. The assistant should leave an occasional round out. Flinching will be obvious by this method, since you will not be expecting an unloaded gun.

Flinching must be overcome through conscious effort. Unwillingness to brake a flinch, and choosing instead to accept and allow for it, will eventually catch up with you.

B.R.A.S.S.

Breathe, rest, aim, slack, squeeze—*B.R.A.S.S.* Do not hold your breath, but breathe normally while consciously eliminating any unsteadiness from anxiety. Think and speak peace to your body while taking aim at the exact spot of your target. On a slow exhale pull the slack (if there is any) out of the trigger, and in the brief calm of the exhale squeeze and do not "pull" the trigger. Do not take your eyes off the target until the projectile has connected, following through. Single-phase triggers have no slack, whereas two-phase rifles such as most military issues have slack. Think realistically but positively.

SCOPES

Telescopic sights have been tremendously improved lately. The various drawbacks which kept the majority of hunters using iron sights have been conquered by newer technology. There are a good many hunters who still prefer to use their iron sights even though scopes might improve their shooting success.

You will hear hunters say that if they had only had a scope they could have connected with a big buck and you will hear hunters state that if they had not had a scope they might have connected. It is a matter of the situation.

The proper scope for the individual hunt character is a matter worthy of considerable forethought. Many deer have been lost because of improper scope size, usually oversizing, or improper mounting to the firearm. In the East, few hunting situations require shots over 200 yards, and most shots at deer are within the 100-yard category. Long-range scopes are therefore unnecessary. Fumbling with scope adjustments to execute a shot can be tedious when the exciting moment arrives.

There are four basic advantages to using a scope:

1. Telescopic sights have light-gathering qualities, which offer clarity in woodland understory, at dawn, and dusk, and on overcast days.
2. Scopes magnify the target, which helps the hunter significantly to positively identify game and to correctly place the bullet.
3. They focus on only one object. When the hunter sights through the scope, he is looking only at the target.
4. The scope makes a fine substitute binocular.

Proper mounting is essential. Select a scope which is made to mount to the firearm you are using. Guns that need to be tapped for machine screws should be tapped by professional gunsmiths only. Some firearms become dangerous if tapped. Also remember that when you put holes in your gunbarrel, you may decrease its value. The best place to select the proper scope and have it mounted is the gunsmith shop. You might find a lower price at a sporting goods outlet or by mail order but you will not receive the attention, skill and knowledge of a smith. He will be able to bore-sight the scope when he mounts it. The gunsmith has already experienced various failures and knows how to avoid them. Remember that bore-sighting is not enough for accuracy. Many hunters have their scopes bore-sighted and head out. Screws should be checked quite often to be sure they are tight. A tiny screwdriver is a good thing to have in your "possibles" bag. Once you are sure that the scope you have is the right one for you, then you may consider putting a dab of super glue in the screws to help keep them intact.

Be sure that the scope is mounted far enough down the barrel so that when shouldered and cheeked the scope will not recoil and blacken your eye.

The scope is an asset in most hunting situations and is a detriment in others. In bean-field hunting in the East and in range-hunting in the West, a scope is indispensable. For close-range hunting in swamps and thickets, it can be a burden. The scope seems to get caught on every vine you encounter. Although quality scopes are designed to be fairly rugged instruments, they still require a little additional care when hunting.

Be sure to read the instructions for care of the lens and use a protective lens cover. A suitable lens cover can be made by cutting one out of a cross-section of bicycle inner tube, which will save you a few dollars.

Some people have eye-sight such that they just cannot connect with iron sights and find a telescopic sight a necessity. Lining up the rear sight with the front sight and lining up the both of them with the target is just too much.

The scope simplifies the matter by allowing the hunter to readily line up the dot or crosshair with the target, a move which amounts to little more than looking through the glass to the animal. Nearsighted individuals need scopes. Farsighted hunters can do without them.

A scope will show you how much you waver in shooting. The crosshairs will move around on the target unless the gun is nearly bolted down. A scope is good for revealing to iron-sight hunters that are attempting a conversion to optics who often think, at first, that this movement is because of the scope and say they don't like them, not realizing that they wavered all along and that the scope just made it evident.

A scope can be used at close range and in brush just as well as on the open fields and plains. A low-magnification scope, such as the popular $1\frac{1}{2}-4\times$, is the most versatile for tighter cover hunting.

For hunters wary of the scope, with its delicacy, its technological alienation from pioneer-style hunting, and its need for rapid focusing adjustments, the see-through mount may be the answer. This allows them to use their iron sights but also have the advantages of a scope. These elevated mounts make it possible to see under the scope and through iron sights. These mounts are difficult to click in, however, and more unforgiving to bumps and other problems of alignment.

RANGE

Range, the distance from the hunter to the deer, can be critical. When properly employed, rifles and other firearms can shoot from point blank to a thousand yards accurately.

Most shots at deer are from 40 to 100 yards with firearms and from 15 to 40 with bows. Unless you are hunting large fields or other open range, your training need not exceed 100 yards with a firearm or 50 yards with archery equipment.

Rifle ranges are available near most metropolitan areas. For small fees, some clubs will allow non-members to use their marked ranges. It is important that safety be considered in testing rifles and zeroing in. Always remember that the bullet will travel a considerable distance unless there is a proper backstop such as a dirt bank.

Do practice at different ranges. Know your weapon. The closer you are to it the better. If you are not confident with your gun or bow, if you feel fear and doubt, then you need more practice.

If you have trouble with range estimation in the field, visit a local football field and study the range markers from the ground and from the stands. Walk all over the stadium and look at the markers from different points so that you will get a feeling for distances. A driving range for golfers can bring some range understanding.

Of course, with a bow, range estimation is crucial. Arrows drop measurably at differing distances. Pin sights should be set at ten-yard gradations from 20 to 60 and these sights should be tested by the archer at different locations, over different terrain, and from different positions.

MUZZLELOADING

Muzzleloading packs some charm into the hunt. The firearms are a lot of fun to shoot and virtually all of them make a lot of noise. Blackpowder makes gunsmoke that sparks the nostrils and stirs the imagination to summon up images from frontier or Civil War days of old.

It is a memorable experience to wait for the fog of smoke to drift away from the flint-lock rifle and see the deer down. This exciting adventure activates the Daniel Boone in us all.

Often these weapons have their own specially designated season. Some public facilities and military reservations have areas for hunting with primitive weapons only. The use of such firearms is regulated to provide recreation for the growing number of deer hunters who become blackpowder enthusiasts.

Muzzleloaders are usually attractive weapons that qualify for display above the fireplace mantle. Many and varied are these guns, for a great many individuals make their own from start to finish. Some start out with only raw materials to build exact replicas of the oldest versions. Kits for assembly and finishing are popular. There are gunsmiths who will custom-fit a muzzleloading firearm to your exact specifications. It is quite an art.

Most blackpowder rifles are single shot. These rifles require exact shot placement the first time, for reloading in the field for a second shot consumes time which is seldom available. The over-and-under and the side-by-side blackpowder rifles are available commercially and are used by a minority of hunters. These weapons, which allow the hunter more than one shot without reloading, help to facilitate a killing shot to finish wounded animals. One drawback to the use of two-shot varieties is that the hunter has a tendency to be less accurate with his first shot when he knows a follow-up shot is available. Historically there were multiple-round blackpowder guns manufactured for military and other use against human enemies.

Through practice you can become quite accurate with blackpowder weapons. A visit to a blackpowder match can be an enlightening experience. The buckskin-clad enthusiasts can often drive nails at fifty yards with hits by their weapons with round-ball projectiles. Scopes are very rare on primitive weapons since they detract from the authenticity of the replicas. For some deer hunters, especially those with eye problems, scopes on muzzleloaders may be in order to make them practical for bringing home the venison during special seasons.

The two basic types of blackpowder firearms are the flint-lock, which is the more primitive, and the newer variety, the percussion. Both varieties require the projectile to be ramrodded into the barrel from the muzzle end after powder has been deposited. The flint-lock requires a channel of powder to be deposited on the exterior of the rifle from the hammer to the load. This produces the cloud of smoke similar to that produced by the old cameras photographers used in the past. In the percussion blackpowder actions, a crimped firing cap facilitates this function with more ease, greater dependability, and less smoke. The modernized firing cap versions are more practical for hunting deer, but many nostalgically prefer the flint-lock.

The standard projectile is the round ball. The exact size of the ball is determined by the individual barrel. Some handmade weapons require handmade balls to meet their custom requirements. There are blackpowder buffs who not only make their own rifles but also make their own powder by collecting natural ingredients, their own musketballs from lead they have mined, and make their own clothing from nature. These people really get into the act.

The buffalo ball, or conical bullet, is generally the preferred ammo for most deer hunts. These cones have a lot of knock-down power and shoot on a plane. The round ball takes more practice to master and requires more exactness in loading. Conicals have a hollowed-out butt which really puts it out there. Additionally, they are available in hollow point to create quite a wad or wallop. Longer range with accuracy can be achieved with the round ball through practice. If deer hunting is the chief reason for muzzleloading, it is suggested that you start with the less complicated conicals and stick with them. They require no wadding. Be certain that your rifle is manufactured for conicals. Barrel rifling determines the most suitable type of bullet.

Sight in your muzzleloader at 13 yards. This near distance will put the bullet slightly high at 50 yards, centered at 75 yards, and a few inches low at 100 yards. The maximum range muzzleloaders should attempt with deer is 100 yards. Most hunters begin their practice at 25, 40, or 50 yards, which will bring more confusion and the need for more shooting with the muzzleloader.

Dies may be purchased for reasonable prices to make your own bullets from salvaged lead. These simple projectiles are the easiest bullets to make, no more difficult than fishing sinkers.

Pyridex is the most commonly used firing powder for deer hunts. This modern version of blackpowder is not as odoriferous as its predecessors and is comparatively smokeless. Pyridex is also less apt to absorb moisture than is regular blackpowder. Since it is a more stable mixture, Pyridex is less dangerous to store and handle. Store owners often stock only Pyridex for this reason.

Still, traditional blackpowder is the preferred charge for many hunters. The potency of the powder is rated fg, ffg, and fffg. Triple-fg is the most powerfully explosive. There is increased spontaneity in the use of true blackpowder. The time lapse between the slam of the hammer and the combustion of the barrel charge is minimized. There is a momentary delay with Pyridex, though this is not a true handicap. Blackpowder of the traditional variety may be harder to find over the counter in your locale. It is legal and can be found with a little telephone searching. The shelf life of standard blackpowder mixtures is limited to one year when properly stored. Pyridex lasts longer. To prevent hunting disappointment, be sure to replace old black powder with fresh.

It is best to go on and fire out your muzzleloader after an unsuccessful hunt. If you did not remember or did not have the opportunity to clear the barrel and are left with a loaded weapon you should stand the loaded gun on the barrel and in a secure corner to prevent powder cramp in the nipple and wax or grease from running into the powder. After your rifle has been stored in this inverted position, it will be necessary to retamp the load with your ramrod to secure the projectile.

Blackpowder weapons must be cleaned after use. The residue builds up and seriously affects performance. Varied cleaning techniques are suitable. Some use dish soap and water down the bore, but commercially available rust preventative solvents are the best current method. Care must be exercised when using oil in these weapons due to the fact that dry powder is poured into the barrel. Any oil residue should be thoroughly cleaned from rifles left in storage before firing.

Speed loads are great to have. These are containers formed with plastic which clip into the shirt pocket like a fountain pen. They have space for a premeasured amount of powder in one end and a bullet and firing cap in the other. These are great for those occasional second shots or for finishing wounded deer. If you are not carrying a finishing sidearm such as a blackpowder pistol, you will need one or two of these. If a ramrod doesn't attach to your firearm then I suggest you buy a ramrod which breaks down for compactness in field use.

If you use firing caps, be sure to carry some extras in your shirt pocket. It is easy to lose one of these little jewels during the excitement. Duds are often encountered as well. The round tins that they come in are noisy so stick loose caps in your shirt pocket. For some of us grasping these primers with our bulky fingers and placing them on the nipples of the rifle is a clumsy affair. They make gadgets to help with this chore but they never seem to be handy in field situations. Cold and calloused fingers picking up one of these primers reminds me of a gorilla eating grapes.

Before going into the woods with your rifle, be sure to shoot a cap through the firing ports without a load and projectile in the barrel to make certain that the port is clear of obstruction. The slightest blockage will cause a misfire. Check to be sure that ignition charges are not hindered by firing the unloaded gun at a piece of paper or a leaf near the muzzle tip. If the cap exerts enough force to move the paper or leaf, you can be confident that the ports are clear. If there is not sufficient air force from the muzzle end, the weapon must be cleaned. To keep the port clear during non-use, place a cleaning patch or ball patch between the hammer and port, letting the hammer rest on the cloth.

When the weather is very humid, muzzleloading is difficult because the powder absorbs moisture. If you have only a short blackpowder season or if your day to hunt turns out to be rainy, do not be discouraged—you may still hunt. Weatherproof muzzleloading can be accomplished with a little ingenuity. To avoid misfires, place a two-and-a-half-inch square from a plastic sandwich bag over the capped nipple and drum, making sure that it doesn't block your view. The weapon fires with it in place. This raincoat snugs down with a twist tie or a rubber band.

*JIM REALLY LOADED HIS MUZZLE
WHEN HE GOT HOME.*

BOWS

The bow and arrow kills deer. Unlike guns, which take deer by impact, the bow and arrow kill by hemorrhaging. Wounding deer with an arrow is no less common than wounding with a firearm. But it is usually more difficult to locate the animal with an arrow wound since death generally comes more slowly. The limited range of the bow requires the hunter to cover his scent and disguise his appearance more carefully than in most gun hunts. Bows are considered more sporting than guns by the majority of hunters. More and more people pick up bow hunting each year.

There is a long-standing feud between some gun hunters and archers. The gap between hunters is being bridged harmoniously in the 1990s as hunters realize they need to get along with each other, since divisions among themselves only kindle the fires of the anti-hunting movement.

It has been said that if the native American had had the compound bow at his disposal, history would have been different.

The bow is without any doubt the most useful all-around weapon ever devised by primitive man, but it was no match for the long-range trajectory of the firearm.

The primary appeal of bow hunting is the challenge that it offers. More and more rifle hunters who desire to add a new dimension to their skills afield are converting and becoming true addicts. Some bow converts who have taken plenty of deer with rifles sell their guns and say "there ain't no sport in it." Others take up the bow to take advantage of the extended seasons and special hunts. Bow hunters can hunt nearer to roads and urban areas since their arrows do not travel far. Also, experienced rifle hunters who have learned to ambush deer effectively and know the thrill of close contact often convert.

Bow season is generally longer in duration than gun season. Most states have bow seasons before, during, and after the rut. This timing gives the bow hunter a great diversity of hunting experiences. Some old trophy bucks simply hide out when they see carloads of gun hunters coming into the woods and hear guns going off as in a war zone. Bow season, in contrast, usually catches them off guard. It is true that when gun season rolls around, deer which have been hunted by bowmen may be more edgy.

Gun season interrupts their patterns, but bow season hunting before gun season consists in more patterned routines and allows them more consistency.

Bows are almost silent. They are not for people who get a bang out of shooting.

BOWHUNTING

Many gun hunters and non-hunters have seen photographs of deer with several arrows in their flesh which were found rotted and wasted by the wayside and concluded that bows are inhumane and a poor way to take deer. Since the advent of the compound bow, it does not take a Hercules to get enough draw and thrust to send most arrows completely through a deer. Providing the arrows found in the deer carcass were not placed there by radical animal rights activists, such findings were the result of the use of the earlier recurve and long bows. Lots of old-time hunters still prefer the recurve bows and can make killing shots quite well with them. They just have to be accurate and build their muscles for more draw. Recurve bows are by no means obsolete. The preference of many archers for them is usually based on their experience with it before the arrival of the compound. Some recurve bow hunters state that they have better success with their arrows not having the tremendous penetration offered with the compound. Target archers don't like to have to go through an ordeal to remove their arrows from haybales where they are imbedded completely. In the 1990s, I suggest that the beginning archer choose the compound bow and be grateful for the fact that he is getting into bow hunting at the right time, after many advances have been made. He will find the compound just as sporting as the other bows since getting a shot off at a deer is the hard part anyway.

Some people think that states should require shooters to take exams before bow hunting (or rifle hunting), just as drivers take license examinations. Such an exam might limit the number of people in the woods who pose a threat to other hunters or wound deer regularly because they don't know how to shoot. This might not be a bad idea, but that we don't need more red tape limiting our liberty to hunt. We already have so many regulations to read and understand that we are somewhat confused. The real hope is in hunter awareness and effort on a personal basis.

On the national average, only one in ten bow hunters is successful in any given season. For this reason it is clear that the longer season afforded the bow hunter does not really give him an unfair advantage over the deer and is not apt to decimate the population.

It is true that a bow will seldom put the beast's heels in the air like a gun will. The arrow has no stopping power on big game.

The bow you select should match your intentions, capabilities, and pocketbook.

The beginning archer who is not planning to shoot in competitive archery shoots and intends only to hunt with his bow should of course select a hunting bow. He should select a medium-priced bow or a top-of-the-line bow, even if it means making a sacrifice. In the long run he will save money, time, and trouble for himself. Dissatisfaction with a particular bow and subsequent desire to upgrade comes inevitably and the bowman has to buy the better equipment anyway, making his previous investment a waste of money. Bows, unlike guns, seldom gain value but depreciate rapidly like cars. As soon as you drive out with your bow, its resale value plunges.

I recommend starting with a 50-pound draw weight. This weight will be set by the archery shop. The bow you should select for whitetails is recommended to be capable of adjustment from 50 to 70 pounds of draw. This means that the actual strength, measured in pounds, needed to pull the arrow from brace height, when it is strung, to 28 inches will require a pull weight of 50 pounds. The draw weight for whitetail deer need not exceed 70 pounds anytime, anywhere. The draw weight can be increased as the hunter develops those muscles (which other types of exercise do little to develop) that help him to increase from 50 pounds gradually to 70. Draws above 70 are for other big game than whitetails.

Go to an archery shop. Some sporting goods shops have good selections of bows and accessories and often good deals with their sales and promotions, but the beginner needs a salesman who is an expert. Archery shop personnel spend all of their working hours dealing with the isolated subject of archery. Salesmen in department stores may seem to be knowledgeable, but many have just learned to make a sale. Select a sporting goods store that is staffed with at least one competent archer for giving beginner instruction and helping in the proper selection of archery equipment. It is worth your while to drive the distance necessary to find a good archery shop. The best ones have indoor archery ranges. It is a good idea to buy your first bow out of season to avoid the pre-season rush of customers and allow the proprietors to spend unhurried time with you. If you must go to a department store for your equipment because the price is right or a time and space limitation, then take someone else along who knows what is going on.

Never draw and release your bow without an arrow. This can cause harm to your bow. It is unlikely that a salesman would allow you to make this mistake, but it may happen when you mail-order a bow.

The biggest pitfall to the beginning archer is inadequate instruction. Instructors can pass on bad habits which are hard to break. Learn from someone you know is accomplished, then find someone else whom you have confidence in, and make a comparison. Blend their techniques with your own thoughts about the way it should be done and you will have an individual style.

Shooting a bow accurately is easier to learn than the beginner may think. Three or four lessons will normally be enough to get the beginner on target. By this time most beginners feel more confidence and have a desire to become better at the sport, which becomes more pleasurable. Bowhunting is not difficult to learn. Mastery is always hard with anything.

The most common target setup is a row of straw bales. Pull the spent arrows from the bales taking care not to bend them.

The beginner must first concentrate on his form, release, and technique at 20 yards. As he gets better he can go farther back. He can learn to shoot from different positions and angles after becoming adept at standard shots. Moving targets and field ranges which simulate hunting situations come last.

Practice should be continued until the hunter knows, not thinks, that he can kill a deer.

Stands for the bow hunter should be larger than those normally used for gun hunting to allow him to stand and fire an arrow steadily. Bow hunters keep their stands lower on the average than do gun hunters to allow bow shots at reduced angles. Bow hunters should practice their archery from the same angle from which they intend to hunt and place their stands where they intend to get side shots. Arrows too often deflect on over-head shots and head-on shots as well as find a smaller target.

Practice often with your bow to develop skill and confidence. This is one place that if you don't think that you can do anything, you won't. Many areas have archery ranges where archers can share information and assist one another. It is good to witness a variety of hunters applying their techniques. Some little tricks or moves may be just the thing for improving your own style. Some beginners learn to shoot by themselves, but this is not unlike jumping into deep water to learn to swim.

The penetration of an arrow depends largely upon having the heads razor sharp. Remember to practice with broadheads before a hunt since target tips often fly a bit differently. Resharpen or replace the broadheads when you are through. Practice with broadheads helps to remove fear or apprehension of their sharpness.

The smallest twig will deflect an arrow, so the archer must get a successful shot by choosing a clear shooting lane. Shooting lanes might be cleared out well enough to allow free arrow flight at select spots about your stand.

Since the arrow at best is only a slow killer, avoid all chancy shots. Running shots are not a good idea. The high ethics of the bowman are his most precious route to satisfaction. Many an archer will turn down shot after shot at his deer simply because the outcome is not certain.

A fanny pack is good for bow hunters since it remains out of the way of the draw in various positions. Bows can hit on body obstructions as arrows are released. Be conscious of baggy or loose clothing which you have not practiced in. Never let the limbs of your bow touch anything when you shoot. You cannot rest a bow on an object for steadying as you can a firearm.

Buy a sight light for shots in the near-dark.

Sights for the compound bow are set up with pins which indicate alignment for the peep sight on the bow string for different yardages. There is usually a pin for each ten-yards of range. These increments may be colored differently by the hunter so that he can make quicker selections and fewer mistakes.

Learn to shoot without the sights for those times when it is just too dark to use them at all. It is also important to learn to shoot without the aid of an arrow-release mechanism for those times when you lose or forget them.

Arrows should have sufficient "spine." Spine is the bending quality of an arrow that allows it to spring out as it passes the bow upon being shot then return to its original straightness when free in flight.

Your bow and your arrow should be fitted to match your arm length. Custom fitting is a service of quality archery shops. Remember your arrow length for future ordering.

Much has been said about deer "jumping the string." This is the reaction of a deer which has been startled by the sound of a released arrow and leaps excitedly—as we do when someone comes up behind us and shouts "boo." Jumping the string was a common phenomenon with the recurve bow since it took a comparatively long time for the arrow to reach the target. Hunters allowed for it. Compound bows do not shoot faster than the speed of sound but they do minimize the time, making the need to allow for the deer jumping less important. Many experts with the compound take no measures at all to allow for this action. I recommend, however, that you have one or two muffling devices attached to your bowstring to reduce this twang. These devices look like rubber-skirted fishing jigs, or spinner baits. These inexpensive devices will serve the purpose of easing the hunter's mind if nothing more. Try anything that is legal to increase your odds.

On the practice range, problems with shooting errors need to be corrected and not compensated for.

If you are consistently shooting arrows low, then you are probably not pulling the bow string all the way to your anchor point or you are letting your firing hand slip forward when you release the arrow. When the arrows are going high, the problem is probably that you are overdrawing the bow or setting the arrow to the string lower than it should be. If your arrows veer to the left, then the arrows have too much spine or you are moving your arrow release or fingers too far away from your anchor point. When arrows fly low and to the left, it is possible that you are dropping your bow arm as you shoot. When they fly high and to the right, you are jerking your string hand back and in on firing the shot. These rules of thumb pertain to right-hand shooting and can be reversed for left-handed archers.

Most bow accidents are due to careless treatment of the broadheads, resulting in cuts to the hands, thighs, or even eyes.

Watch for cracked arrows in the spines or nocks. Do this before loading any arrow. These defective arrows are very dangerous.

Tape off the rubber cord used to line up the peep sight to prevent possible injury to your eye. A couple of loops around the limb with electrical tape will suffice to assure that the suction cup doesn't come loose. Check the cord regularly to be sure it is in good shape, free from nicks and signs of weathering. This problem, though seemingly small, is preventable and may be just the thing that ruins a good hunt. Problems with the cord usually occur in colder weather. Not all bows have these features and some archers remove these alignment cords when their string and sight develop a memory. Indeed, many hunters use no sights at all.

An armguard will save you some bruises, some of which can be very painful. When you are practicing these are particularly nice to have to prevent soreness from repeated string taps to your holding wrist. In actual hunting you can leave this extra equipment at home since you won't notice the pain.

An arrow-release mechanism will make it easier on your fingers in practice. The arrow release is generally considered better for accuracy than a finger release.

Carrying a spare bowstring is a great idea providing the hunter knows how to put one on without risking personal injury. The spare string shouldn't be needed if the string is in good condition before the hunt and if it is treated without such negligence as letting it get severed by sharp objects bouncing around in the bed of a pickup.

The size of the hunting bow in relation to the size of the archer is relevant. Bows can be fitted to children. Bow size is figured by the bowman's reach, which in turn determines arrow length. Reach is the distance from the archer's shooting eye at shooting stance to the knuckle of his opposite index finger minus one and a half inches. The pull, which is called the "weight" of the hunting bow, is determined by the strength and experience of the archer and the hunting regulations of the individual state.

The "quiver" is either a tube-like pouch for holding arrows which is carried by a shoulder or waist band or it is a device which is attached to the bow itself. You will need some kind of quiver for convenience and also to keep your arrows straight. Arrow straightness can be checked by removing the broadhead or target point from the tip, and with the fletching hanging freely over a table edge, rolling the arrow shaft to detect irregularity.

When you hear the peculiar "chunk" of an arrow meeting flesh, you are set to experience an equally challenging part of bow hunting—finding the deer.

SPEARS

What a challenge it would be to spear a deer. Many has been the time when a hunter could spear a deer from his tree stand. Close encounters on the ground also offer the opportunity. It seems saddening to take a deer with a long-range weapon when a spear is all that would be necessary. To spear a deer would be a truly exciting primitive experience.

I myself have two spears. One is heavy, made from steel, one-inch pipe, hollow, with a large spearhead forged onto it with barbs. The weight of the spear would nail a deer to the ground when thrust from an elevated stand. This may sound barbarically cruel to some, but if the hunter did connect with the deer it would not run off to suffer and never be found. The heavy weight of the spear makes it useful for throwing directly beneath the tree, which is a hard shot with a bow. The thrust is tremendous.

The second spear consists of a stainless steel hunting-knife blade inserted into a solid aluminum shaft. The knife blade has been barbed. This well-balanced and lighter spear can be thrown accurately at 20 yards. Although I have not tried this, it is probable that using a sling to launch this spear would increase distance and thrust.

A deer speared with either of these weapons would stand very little chance of disappearing through the thickets with the spear banging against trees and bushes.

At times you will get close enough to deer to reach out and touch them with your spear. The hunter skilled at the art of concealment sometimes even has to make evasive moves to get out of the deer's way.

The only problem with my own spears is that I cannot legally use them on game. It is legal to hunt with a gun, but not with a spear, or a rock, or a hammer for that matter. What a wide-open field of hunting experiences the spear holds for the future. If enough hunters got together and enough signatures were collected, wildlife legislators would accommodate them and spear hunting would be allowed. New products for spear hunters would be a booming marketing industry. I began the process of having spears legalized in my home state of Kentucky in 1989.

Perhaps the legislators are afraid that hunters will get carried away with spears, or that if spear hunting is accepted, hunting with bolos, sling shots, blow darts, boomerangs, lasers, and traps will be proposed next. In fact, the Cherokee Indians used blow guns among other tools, something that few are aware of. They also used spears, of course.

Incidentally, if you like to eat squirrel and squirrels are allowed to be taken during deer season in your area, a slingshot can come in handy when you are taking a stand in a tree. Squirrels do not expect hunters to be in trees.

CROSSBOWS

Crossbows are popular in some areas. A crossbow is a marriage between a bow and a rifle. Using this weapon is thus easier for a rifle-indoctrinated hunter than learning marksmanship with a bow. The conversion is only half way. By taking up the crossbow, the hunter can take advantage of special crossbow seasons.

Many sportsmen have misconceptions about crossbows. Because they are silent, they are the perfect weapons for poachers. Thus many hunters appear to view the crossbow as a dark and medieval instrument used by cheaters. The crossbow does not deserve this negative reputation. The modern crossbow is a true work of art in design and workmanship and is no less sporting than any other weapon used to take deer.

Crossbows can be used very accurately with minimal practice. Their use is not as demanding as that of other types of bows. Crossbows have only one disadvantage: a comparatively long time is required to cock the bow after each shot. With a little shopping, the hunter can find models that have minimized this pitfall. A repeating crossbow can shoot five bolts in four seconds.

An accomplished crossbowman can place all his bolts in a 24-inch target at 100 yards with consistency. Not all crossbows have this range. When choosing a crossbow, the buyer should try to find an experienced guide. There are many types available with some significant differences.

A used crossbow will decline in value quickly, like any bow. It is best to find the one you will stick with the first time around.

Crossbows are still illegal in some states. These states see no need to allow them since liberal gun and bow seasons are already available. It is likely that these restrictions will change in response to the growing number of hunters who will choose this hunting medium in the 1990s. The truly avid hunter is eager to explore all the ways to hunt and to vary his or her experiences. At present, Alabama, with a most generous buck-a-day deer limit for several consecutive months, disallows the crossbow.

Vietnam veterans who spent time in the jungles near Laos and Cambodia will seldom underestimate the ability of the crossbow. The Montagnard Indians there taught many Americans how to use them. Some combat Americans were issued crossbows in Vietnam for ambush (the most popular and successful method of taking deer) and the firing of certain other interesting projectiles silently.

HANDGUNS

Handgun hunting is the easiest method. The handgun is highly portable. A shoulder or hip holster allows free movement of both hands and makes tree, rock, and dirt-bank climbing easy. Long-distance walking is less demanding when the arms are free to swing in stride. Hunting with a pistol is very satisfying. Shots from 100 yards are not too much for most magnums. Handguns are very appropriate for still-hunts. There is a feeling of accomplishment in successful handgun kills.

Scopes are available for those for whom iron sights are not enough. The pistol scopes that have a red dot for focusing on the vital area of the target are the most functional for the deer hunter. Some handgun shots are quick, making alignment of crosshairs slow and unsteady.

Many hunters carry a handgun as a secondary or auxiliary sidearm for use in close-range situations or to finish off a wounded deer.

Handguns clean and store easily. They are considered very sporting in whitetail deer hunting. Target practice is recreational. These guns are also relatively easy to conceal from thieves or children. Remember to separate ammunition and weapons as a safety precaution with children in mind.

The legality of their use varies from state to state. Limitations generally deal with calibrations and barrel lengths. The hunter should be certain that he is aware of the law so he does not risk having his pistol confiscated. Concealment laws vary greatly. It may be a violation of the law to have a handgun hidden from open view or to possess one period. Indiana presently allows handgunners to use their equipment for whitetail but does not allow the high-powered rifle. In 1990, all but four states allow handgun deer hunting.

A .41 magnum Smith and Wesson with a 10-inch barrel fitted with combat grips and no scope is my own handgun of choice and my preferred close-range hunting weapon. I have taken several deer with the revolver and have as much confidence in thicket hunting with it as I do with any other type of firearm. The .44 magnum is more widely preferred and has slightly more knockdown power. However, I have found the .41 easier to handle and sufficient. It is said that if Clint Eastwood movies had not made the .44 so popular, the .41 would be in its place of status. The .357 magnum is commonly a preferred pistol, and there are numerous other choices. The Thompson Contender is available in many setups with interchangeable barrels, which make it a contender for the title of most versatile and accurate small arm available.

I have one of the fingers of my right hand missing, which makes it a bit weak. I shoot better with one hand instead of two hands like they do in the cop shows. Being right-handed, I fortify my weakness by holding an extended milkjug filled with water to build my shooting arm, shoulder, and chest muscles.

TALKING, COUGHING, SNEEZING

For some strange reason it seems that virtually everyone is inclined to clear his throat in the woods at just the wrong time. It is common phenomena for hunters to cough as soon as they begin to enter the woods. No doubt we do this unconsciously at home or at work where the action will have no consequence. But in the quiet of the woods, we are aware of the sound and it has a new relevance. Whitetail hunters must make a conscious effort to avoid or suppress the cough.

The cough, the sneeze, and the clearing of the throat are strictly homo-sapiens noises. These are foreign to the deer. Clear your throat well before you enter the woods, or better, before you leave your car. Suppress coughs and sneezes by holding your hand over your mouth or nose. Muffle any sneeze with your hat or jacket sleeve. The muffled sound may more nearly sound like that of a deer than that of a hunter. Try to throw a little deer sound into it by getting more guttural as you find yourself unavoidably producing one of these sounds. In the hunt, a cough or a sneeze can cost a whole day. Alter it! Adapt it! If you have a continuous cough which cannot be suppressed then keep a grunt call in your mouth.

The human voice is easily recognized by the long-eared deer, most of which have heard it before. Be assured that deer are more aware of our vocalizations than we are of theirs.

Deer that hear human voices at a distance are comfortable in knowing they are a safe distance from their potential enemy. Deer will move more freely and with less caution when they are able to pinpoint the location of hunters. Thus a hunter can take advantage of others at a road or campsite by taking a position on the fringe of that area. Hunters who are talking together often sight deer moving about freely. There are times when hunters who have hunted diligently all morning meet each other to discuss the obvious absence of deer and are surprised to see deer that feel safely distanced walking about like zoo creatures after having found out just where exactly those human scents and sounds were coming from.

NOISE ATTRACTIONS

The ears of the whitetail deer are large in size, cupped, and highly mobile as they pivot on their flexible bases of cartilage. Watch a deer feeding in the wild. These consistently nervous deer will point their ears forward, to the sides, then backward, turning in every direction. At the slightest sound, the whitetail will swivel its head and cup its ears toward the suspected source. The deer will spend as much time as it feels is necessary to determine the source of the noise before resuming feeding.

The old saying "No noise is the best noise" is applicable the majority of the time in deer hunting. Every attempt to evade those acute sound detectors which are so close to the thinking center of the deer is good practice. Learning to stalk and still-hunt without making noise or to sit quietly in ambush is an art in itself.

There are other ways to utilize sounds which are worth mentioning. Deer are attracted to music. Deer will venture close to farmhouses and hunting cabins to enjoy the music, and they listen to music at a distance. Temporary residences such as an R. V., hunting vehicle, campsite, or otherwise new sources for the music, will find them interested but keeping their distance. A transistor radio tuned into mellow music and placed strategically will lure deer. The hunter may want to place the radio in a valley and position himself in a tree stand on the valley rim to observe or hunt the inquisitive whitetail which come to sneak a peek below. Chainsaws and tractors idling, bulldozers, a music box, a set of wind chimes, or even a tethered goat bleating will produce a good sound lure by arousing the curiosity factor of deer. Deer want to know what is going on in their territory. The whitetail will seldom go right to the object but will check it out from a safe location.

Deer associate chainsaw noise with food. Although the noise and commotion will run deer off temporarily, they will not abandon the area and will wait for the noise to stop and the loggers to leave. The deer then come in to feast on the tender tips of limbs, leaves, and the lichens that the fallen tree-tops make available in profusion. I met a logger that shot a fine deer five minutes after he shut down his log skidder.

A noisy brook will help to cover your sound when you are traversing the woods, but do not expect to see many deer near such places. The deer prefer to avoid areas where noise detection is more difficult. They themselves can be as quiet as they wish and feel very uneasy if they cannot use their acute hearing to detect predators. Noisy brooks are good routes for going from one point to another, but they are not good places to hunt.

A good still-hunt can be made near a highway with regular traffic. The hunter takes advantage of the sound of vehicles passing to muffle his sounds in the leaves as he walks over normally telltale terrain. The hunter moves when a car or truck passes, an airplane flies over, a train passes, or the wind gusts, all of which create cover noises which he can take advantage of.

In the West it is common practice to throw rocks into the thickets of canyons to flush deer below. This technique is useful in the East as well. There are times when throwing a rock or stick into a thicket is just the right move to make.

A hunter can throw or drop acorns or pebbles from a tree to

lure visible deer in closer for a shot. The deer comes in to feed on the acorns or persimmons that it thinks it hears falling, but only if it detects no hunter movement.

The sound of a two-legged hunter puts the deer on alert. The hunter who cannot go through an area such as the dry-leaved floor of a forest without making noise should make an attempt to disguise his sound. Walk with a stick to rearrange the sound of human steps by creating an extra leg. Pause and scrape a few leaves around every now and then. Vary your footsteps from the normal pace. Deer have been known to actually be attracted to the noise of hunters walking in such a manner, probably thinking they have found another deer.

Deer are unaccustomed to hunters doing much other than sneaking. There is a time when the hunter might make an appropriate choice to run through an area to get in range or to make himself otherwise obvious. If you have spotted a bedded animal which you think might be too difficult to sneak to without detection then you might try to near the animal by walking indirectly to it but closer than you are without ever looking in the direction of the deer and without hiding any noise or moves while walking at a normal stride. The deer will be unlikely to flee when it thinks that it has gone unnoticed.

Where wild turkeys are found, the hunter can use a turkey call to effectively deceive the deer. Deer and turkeys have an affinity for one another. Scratching around like a turkey can bring them in.

Indigenous scents can be used to advantage in the deer hunt. Hunting near a tobacco barn will help disguise the smell of a chewer or smoker. The smell of a paper mill filling the woods can lower the odds which normally favor the deer. Hunting near an oil well may be particularly useful for a mechanic or someone who has worked on his vehicle before the hunt. Hunting in an area covered with the scent of pine or cedar may tend to favor the hunter as well.

DEER BELLYING, SNEAKING

The whitetail is an escape artist. A little experience will soon teach the hunter respect for the cagey whitetail. Some hunters with many and varied experiences lean toward the belief that big bucks know how to vanish into thin air. I will not go so far as to insinuate that deer are supernatural creatures but will readily state that as natural animals they can be quite "super."

"Houdini" deer vanish at times by crawling on their bellies. Deer have been observed crawling on their bellies for considerable distances to escape a hunter or to investigate one. I once observed a buck in rut crawl a hundred yards to reach a hot scrape since he knew a hunter had built a stand in the area. I had waited patiently for three days when I saw a tiny little animal crawling in the woods like a mouse toward the scrape. The small animal became suddenly very large when it came upon the scrape. The deer made itself appear small, knowing it would be hunted for its size.

A very small drainage rut, only a few inches lower than the rest of the terrain, can be used effectively for crossing a field by bellying and evading viewing by hunters. A big-racked buck can belly through a briar tangle passageway which looks only large enough for a rabbit. A 200-pound deer can look like a rabbit going through a rabbit run under the thickets. The deer knows how to "get small."

They can sneak as if they were wearing sneakers. A dry-leaved forest where a squirrel moving can unnerve you and be heard for a hundred yards can be traversed by a deer without the slightest revealing noise. This is the case when the deer smells human intrusion or knows it is passing in view of a tree stand that is sometimes used by hunters.

It will seem at times to be the only statement to be made about the whereabouts of a deer which was clearly standing right in the middle of a field or forest before you to say "it disappeared." It became invisible. It will make you wonder if the deer was a "for real" ghost.

*ABLE TO SNEAK LIKE A MOUSE, THE FLEET-FOOTED
DEER CAN RUN AT TERRIFIC SPEEDS AND JUMP
OVER TWO AUTOMOBILES IN A SINGLE BOUND.*

BAITING

Baiting is illegal in some instances, however providing adequate wildlife habitat is encouraged. Your area may not allow baiting. Most people presume that baiting is illegal and are very surprised to find that it generally is not.

A farmer's crop is never illegal baiting. A pile of the farmer's crop dumped purposely in the woods and hunted over is. Be sure to investigate local regulations before attempting to feed deer at a spot you hunt. Many laws have been updated to allow baiting now that the herds are established and need hunter control measures.

Salt is generally not allowed. Deer may utilize blocks placed for livestock, however. A salt block placed solely in the woods for a hunter's purpose is not allowed some places. Salt blocks, deer food, and the like are not illegal in themselves, but hunting over them is. Some state regulations allow deer hunting over baited areas when the bait has been removed for a specific amount of time prior to the hunt. Find out exactly what is the truth for your area by contacting a game warden.

Deer will avoid block salt for a couple of months. Then they will turn the block over and lick the ground beneath them, or lick all around them if they are too large to topple. Only much later and usually after block replacement, do they decide to actually use the block itself for licking. From that point on they will visit it frequently. To draw deer more quickly, sprinkle rock salt on the ground while wearing clean rubber gloves and boots. Bucks use the licks less commonly than do does.

Natural salt licks are abundant in many areas. They are inconspicuous for the most part, not readily apparent to the untrained eye. The natural salt lick is usually an eroded spot on a hillside with a lot of hoofprints. It has a briny look, and the earth nearby tastes slightly salty. In the past century many of the mass quantities of deerskins that were sent to England from this country were taken over these natural salt licks.

If you are going to provide salt for deer, choose the mineralized blocks over the plain white ones. These additional minerals promote antler growth and general health and are more like the natural licks. The deer need the minerals more than the salt, and buck deer seem to know this, tending to visit the mineralized blocks more often.

Some hunters bury the entire block. This causes the deer to scrape away and paw the earth, creating a sizable lick. As the block deteriorates and penetrates the soil when it is eroded by rainwater, a more natural type of lick is formed.

Deer mainly visit salt blocks at night. Salt stands are generally a poor choice for daytime hunting. Salt is less attractive to deer during the cooler parts of the year than in the summer. It is in the heat of summertime that the deer hit salt like crazy. Although hunting salt in the late fall deer season is not the best course of action, having placed salt in the area will have served to attract deer to the general area and to supplement their health.

Planting crops with the intention of luring and also nourishing deer is a good and ethical idea. Providing food for the deer is a matter worthy of your energy as a giver and taker of life in the woods. You sow the crop, improving the deer's nutrition, and for your efforts you reap a better-quality animal. Good crops to plant for improving the whole herd are red clover, sweet corn, alfalfa, turnips, and any legume such as beans or peas, lespedeza or sorghum millet.

Honeysuckle stands can be improved by cutting out some of the overstory and the trees on which the vines climb to keep the mass nearer the browsing height of the deer.

When trees that have become too tall for the deer are cut back to force suckering of tender shoots at forageable levels, deer are strongly attracted. Stands of saplings can be cut back with the aid of a machete in late winter to make bushes of quality browse in the spring. It can't get too thick for the whitetail deer.

Fruit-tree plantings are excellent attractors. Deer will come to apple trees from miles around. Old apple orchards are sought out by hunters everywhere as favorable places to hunt. A deer which has feasted upon the delicious, teeth-cleaning apples is unlikely to forget the experience and will return to the site repeatedly. The old-fashioned crabapple (the large kind) is great for deer and other wildlife, but any apple will do just fine. Deer will eat apple bark, so cover young trees by a wire enclosure, with drainage tile, or other similar material until they reach maturity. Bars of soap left unwrapped and hung from immature trees by a wire or a string run through a hole bored into the bar will usually keep the deer away from the tree until it is hardy.

Remember that it is improper and often illegal to bait deer for shooting, but it is entirely ethical to provide the deer with adequate food supplies in order to promote general herd healthiness and prosperity, which in turn provides for better harvests. In any case, baiting is a less satisfying method of hunting. Those who hunt over baits may enjoy regular success and with comparative ease, but they miss out on true adventure.

Baiting is relatively unsuccessful when deer browse is abundant. Baiting is a good method for attracting deer to the handicapped hunter and to youth.

In my home state of Kentucky, where I own a small tract of land inside a very large tract of uninterrupted deer habitat, baiting for deer is completely legal. Shooting a wild turkey at a bait station is subject to strict penalization and reproach. If I cared to, I could take a dumptruck full of apples and sweet feed out there and hunt right on top of it. I can bait all I want to, but when the rutting season is in progress the only reason a buck will come around a bait station is to look for does. Acorns are nearly always abundant that time of year and the deer would rather have them than the shelled corn I offer.

DEER CALLS

Deer calls have been around a long time but have received very little attention. Recently they have regained popularity and are fast becoming a necessary addition to every hunter's bag of tricks.

Their value to the hunter is a subject of debate. Some hunters attribute their success to the use of calls while others are confident that the contraptions deter success. The value of a call is dependent upon many variables. The ability of the hunter to employ the call, the call design itself, the timing, and the individual character of the particular deer are all subjects which influence the usefulness.

Deer make several vocalizations. Currently, the language of deer is the subject of extensive studies.

The various utterances of the whitetail deer can be described as the bleat, the bellow (the deep, throaty, continuous noises that seem to fill all the surrounding space), blows, low whining noises, shrill whistling sounds, low snorts, and louder, coarser snorts of challenge, bawls, skews, squawks, or raucous whistling squawks.

Commercially available calls are presently separated into two types for hunter use, the bleat call and the grunt call. By experimenting a hunter can learn to make most of the other utterances with them. They are great for disguising a persistent cough.

Some of the louder noises deer make can be heard by the human ear for hundreds of yards under the right conditions, while the lower-pitched noises are likely to go unheard. Some hunters experience only the snort or whistle of alarm or the bawling of a wounded deer. Many hunters have never experienced deer vocalizations in several years of hunting. As a rule, deer pursue their ways in quiet. They have voices, which they use when they need to, but mostly they rely on other means of communication. The eyes, the nose, and the ears and also body and hair movements are usually expressive enough.

Most of man's trouble in recognizing the vocalizations of deer comes from his own inability to sit quietly long enough to catch and witness the sounds. Here, as in many other aspects of whitetail deer hunting, patience will be rewarding.

Deer calls are not as important in the silent world of the deer as the commercially-responsive hunter may be led to believe. Sure, understanding deer vocalizations is an integral part of the hunting experience, but commercially produced aids have been given more emphasis than is due. The beginner should experience the calls firsthand by spending time with the deer before using deer calls himself with too much zeal.

The truly accomplished hunter has witnessed the calls of deer enough times during woodland experiences that he can reproduce the sounds himself without mechanical aids.

One of the most widely accepted uses for a call is to get the attention of a departing deer. A deer spooked by movement or noise that has not had the opportunity to smell or clearly see the source might stop in his tracks when given a correct call and sometimes even return to investigate.

It has been successful to whistle at a departing deer as one might whistle to call a taxicab. This very foreign sound temporarily halts the fleeing deer as it sorts out the surprising sound in its brain. A handy call will serve this same function and hold the deer longer since the deer is familiar with the sound. Some deer hunters actually carry a police whistle for momentarily stopping running deer for better shots. The whistle also serves the purpose of communicating with other hunters.

Deer "grunt" with deep guttural belches to assert masculinity at fight time or in response to dominance challenges. Grunt calls are corrugated tubes fashioned in plastic which are modeled after the actual larynx tube of a deer. The end of the tube is fitted with a reed-type device that reproduces the shape of the deer mouth and tongue in order to conduct the sound. When you field-dress your deer, be sure to take a look at its windpipe for a better understanding of grunt calls. You might even attempt making your own call from the deer part. Before grunt calls became popular, hunters often fashioned their own. Methods of creating the calls included such improvisations as using the funnels with corrugated nozzles designed for filling automobile transmissions, with the funnel flare end reduced in size then held to the chest of the caller for guttural muffling. The grunt call is the best call for turning deer to "bring them in" for a shot when they are spotted out of range. Combined with rattling antlers to attract bucks, the grunt call works better than the other calls.

*SOME DEER UTTERANCES ARE PECULIAR
TO THE RUT.*

A buck chasing a doe will also now and then utter a short series of guttural grunts. This sound is made by the buck with his
mouth either closed or only partially open and sounds like an
"Uhh-uhh-uhh." Another grunt associated with the rut, which is
uttered when two bucks fight, is a rather loud, abrupt "blatt," like
an explosive "bah." Bucks trailing does in the fall often give less
dynamic, short, and repeated "bla," "ma," or "ba" sounds with
guttural grunts. All grunting sounds are masculine-sounding and
attributable to buck deer. The older and larger the deer, the more
depth and resonance there will be to the sounds. Does are just as
capable of emitting grunt sounds but are rarely observed doing so.

Don't worry about a stomach growl betraying your presence —it sounds just like a buck's grunt! Use it to your advantage.

All deer make bleat sounds. Big bucks in rut are not likely to utter them for fear of being considered wimps. The bleat call is therefore, for hunting purposes, primarily for attracting does and smaller deer. Does attract bucks, let us not forget, so the bleat is useful.

A fawn has a gentle bleat which it sometimes uses to attract its mother's attention. The fawn uses a louder bleat to call its mother from a distant point. A doe has a mere murmur when speaking to its young. A fawn moving through the woods constantly bleating loudly will not be answered with a vocalization by its mother. The mother will most often merely procrastinate in her travel and wait for the fawn to catch up. Does will sometimes bleat when they have lost contact with a group of companions and wish to rejoin them. Most hunters will never experience the vocalizations of adult deer, however, since the deer prefer silence. When in pain, as when shot or in the grip of a predator, a doe will bawl loudly like a calf in pain, as will any deer.

The bleat of a fawn is a "wah," rather sharp, or a "ska-a-w," in series spaced 10 seconds apart. It sounds like a goat crossed with a tree frog. It is not the sound of a goose with aluminum foil stuck in its throat that you will first get out of the marketed bleat calls. These bleat calls are difficult to use and often only call in dogs, which come to investigate.

One of the most startling deer vocalizations is the loud "blow" made by startled animals of either sex. This is a warning noise generally emitted when the deer is worried or is unable to distinguish the character of something it has just scented, heard, or seen. The blow serves to alert other deer within hearing range to the presence of some foreign, and potentially dangerous, object or animal. The "blow" is commonly termed the "snort." A snort can be quite a surprise for the unsuspecting hunter who has not detected the presence of a nearby deer, particularly a big male. Normally the hunter hears the snort immediately before the animal departs at a rapid pace. Kick up a bedded buck, and he will shock you with his snort. It can leave you breathless and unable to function until the deer has vanished. Most hunters consider the "blow" to mean the communication between deer for alertive responses and the "snort" to mean the communication between man and deer or predator and deer—like the snort of a bull to the matador. The snort call is of no value in attracting deer since it indicates suspicion or fright, which the hunter doesn't want to arouse.

Two important things to remember when using calls are not to call too much and never to expect a vocal answer.

STOMPING AND TOOTH CHATTERING

Big deer at times communicate by stomping the earth with their hooves, producing a sound that is modestly detectable to the human ear and detected well by other deer. Remember the old westerns when the Indian scout put his ear to the desert dust and warned of approaching horses or nearby buffalo? It is unlikely that you will ever do such a thing in deer hunting unless you use some futuristic instrument, but the same principle applies to hearing the sound. Deer stamp their hooves on the ground to send messages to other deer which, in turn, pick up the message through their gelatinous-filled hooves, their receivers. Be aware of this rare sound as it may betray the presence of a big buck which is trying to communicate with the deer whose scent you have simulated through a doe-in-heat or other matrix lure. When you hear this sound (it is sometimes possible in the right conditions), it is a good idea to give a deer bleat call motionlessly and lightly. The call may bring the deer in.

Stomping is used by hunters when rattling antlers from ground blinds. The antlers are thumped on the earth, loose rocks and gravel, or sand to reproduce the foot-stamping action.

Humans who stomp on the ground or on a brushpile to flush a rabbit of bird are doing the same thing a deer does when it stamps its hooves. It is trying to get the hidden creature, in this case, the hunter, to move and expose itself.

A deer which has seen a hunter but cannot clearly determine that it is indeed a hunter will usually stomp its hooves first to get the hunter to move then will sometimes rear up and flail the air with its forelegs to really show itself. These actions are sometimes accompanied by tooth chattering. When a doe exhibits all three of these actions, you can bet she is protecting a buck hidden nearby, and you should not move at all. A modest bleat is the only suitable hunter response. With luck, this may expose the buck.

Stomping in this case is a technique used to attract deer. Stomping through the woods and fields to hunt is not. When walking in the hunting area, whether it be to a stand, in a still-hunt, a stalk, or back to camp or vehicle, the hunter should walk sharp-toed like a deer. Put the weight of your step on the front of your foot and not on the heel, which makes the sound of your steps less like the sound of human feet. At first this way of walking may be difficult to maintain, but with a little practice, you will find that you suffer less muscle strain and you see deer more frequently.

FLAGGING

Deer signal with their tails. They send many messages with their large, feathery plumes which are bright white and highly visible to one another.

The hunter who catches sight of the fleeing white plumage has usually hunted too fast. The deer bounces off with its tail aloof and the hair feathered out boldly. It is hard to believe that such a small tail can look so large. Special muscles in the tail make the hair stand erect. A flagging deer tail can appear to be three feet high and a foot or more wide as it floats through the air with hypnotic grace. The whitened hide of the haunches contributes to this as does the white underside of a bounding deer.

A fleeing deer tail makes a good shot for a deer rifle but shots like this are very dangerous since the area of passage for the projectile is seldom scouted and is usually at ground level. When you have the opportunity for a jump shot, hunter safety should be your primary consideration and shooting the deer only secondary. Sometimes bedded deer can be safely hunted like big rabbits, as when headed downhill with the terrain clearly visible all the way to the bottom. This type of hunting is rarely safe, however, and is not recommended as a general hunting technique. It is far better to plan out a hunt, look ahead, think ahead, and pre-plan each shot.

Deer signal danger with their tails and also signal safety. The hunter can use a slightly unraveled white dishtowel or handkerchief to attract a deer by flicking it up and down while holding one corner. A deer which is modestly spooked by movement but has not clearly identified the movement by sight or scent can be halted or even drawn back by the use of a signal flag. The signal flag should be concealed in a pocket which is easily accessible when such a need arises. The signal flag can double as an actual handkerchief, of course. Its uses are many in still-hunting and stalking. Of course, acting like a deer can get you shot, so be careful to wear hunter orange when using the flag. If you are hunting in camo, then put the orange on the signal flag and avoid hunters who shoot at anything white they see.

When deer see the flag, they think the sound which alerted them was not a hunter after all but another deer. The escaping deer will nearly always look back as it moves away. The hunter should gently swing the white cloth from side to side after he has caught the attention of the deer with the up-and-down motion. This sideways swing means "all clear."

Another side-to-side swing of a deer tail, when not shooing flies, is used to caution following deer. It is like the hand signals of the point man in a jungle patrol. This is a twitching motion from side to side with the tail down. A caution twitch is a stiff twitch. When you observe such a movement, be certain that the deer are looking for you and that you should be very still and quiet.

When deer feed, they twitch their tails before they raise their heads to check for danger. If they are worried, they raise and cock a front leg and flair the tarsal hair. If their suspicions mount, they stamp their cocked leg while abruptly twitching their tail to warn other deer. A dependable sign that a deer is about to depart, especially a buck, is laid-back ears. If the deer detects no danger, it lowers its tail to the normal position and resumes feeding. This is when the hunter chooses to shoot, since the deer's reaction time is minimized.

Occasionally you will see a raised-tailed buck that you are sure was not spooked trotting along unhurriedly through the woods. Such deer will have their mouths wide open and even sometimes have their tongues conspicuously hanging out. These bucks are chasing a doe in heat.

Bucks don't usually flag—check that deer out first for antlers when you jump a group. Look for the one that doesn't send up the distracting flag.

RATTLING

Antler rattling is a means of luring deer by imitating a territorial or dominance battle between two bucks. This is a highly effective method of attracting mature bucks. Not just mature bucks appear, but all deer turn out for the fight. It is a phenomenon akin to that moment in grade school when someone yelled "Fight, fight!" at recess.

Rattling or "racking" as it is termed in some locales, is most effective just before the rut and during the rut peak.

Fresh antlers carry the most authentic tones. Antlers for rattling can be frozen in sealed bags for use the following season. Old sheds are sometimes reconditioned by boiling in linseed oil. Almost any antlers will do, since no specific tone is needed to reproduce the actual sound of racking deer. I have seen successful rattling performed with sheds from spikes to 10-pointers several years old, as well as those which were fresh, frozen, water-logged, or boiled in linseed oil. Plastic limitations even do the job. Artificial antlers with excellent resonance are easy to obtain. The trick is not so much in the materials used as it is in the application of the technique.

Dry, old sheds may be too brittle and simply break, which makes boiling in linseed oil a good idea. Freezing does enhance tone quality but also serves to preserve the antlers.

Authentic antlers for rattling purposes can be purchased via mail order. Another source for antlers is road kills. You may pick up a rack from a packing house.

Big racks are burdensome. They usually wind up on trophy mounts anyway. Smaller bucks don't want to tangle with the big ones, and though they may be lured to large-sized antler sounds, they will remain shy and distant. Big ones do bring in the biggest bucks with the most consistency. If you want to see more deer, though, a medium-sized rack will do best. These will offer some challenge to the subordinate bucks while also bringing in the big boys.

Small racks will do fine. A pair of nice forks or spikes fit into leg pockets well and can be used effectively if the hunter has adequate knowledge of the sounds. My best success has been with spiked antlers. They are no burden and have brought in big bucks.

In this subject the whitetail is variable according to individual personality. If the big buck has suffered wounds from antler bashes, he may shy from the sound of a large rack. A large rack being rattled may repel him completely.

It is popular consensus that an eight-point rack in the medium range is the most suitable to use when there is a choice.

The best way to learn the sound is to hear it in the woods. Such sounds are more frequent at night. This sound is surprising to the novice because the sound is more mechanical than he might expect. The first time I heard the sound I suspected it was the noise made by a clicking oil-well pump line and only realized it was fighting deer when I actually saw them. At night deer are more active, and the wind has usually subsided enough that except for the noises of crickets, frogs, locusts, and owls, the woods are quiet and sound travels far. When the ground is moist and frozen and all the chirpers are hibernating, encounters are most frequent.

Actual sound simulation of a pair of battling bucks is very difficult to achieve no matter how much you study it away from the wild. Good videos are available for help. But when the viewer witnesses another hunter racking in deer, it is likely to be in a hunt situation very different from the scene in which he is going to hunt. A lot of success can be had by rattling at a game farm where the buck ratio is high and hunter pressure is minimized. These videos are indeed good for initiation into rattling, but they are not capable of producing instantly successful rattlers. If rattling for bucks doesn't work like it did for the fellow on T.V. for you, it doesn't mean that rattling won't work in your area. It would be hard to sell a video in which the viewer sits there patiently watching for a couple of hours or more before having any success, or even all day with no success at all. No thanks, you say.

Deer don't butt heads like bighorn sheep. They do more jousting and pushing. They rub and mesh their antlers together while pushing in a test of strength and endurance with little butting after initial contact. They lock, push, and rub, and that is it. They do not intend to hurt one another, since they are not enemies. Injuries do take place, but usually the only thing hurt is the pride of the loser.

Bucks are sometimes found with their antlers locked together. Hunters have stumbled upon bucks dragging around other bucks with a broken neck and locked antlers. One hunter found a buck with the head and rack of another buck attached to his own. Most likely the two bucks had locked horns in battle, and the bodiless buck was taken by predators while the live buck fought to free itself. Breaking the neck of an opponent during the rut is very uncommon since nature has provided the deer with swollen necks which really brace them up during this period.

When rattling you can run off the deer by being too enthusiastic. Firm your antlers together abruptly to make initial contact then mesh them together systematically while varying speeds. Rattle for awhile and then pause for a significant length of time while looking for deer. You can blow it by coming on too strong at first if deer are nearby. Follow instinct. Feel it out. Rules about how long to rattle or how long to stop should fluctuate with different situations. Generally the hunter rattles for less than 60 seconds and pauses for fifteen minutes or more.

Harder and heavier rattling can be best accomplished by two people. In this case the person doing the rattling, often a guide, conceals himself in a ground blind while another person, the hunter, perches in a tree motionlessly.

Rattling done right will allow you to see the local bucks. Rattling is a good way to get them out of the thickets, beds, and hiding places of their daytime haunts. Effectiveness is decreased where a lot of hunters practice the technique. Deer learn quickly.

Rattling is a very satisfying experience, more exciting than ambush without it. The buck often comes out swinging his antlers from side to side in swoops like a boxer swinging his gloves at ringside. Some will barnstorm you fully intent upon proving their dominance and upset over the fighters intruding in the area they think they own. Some subordinate bucks will come in with the intention of running off with the does the older bucks are fighting over while the bigger deer are battling.

When waiting for a response from a dominant deer after rattling, watch for does, spikes, and other smaller bucks looking over their shoulders and seeming uneasy. This is almost a sure sign that a larger buck is moving in. The other deer are intrigued but do not want to get in over their heads, so they wait for the dominant buck to appear. They will egg him on, further tempting him to do something about the situation.

The rattling technique works best when the hunter makes the sound at ground level. The sound is more authentic nearer the earth. While on the ground the rattler can stomp and beat antlers on the forest floor. He can rake bark, leaves, and gravel and grunt. Such movements are more conspicuous in a tree and if pinpointed to be coming from such a source will be ineffective.

Rattling antlers should be painted orange or taped orange. A hunter banging antlers in the brush or carrying antlers over his shoulder is a likely target for another hunter. Many are the hunters who would shoot into a thicket upon the sight of an antler.

Cutting off the brow points and grinding down the sharp edges will make the tines more comfortable to handle and prevent accidental hand injuries. Some hunters prefer to cut off the tine ends to make handling easier. This, however, makes it difficult to gently tick the tines together to pull a buck in a little closer for a shot.

Bicycle handlebar grips placed over the ends of the antler bases work well for softening and warming the hand grasps. Dipping antlers in liquid rubber which is commercially available for dipping hand tools is good also for hand grips. Duct tape will suffice but can be a burden if it should start to peel off in extreme heat or cold.

Drill a one-eighth-inch hole near the base of the antlers through which to tie a length of rawhide or a boot string for carrying the antlers over your shoulder in transport. This will also keep you from dropping an antler and losing it.

Once again, the beginning hunter should not overemphasize the technique of rattling antlers as he attempts to take his first deer. The silent and still approach at the proper location is difficult enough to be successful at. Take the antlers from your first buck and use them when you go after a bigger one later.

CAMO

Some successful deer hunters insist that they can wear a flashy business suit deer hunting. Such opinions are advanced by hunters whose techniques involve hunting from shack blinds or long-range rifle hunting. The hunter who downplays the value of camouflage seldom experiences the closeness that makes deer hunting a real conquest. Long-range rifle hunting is more of a "shooting" sport. Shooting accurately at longer ranges is an objective of considerable merit, of course, but differs in difficulty from close-range deer hunting.

The whitetail hunter must always think in terms of becoming part of the landscape in an effort to surprise the deer. The concept of "environmental blending" is based on trying to utilize landscape features in combination with personal disguise to avoid being a new or unnatural spot in the scenery.

Whitetails living in any particular area are intimately familiar with every stick, stone, tree, and bush. They can readily identify anything out of place. In the same way, when you arrive at your home from a day at work, you would be certain to notice a piece of paper in your driveway or an aluminum can on your lawn. It would be a real surprise to see a new deck or front porch.

Camouflage has become fashion. Many commercial varieties are available. One should consider his environs before he selects his camo clothing on eye appeal only. If green is out of season in the fall in your area, then green is only going to be useful in evergreen stands. Brands that resemble tree bark are excellent for hardwood stands. Leafy camo is best in fall when leaves are clinging to the trees and in ground blinds. White-blotched camo is for snow. Camo can be found with patterns for vertical or horizontal blending. Choose the right design and color for the individual hunt situation.

You can always make your own camouflage. A bedsheet with a neck hole to form a poncho-type covering will suffice for snow hunting. You can make any sort of clothing by sewing, painting, staining, or otherwise improvising a camo design.

To simply have one color intensity for the bottom half of your torso and another for the top is a good step in breaking the outline of the human form. The buckskins that pioneer hunters and Native American hunters wore had fringe, not because the frilly appearance appeals to humans, but to break the outline of their garments when hunting. Color itself is important but not as important as color change to break and blend outline.

Camouflaged clothing should be as quiet as possible. Nylon and other synthetics are good for stopping wind and repelling water, but they are noisy. They are just the thing for goose hunting but are the wrong apparel for deer hunters. Quality hunting apparel might be expensive, but it will prove its value in the long run. Cheap hunting clothes sometimes don't even make it through a season.

Wool is best for cold climates. It will retain heat even when wet. Wool is quiet. Cotton is the best fabric for warmer hunts. A limb rubbing against one of these natural-fabric garments will make minimal noise. These limb swipes are high-frequency sounds detectable by whitetails from afar and distinctly human noises. Animal fur makes no such sounds. Noise reduction is one of the primary considerations in selecting hunting apparel.

Deep pockets are a plus in jackets, coveralls, and trousers. You will probably have good uses for every available pocket.

All clothing should fit loosely to allow for layering of undergarments and agility in climbing trees. Looser clothing might also break outline somewhat.

An often overlooked part of hunting apparel that needs some environmental blending is the boot sole. Hunting boots are offered in a wide variety of camo colors but are often made with somewhat standout material for the soles, which may be highly visible when viewed from below. The glistening, creme-colored boot sole shape is quite alertive to deer, which are familiar with the shape and associate it with threats to their survival.

Totally avoid shiny garments that produce a glare. The glare can foil all efforts at concealing your identity. Some of the camo design hunting clothes produce a strong glare under sunrays. Blacken your zippers with a magic marker. Deer are unimpressed with diamond rings.

If you elect to paint your portable or permanent stand, then do so long before the hunt to minimize scenting.

Among most wild animals, there is nothing more terrifying or distasteful than a human face. Hunters should make every effort to hide them. Camo headnets can be used, but they are more practically associated with turkey hunting than with deer hunting. Although they do function to conceal the eyes of the hunter (the most frightening part of the face), work as mosquito nets, and are easily stored and removed, they are second choices for facial camouflage. Deer hunters need unobstructed vision.

First choice is camo face paint. The colorants should be dull and lusterless, disguising the normal glare of your face. Just black will do. Shades of green, brown, and grey are useful but not as essential as black. Apply a dark streak beneath the eyes to make them less noticeable and also to reduce sun glare for better vision—just as football players do. Put a little dark camo on your closed eyelids. This will keep you from drawing attention to your blinking. Consider your shiny nose, your ear lobes, and your hands. Don't overlook the spaces between your fingers.

If you have no commercial face paint, use dirt, charcoal, fire ashes, or berries for this purpose. Burnt cork is an old-timer. If you have a black complexion use some motley white.

One problem with face paint is that the user often suffers ridicule from other hunters who consider it unnecessary. Such mockers just have not experienced the virtue of face paint themselves. It can draw a lot of attention in public places too. Some people seem intimidated by it. To solve this problem, a few moist towelettes from the chicken place, some handcleaner and a rag, or soap and water for removal are in order. You may want to wait to apply the paint until just before entering the woods and clean it off upon leaving them.

If you want to get close to deer, apply face paint. It is a definite advantage, and in some situations it is a major success factor. When you are properly camoed and blended in with the base of a tree, when your scent is subdued by masking and using the wind, deer will come very near you without detecting your presence until you make a gesture or a sound to get their attention. You can actually smack a buck on the rear as it walks past you. You can become invisible. At such close range you will have to squint and peek through slit eyes to avoid eye contact. It is great fun to fool deer in this manner. These games are good for off-season deer hunting especially. The young deer learn a survival lesson quickly, and the older deer are shocked that they let themselves be fooled. In deer hunting there is an unequaled feeling of accomplishment in having fooled an old buck and let him go. I think that most of them would rather be shot than suffer such a disgrace. It *is* a shot—to their egos. It is a lot easier to let the deer come upon you than for you to come upon a deer and get close enough to touch it. You have truly mastered the art when you can go to the deer and shame it. It is an accomplishment to get close to a deer anytime that you are on the ground. Unless the deer makes an unusual blunder, it is unlikely that you could do this without camouflage that is appropriate.

Some hunters grow beards for their hunts. This appears to be a male ritual with many groups. In one factory where I worked it seemed that the hunter with the best beard was destined to bring home the best buck. Beards are warmer in the cold seasons, retaining heat and repelling wind somewhat. If the beard is not the soft variety but is coarse, it may be noisy when rubbed against the collar of your clothing. A beard stubble rubbing your collar as you turn your head in a stand can be astonishingly loud on quiet days. Either soften up the beard or shave closely to avoid this aggravating phenomenon. In a really close encounter with a deer, a beard stubble can be the decisive factor. It does interfere with the hunter's hearing ability as he slowly turns his head in the stand since the hunter is so intent upon zoning in on the finest of sounds he hears in the woods. The razing sound of beard stubble on the collar or neck gear of the winterized hunter is made near the hunter's ear and interferes with his hearing the sound in the woods that he wishes to identify. This may sound like hogwash but I have found it to be important. Beards grown for camo purposes can be replaced by camo paint. If you think it is absurd to believe that the prickling of a beard can be a loud sound, then wait until you try to quieten your heartbeat in the mysteriously quiet atmosphere of the cold woods. Things get so quiet sometimes that your heart will sound like a drum.

Remember not to wear too much black where black bear are hunted and to always have some hunter orange available for walking through the woods. When hunting in full camo, be continuously on the lookout for other hunters and have some hunter orange ready to display promptly.

COMFORT

Armchair executives or certain others who enjoy comfort as the norm sometimes like to rough it on their hunting trips. There is a right place and a right time for everything under the sun. However, the first time I sat perched in a tree fork for a length of time, I became aware of the possibility of making it a little easier on myself.

Some hunters go so far as to place easy chairs in their stands. Such extremes may be appropriate in some instances. Or there may be no need for any convenience other than a plastic bag to protect against moisture and keep hunters from "taking root" while sitting on the ground. A waterproof pillow filled with pine needles will do nicely and can be made with a trash sack. Styrofoam-bead filled, orange, or camo-colored vinyl pillows which attach to the belt do a great job of retaining body heat and providing a comfortable seat but make too much noise on quiet days at close range. Styrofoam beads move when the hunter squirms or shifts position. Carry something with you for sitting, whether it be in a tree or on the ground, and choose what is appropriate to your hunting situation. If you expect shots at ranges 50 yards or more, then the faint sound of plastic rubbing or beads moving will not hinder you. Find a good thermal cushion commercially available or improvise one which will be scent-free, waterproof, noise-less, and easy to carry in the woods.

Wear comfortable clothing. Trousers which are too tight, long underwear which has shrunk in the wash, socks which have lost their elasticity, none of these has a place on a hunting trip.

The more comfortable you are, the better your chances of remaining still and alert for as long as it takes to bring home the venison.

ENERGY FOODS

When out there in a hunt you need energy to stay alert and fight off chill. High-caloric foods which are quiet-wrapped, natural scented, and noiselessly consumed are appropriate snacks. Peanut butter and jelly sandwiches in baggies are good choices to calm a woods appetite. Avoid foil wrap, as it is much too easily spotted as foreign material by deer. Cellophane is often too noisy. Chocolate, peppermints, butterscotches, and other foods with strong odors should be left at home. Think about your food. It is better to have your food with you than to have to leave the hunting site to go get it.

WATER

Water can be carried in a canteen or pocket jug. Army surplus stores, Boy Scout suppliers, or sporting-goods stores are likely sources for this handy commodity. Boxed, hole-punch fruit drinks are handy. Pop-tops are alertive to deer. The spew is an attention-getting noise. Drinking water from a spring may be part of your outdoor adventure. Water from ponds, lakes, and streams is some-times pure enough for drinking, but the hunter should be certain of the purity of water taken from any outdoor source. A cow field above the source, for example, could give you hepatitis or some digestive disturbance. Just one drop of animal scat upstream from you in the pristine wilderness of the highest mountain streams can cause infection with harmful bacteria, virus, or parasite.

Overall it is best to get your water from a reliable source and carry it with you in a lightweight container. Extra water in camp or in your vehicle is a good idea too. This may refill your canteen and prove useful for cleaning purposes.

Too much pre-hunt coffee can make you have to urinate too often to sit still. Limit fluid intake to avoid unnecessary movement. Excessive intake of caffeinated coffee can constrict blood vessels, making the body chill while warming the stomach.

PEEJUG

A urination vessel is a necessity in a tree stand and for general hunting. A plastic pocket jug with a cap opening is recommended. A thoroughly washed fabric-softener bottle, orange-juice jug, or cola quart will do. Such a jug will allow you to eliminate urine without repelling deer from the area. The volume of the jug should correspond with the amount of planned fluid intake with allowance for length of hunt. Remember that human urine down the side of a tree releases a wide band of scent stream into the air and can foul a select stand for weeks. If you urinate on the ground, be sure to kick leaves, dirt, or dust over the area to minimize the scent. There is no logic in deer hunting that suggests that marking your position with urine is in any wise productive.

YOUR SCENT

Take a good bath or shower before you hunt. By all means avoid scented soaps, shampoo, and conditioners. Unscented soap may be purchased at sporting-goods stores. Product availability is increasing as more hunters learn the value of the age-old concept of "invisibility." Drugstores carry low-odor germicidal bathing cremes which kill odor-producing bacteria for several hours. It is largely the bacteria which produce body odor by emitting gases. Phisohex is superior for anti-bacterial bathing. It is currently not available over the counter and requires a doctor's prescription. The less potent Phisoderm is easy to get but is considerably less effective although still a good product. Scent Shield is a valuable new product for covering these body gases. Chlorophyll and baking soda mixtures are effective. Baking soda itself is the most often used detergent for body and clothing. Betadine surgical scrubbing soap is a good idea for a wash in cases of extreme scent due to bacterial exposure. If any of the cleansers you chose to use have the slightest scent to them you should rinse them off thoroughly.

After the bath, avoid sweating as much as possible. Underarm deodorant is recommended providing that it is unscented. Of course, after-shave or cologne of any kind is taboo.

Clothing should be washed thoroughly using an unscented detergent or baking soda. Use no fabric softener. If detergent is needed to remove soils or stains, then clothing should be rinsed a couple of times more than usual. In the 1990s we will see great expansion in the kinds of soaps available corresponding to the increased number of people getting into bow hunting and also reflecting a trend toward more natural skin care due to the increase in skin cancer.

It is a good idea to place all your clean, well-rinsed, dried garments in a plastic bag with green cedar, absorbent sweet or black gum, pine needles, or whatever is natural to the area you have scouted and plan to hunt. Keep the bag in a cool location out of the sunlight. Some plastic bags give off distinct odors right out of the box. Most plastic bags are acceptable unless they are heated in some manner. A grass sack, cloth laundry bag, clothes hamper, cardboard box, or cedar chest may be a better idea for the hunter who has developed a scent consciousness. Keep an eye on sealed bags to be sure the clothing inside does not mildew. A little mildew may create an earthy smell which is acceptable, but too much can repel deer and ruin clothing. Airing out your clothes helps. Hang them out in the fresh air the day before the hunt.

Some hunters leave their hunting clothes and boots hanging out all year in their barns, on porches, or in other places where they will take on a natural scent.

Avoid being around smokers in confined places such as at breakfast bars or in automobiles. If your hunting companion or you yourself choose to smoke in your vehicle, then open a wing vent and try to keep the smoke moving away from your hunting apparel. Tobacco smoke literally clings to whatever it comes into contact with.

Gas up the night before you hunt while in regular clothes and shoes in order to keep filling station odors from your clothing and boot soles. Oil and gas smells are only permissible when you are hunting near an oilfield. Incidentally, avoid hunting on top of those temptingly elevated oil storage tanks. They may be unsafe. Some have inside ladders and others do not. Sometimes the tops have rusted out enough that people can fall through even though the exterior surface gives no indication of deterioration due to a good coat of spray paint. Trying to get out of that mess could be a real horror.

Keep at a distance from your pet dog as you leave the house. A friendly hug from your canine companion could cause you to blow a lot of preparation since dogs are natural enemies of deer all the year.

Use rubber boots and wash them on the outside to remove all previous odors. Put a liberal amount of baking soda into the boots. This will reduce lingering odors that might puff out with every step you take through the woods. Take along a change of socks and a plastic sack for the old ones.

Your breath needs tending too. Brush your teeth and gargle. Thoroughly rinse out toothpaste and mouthwash odors. Saltwater or hydrogen peroxide mouth gargles for a few days before the hunt will help solve the breath problem. Baking soda, the old reliable, is in order for the mouth as well. Do not chew gum in the stand as this is too much movement and introduces a foreign scent. When deer encounter a discarded cough drop wrapper or chewing gum wrapper on the trail of a hunter they know what to scent for in attempting to locate the predator and avoid it.

SUCCESSFUL HUNTERS PAY ATTENTION TO THEIR INSTINKS, JUST AS THE DEER DO.

Your ears give off more scent than you think. (If you think that your ear cavities don't smell, then insert your little finger in your ear, twist, and smell.) This smell can be reduced by pouring a small amount of hydrogen peroxide into the ears the night before the hunt. Lay your head on a table and treat one side at a time. This kills bacteria which inhabit the sheltered areas inside the ears and also helps to remove wax buildups, which can impair hearing. Since peroxide does not readily evaporate but turns to water after bubbling, it needs to be carefully removed. To remove all water, thump the opposite side of your head with the palm of your hand while bending the treated ear toward the ground, then dry the ear with a soft and absorbent towel. Deer lick the ears of one another to remove ear mites as well as to groom the ear.

The hunter should take measures to avoid the need to expel repellent internal gases. The deer will recognize this sound and odor as distinctly human. Try to refrain from eating beans or other known gas generators before the hunt.

The hunter should allow ample time before the hunt to re-move waste material from the bowels. Human feces left in the woods can foul a hunting area for a considerable time. If you must empty your bowels while on the hunt, it is best to leave the area to do this. Bury the waste material. If you don't have access to a shovel, cover it well with leaves, dirt, or sand. Carry a little toilet paper or paper towels in case of such an emergency. Wiping with leaves is just fine if you know the leaves. But poison ivy or oak rubbed into the rectum can hospitalize you in misery.

Urine scent is contained in the peejug already mentioned. Remember that human elimination scents are notable deer repel-lents. Animals mark their territories with such smells. For a human to deposit his markings means to the wildlife that they are in very dangerous territory, and they will retreat. Some hunters walk over an area to scout it, take a stand in the middle of it, and wait unsuccessfully for deer to come in without realizing they have put a barrier of urine spots all around to warn deer and forbid them entrance. Deer have been observed sniffing human waste in the wild, but rest assured that such a deer is nervously educating itself to "know the enemy." Once it has determined in what direc-tion the human went, the deer will head in the opposite direction. The fact that human scent, and most especially human waste scent, is a deer repellent should be taken seriously by the hunter.

All apparel, your torso, and all the contents of your pockets and pack should be deodorized. Your firearm or bow and arrows should be scent-free also. Clean the bow to remove old perspira-tion film which you left while practicing. Wipe excess gun oil from your firearm. If your intention is to outwit a mature buck deer then you must outwit his nose.

For many years, hunters have used chlorophyll tablets for "internal camouflage." The idea has considerable merit. The tablets are available as supplements at health food stores and some drugstores.

Always take care to avoid sweating. The only time a sweat

may be necessary is when you are hauling your deer from the woods. Too often the hunter is adequately clothed for the cold when he enters the woods but begins to overheat on the trek to the hunting site. The best idea here is to remove some of the clothing for walking then put it back on once you are settled down. Slow down. A slower pace will be less frightening to wildlife, safer for the hunter by helping him to avoid eyepokes and stumbling blocks, and useful in keeping scent and wetness down. Take your time. Don't get excited. "No sweat."

Many hunters think these extra steps to avoid scent detection are unnecessary. They may be successful at longer ranges when the wind is in their favor, but they have little luck when the wind shifts or at closer ranges. Virtually all bow hunters are meticulous scent watchers. A deer can smell a hunter a mile away under the right conditions. In situations where a whole lot of hunters are moving around the area and subsequently leaving scent everywhere, watching your scent is less important since frightened and confused deer are less cautious.

SCENTS

Deer have a nose equal to or better than a bloodhound's. Their sense of smell is at least 100 times better than that of a human. Deer live by their noses. They train their noses. The older and wiser they become, the more they are able to use this survival tool. Scents that are undetectable to our noses may be intensely strong to the deer. The hunter can better understand the powerful deer nose if he takes the time to boil a deer skull to remove flesh and cartilage. The many chambers of the deer nose for collecting scent are thus exposed. The thin bone divisions of the nose section are generally removed when skull wall mounts are made to improve the looks of the skull, so don't try to see the bone divisions in a finished, European-style mount. The many scenting chambers lead directly to the interpreting center of the brain.

There are two main types
of scents for hunter use. First
are the "cover" or "masking"
scents. Second are the "sex" or
"matrix" lures. Combinations
of the two are also available.

A. *Cover Scents*

An assortment of cover scents are on the market. There are
also a host of materials in the woods, fields, and your own backyard that you could use to prepare cover scents at home. These
scents are called "cover" scents because they cover up human
odor and "masking" scents because they pull off a masquerade,
with the hunter smelling like something other than what he is.

Some hunters insist that they do not have odor problems and
find the idea that they might need something to hide their personal scents a blow to the ego. But any hunter who thinks his
scent is not detectable by the keen nose of the whitetail deer is
mistaken. Covering your scent is useful in all deer hunts and absolutely necessary in some.

All scents must be carefully considered before use. Misuse of a
scent can cause the failure of a hunt. The hunter should analyze
his hunting environment well before using a scent. Common
sense must be applied. To use pine for a cover scent where there
are no pines will fool only foolish animals. Another example might
be peppermint, a deer favorite. Peppermint could be inappropri-
ately used by a hunter on a hilltop, for the deer know that in their
habitat, peppermint only grows in low places. The same odor used
in the proper, lowland location but used in excess would be another mistake. Deer are alerted that something with large, mash-
ing feet must be passing through the peppermint in order to release so much odor. Deer are dainty walkers, especially through
their food supply. Proper use of the example, peppermint, as a

masking odor, would be to rub a small amount of the crushed herb on your clothing when you are hunting over a patch of peppermint. You might also place a sex or matrix lure within gun or bow range at a spot from which to harvest an investigating deer. The peppermint mask would not draw attention to the hunter but would instead camouflage his predator's scent. The matrix lure would capture the incoming deer's attention.

Honeysuckle may not bloom in the late fall season of your locality. This is an inappropriate scent for that reason. The apple scent is very productive early in the season near orchards, but apples are generally long gone in late season. Any scent is likely to arouse the curiosity of the whitetail, even some of your wife's perfume. But to count on the curiosity factor bringing home the bacon is to gamble, because the deer will investigate cautiously and at a distance. Reckless curiosity is the exception to whitetail behavior, not the rule. The deer which has chosen to locate a foreign scent will be so keyed up and alerted that your chances of avoiding detection are minimal.

Cedar oil provides excellent masking. Deer use cedar in many ways, and cedar of some sort is prevalent in most geographical whitetail ranges of North America. In some northern regions the white cedar is a preferred food. Although not at the top of the menu for whitetail consumption elsewhere, the other cedar varieties do possess qualities which attract whitetails. Bucks often rub against cedar saplings, and they use the cedar scent as a perfume for mating and as an insect repellent. Cedar is a good, pure scent to use as a masking odor and ranks tops overall in my book. A bough of cedar broken from a tree and placed on top of a stove in a hunting cabin will fill the room with a cleansing odor and drive out foul odors. It is a great air freshener. Cedar foliage stuffed into the pockets of hunting garments will scent the garments well. Cedar is of particular benefit to the hunter before and during the rut. Since bucks often favor cedar for making rubs, the fresh scent of cedar disturbed arouses his territorial instincts and sends him to investigate the intruder, which he envisions as another buck "bucking" his territorial rights. The only place cedar is of no value is in those few locations where no cedar trees occur naturally. Bottles of cedar oil may be obtained from botanical gardens by mail order, from sporting-goods stores, or from craft shops which sell the oil for use in making potpourri. One bottle should last several seasons. You can find fresh cedar boughs somewhere in every city of the United States.

Animal cover scents work well in still-hunting, stalking, and for covering your trail to the stand. Fox and skunk are popular. If you should see a road-kill fox while enroute to your hunt site, get out of your vehicle and rub your boots on it. Of course, avoid blood. The highly scented fox tail tied onto your boot laces and used as a drag will really do the trick of masking your tracks. You must be certain that the fox is dead, of course. Foxes and skunks are the most common carriers of rabies. These animals sometimes go to the roadways to be killed when they are in pain. They commit suicide in their crazed suffering. You might encounter a dazed fox that has not been hit by traffic lying next to the road. I once witnessed a handsome buck following my precise trail when I had secured a red fox tail to my boot and rubbed my boots against the fox.

Deer do not fear foxes and even benefit from sharing the woods with them. Foxes are keenly aware of hunter intrusion and avoid it. Thus deer feel comfortable with the scent of fox around. They will follow a fox trail knowing that the fox is headed in a direction safe from man. If a deer comes upon a trail where the scent of fox has been used to mask human odor and detects human scent due to a lack of thoroughness on the hunter's part, the deer registers "fox-man" and is repelled. Deer will soon learn to associate fox urine with man when several or all hunters in an area use it.

A minimal application of skunk odor is useful cover scent. As with any other scent, too much is unwise. A powerful skunk odor comes from a skunk which has been disturbed or threatened, and deer realize this scent represents danger.

Some of the stronger commercial scent combinations on the market are so useless that one might think an anti-hunting organization came up with them to cut down on hunter success in killing deer. The hunter, presumably buying an attractant, is actually buying a repellant.

The best commercial scents are in glass containers. Glass is odorless, while plastic tends to let off odors when overheated. Direct sun, body heat, or the auto heater can alter the contents of a plastic bottle considerably. Glass will break and make noises when in contact with other items. Plastic will puncture. Glass will allow some contents to collect ammonia since the material blocks the passage of air. Plastic has a modest breathing ability. Whichever container you choose, be sure the contents contain no alcohol.

Some hunters carry used tampons, supposedly to attract deer during the rut. Since blood itself is not a deer lure but a repellent, I do not recommend this practice. It is unlikely that male deer confuse the scent of does with that of a human female. Deer which have been taken in by this method might have been merely curious.

Cow manure is a great scent to use when you are hunting near cattle. These animals occasionally stray into the deer woods. Their droppings are a familiar sight to the deer and are easy to obtain for the hunter (sometimes too easy). Use horse manure near horses, goat manure near goats, and so on. Simply step all over the manure. Don't worry about tracking it home because it will all rub off while you hunt. If there are many deer around, you will find deer droppings. These are quality masking scent but may draw the deer's attention to the hunter, a situation which could be positive or negative, depending upon the game plan. You would not want to use the droppings of a particular deer in hunting that same deer.

A good cover scent is the odor of deer. If you run across

someone with a harvested deer, rub your clothing on the deer skin to transfer scent. Rub your boots all over the hair tufts on the inner sides of the legs of the deer. Rub your gun muzzle or bow on the forehead of the deer between the antlers and your sleeves along the eyelids. Get the saliva on your garments. Get the deer smell all over you, carefully avoiding any blood. Deer have a strong, pungent odor. Squeeze out the urine from the bladder and save it for good scent. If you are planning to hunt from a tree, you may not want to have any deer scent directly on you. This will only draw attention to you. Strong scent placed on your person is useful only in still-hunting or hunting from ground blinds. To use the salvaged urine or the bloodless metatarsal glands as cover scents, place them away from your tree stand and near where you expect to shoot a deer. The hock glands and the urine can be frozen for future use. The release of scent contained in the metatarsal glands of deer is a warning signal used by deer to communicate a threat of some sort. The only time that the use of these salvaged odors is of any benefit to the hunter is when he is hunting a dominant buck which might assume the warning to be directed to him by a subordinate or a challenging rival. Any other time metatarsal scent is repellent.

Scent pads are useful, and more products become available each year for cover scent purposes. A sheepskin boot strap is an old favorite for scent retention and distribution. The wool is carried between the heel and the sole in the arch of the boot.

Be wary of commercialization. The profit motive is the chief one behind much deer-hunting gadgetry. You may not need all this stuff. Too many helps may be a hindrance.

The old school teaches "No scent is the best scent." The new school teaches "Moderation in all things." There is another school down the road which ascribes to the doctrine that "More is better."

As more and more people employ cover scents the deer will evolve a suspicion of them. In a short time deer learn all the tricks.

When this happens, the scent-free hunter will be the most successful, if he wasn't all along.

The Native Americans used scents appropriately. In addition to using vegetation for masking, they collected odors from the deer themselves. One scent commonly used by Native American hunters was the gummy substance from between the toes of the whitetail.

B. Sex and Matrix Lures

Sex and matrix lures are odors taken from does in the estrus cycle. Proper use defines success. Place small amounts of these scents where you wish to attract bucks for shooting. Never place them on your person or on your stand. This could help the deer to spot you when he is looking for his girlfriend. His girlfriend is never to be found up in a tree and it might be a bitter disillusionment to stumble upon a man in a ground blind when expecting a sweet doe. It can get you gored. A good way to use these lures is to place a drop or two of the scent from a doe in heat on a cotton ball in a film canister on the ground on a good shooting path 40 or more yards from your tree or blind if you are using a gun and 20 to 30 yards if you are using a bow. When you leave the stand, you can collect the lure for future use. Leaving it out there will educate the deer, and they won't fall for that one again. To pour the fluid from your tree or spill it on the ground is unlikely to bring a good response and will decrease the effectiveness of using these lures in future hunts. Sex lures are not cover scents. They are useful only during the rut and the periods immediately preceding and following it. Gun seasons usually coincide with the expected rut period. The buck/doe ratio is a factor in the effectiveness of matrix lures. If there are a lot of does, their usefulness declines.

*DON'T COUNT ON MASKING AND SEX LURES FOR A
FULL MEASURE OF SUCCESS.*

Except during the rut, better lures for the hunter are the deer's preferred foods. Persimmon is a great lure of this type. The hunter can collect persimmons and freeze them for use the following season. This is considered baiting in some areas, while the use of commercially prepared persimmon concoctions is not. Naturally occurring persimmon stands are a good place to set an early-season stand. Know the bark of the persimmon tree so that you will not have to stumble upon the fruit to identify the trees. The fruit is voraciously consumed by deer, opossum, fox, and raccoon. Partaking of the fruit yourself is rewarding. Just be sure that the fruit is soft, which usually happens after a frost.

Acorn lure is good if there is a limited supply of these favorite deer mast foods. In an "acorn year," acorn scent may be used as a mask.

MEAT ABSTINENCE

Deer are vegetarian. They chew on bones and discarded antlers and drink milk when young. Otherwise they are complete vegetarians. Blood is thoroughly repulsive to them. For this reason, blood meal is an effective deer repellent for crops. It has the same effect if found on your hunting clothes.

Some hunters choose to eat only vegetarian foods for a period prior to the hunt. In fact, meatless spaghetti is on the menu at some hunting lodges the night before the hunt. Eliminating meat and other strong-smelling foods from the guests' systems may help to reduce their predator's scent and promote success. Serious proponents of this practice think three to five days of meat abstinence are adequate to eliminate most carnivore scent if cleansing fruits and liquids are used in the diet.

If you want to get really close to deer, abstaining from meat eating is a noteworthy practice. For most hunting, when the wind direction is favorable, the practice of vegetarianism is unnecessary. Doing without meat for hunter scent control is a practice for only the most serious of whitetail hunters. For you, doing without garlic for a few days may be enough sacrifice.

American Indian hunting parties often fasted from meat before they hunted the whitetail. The practice no doubt originated in the depletion of meat supplies, but there was a spiritual aspect involved as well. Few will discount the Native Americans as inept hunters whatever their reasons for fasting from meat.

SMOKING

I am sure you have already decided that this chapter is another anti-smoking lecture. It is not. It is concerned with deer

hunting and deer hunting success in particular. To many
hunters, lighting up a cigarette in the woods is a pleasing experience. Enjoying your deer hunt is more important than success. If
you must smoke to maintain composure, then go about it in
ways that will reduce the detrimental effects upon your hunt.
Cigars and pipes are out. Smoke them afterwards. If you use
cigarettes, snuff, or chew, do so cautiously.

A survey of a broad number of
individuals who took exceptional
whitetail trophies showed conclu-
sively that none of the successful
hunters smoked.

Indeed, any attempt to downplay the offensive and foreign
odor of burning tobacco is to deceive oneself. Deer can smell it
from long distances and will become uneasy, hide in thick cover,
or flee the area as a result. The truly serious hunter is better off
ending the habit before pursuing whitetail deer. If the hunter is
not inclined to give up smoking, then he should make every attempt at reducing his inclination to smoke during the hunt itself.

In all honesty, very few deer hunters who smoke will not be
able to recall the loss of a deer which they attribute to smoking.
Such recollections do not account for all the deer never seen.

A hunter can sit in a stand waiting ever so patiently for a deer,
allowing ample time for the deer to check out the area in its normal, cautious way before entering it, and just as the deer is about
to make an appearance, light up a smoke. The deer is never seen.
The time span involved with waiting for the deer often directly
corresponds with the time span involved with waiting for a
cigarette. Essentially, the hunter has repeatedly exchanged success for a cigarette.

Deer do not smoke. Smoke is a danger alarm for wild animals.
It is not alarming to backyard bucks who have become accustomed to the smell of smoke from wood-burning stoves or coal-
fired furnaces. The same is true near some factories. Except in the

unusual circumstances in which smoke is a regular environmental factor, smoke of any kind is a deer repellent.

From the positive viewpoint, cigarette smoke, with its lighter-than-air vapors, can be used constructively to gauge wind currents and show the hunter where his scent is being carried. I know of no better method of making air currents visible. You need not look for deer in that direction until the smoke has thoroughly dissipated.

Cigarette butts should be disposed of in the peejug. This confines the scent of the foul-smelling butt and is a great precaution against fire. Do not throw your butt on the ground where the scent will linger. Ground scents persist much longer and are generally in the scent line of deer. Likewise, the odor of a cigarette stubbed out on a tree limb lingers high in the air and emits a continuous stream of scent in the downwind direction that fans farther out. Bury your butts if you can.

The odor of cigarettes is so strong that I suggest you keep the pack sealed in a baggie and make every attempt to keep lingering smoke from touching your clothing. Only near tobacco barns is this scent acceptable. We have all noticed that a nonsmoker can smell the strong odor of tobacco on the clothing of a smoker.

Be very careful about fires. Since disposable lights have become commonplace, the danger of matches causing leaf fires has decreased. Still many fires are caused by cigarettes themselves. In the excitement of your hunt, you may abandon all precautions unless you are extremely fire conscious. No deer is worth the destruction of decades of nature's handiwork.

Light your smokes with well-sealed butane lighters. Do not use lighter-fluid lighters with their stronger smell, or matches, with their strong sulfur odor. Filter cigarettes will keep some of the scent off your fingers. Any cigarette smoke will foul up your hands if the smoke is allowed to touch them. So keep the smoke away from your person and up in the air.

Deer do munch on the green leaves of tobacco, ingesting

small quantities. In the fall season after field tobacco has been cut from stalk and housed, deer are frequently observed dining on the suckers that emerge from the remaining stalk base. The deer do this to experience mild hallucination and to expel worms.

The nicotine in tobacco has an effect similar to that of extreme cold, in that it pinches or constricts the small blood vessels and slows down the return of normal skin circulation after exposure. Smoking will make you colder while hunting.

MOCK SCRAPES

A trick often employed to bring a buck to the hunter is to create a simulated, "mock" scrape during the rut period. These manmade scrapes are becoming popular with hunters.

To make a mock scrape the hunter clears an area in the leaves approximately one and a half feet wide and three feet long by raking back the forest cover with his unscented rubber boot, rubber gloves, or a tree limb. The hunter would do well to move the leaves back in one direction as a pawing deer would. The spot should be cleared deeply because the fresh earth scent is as good a lure as any. In harder soils an inch of depth will do. In less difficult soils you should loosen the soil two to three inches, raking a good bit of it out to one direction.

The next step is to lightly sprinkle doe urine on the scrape. Dribble deer urine away from the scrape and past your stand site but not up to it. It is best to "freshen" the mock scrape with urine at different times during the week preceding your hunt.

Creating a scrape that will lure a buck to the spot requires considerable expertise. You must think like a deer but also use your superior reasoning to outfox him. The mock scrape must be placed within range of a stand which is positioned with wind direction and air currents in mind. Having two or three stands can help you adapt to wind changes.

The scrape maker in search of perfection can place a licking branch overhead. This branch is usually chest to head high on the hunter and directly above the scrape. A young white oak is a good choice for such a branch. The leaves of a young white oak are usually still hanging onto the tree in the fall (without coloration), providing some cover for the security-minded whitetail buck. The branch is roughed up near the tip, and deer saliva mixed with pre-orbital musk is used to scent it. Commercially available scent for licking branches is hard to get at this time. At present, the scrape-maker must collect his own. Being careful to maintain sterile conditions, he may collect these scents from a fresh road-kill doe, a deer he has harvested, or someone else's kill. When you encounter natural scrapes in other hunting locations, you can carefully remove the licking branches and transfer them to your mock scrape. Some hunters enjoy tremendous success by tying several natural licking branches above their scrape. This really drives dominant bucks wild with competitiveness.

Beat the new scrape with tarsal glands tied to strings (from the front legs of a doe), then drag the glands past your stand. A paw print from a salvaged deer foreleg placed right in the middle of the scrape puts a scented signature on it. Many are the times that you will encounter a fresh natural scrape with a singular, deliberate, and distinct paw print centered in the masterpiece. Rattling antlers can be dragged across the fresh earth to arouse the territorial instincts of a buck and make his hair stand on end, his chest puff out, and steam jet from his nostrils.

DECOYS

A hunting method which is gaining in popularity is the use of life-like deer figurines to lure other deer into range. Nothing lures deer better than other deer.

Native Americans used stuffed deer hides as decoys and also

wrapped themselves in the skins to stalk venison. Things were quite a bit less dangerous back then. Currently hunters use expensive, whole-body mounts prepared by taxidermists (these cost from $700 to $1,000). Only a few can afford such mounts and those few use them in very controlled situations far from public hunting access. Inflatable, collapsible vinyl does are available by mail order and in numerous sporting-goods shops. These are blown up on the spot like water rafts. You can make your own deer decoy by forming a torso from chicken wire and wrapping it with brown *papier-mache*. To save money you can use wallpaper glue and grocery bags or newspapers over chicken wire, paint it with latex paint and cover it with a satin marine varnish for protection from the elements.

Decoys are dangerous, and hunters should be most careful about using them. When transporting decoys through the woods, wrap them in a bed sheet dyed orange. Keep the orange sheet on the deer until it is in place. Remove the sheet only when you are prepared to make an immediate exit. When through hunting, return to the decoy with the orange sheet obviously displayed and recover the decoy. If you want to reduce the chance that your decoy will be shot, put an orange collar on it. A length of orange surveyor's tape will do nicely.

Lifelike deer decoys prepared by the taxidermist will draw and hold deer so well that hunters using them have actually seen bucks attempt to mount them. With less authentic-looking decoys, be prepared to shoot well before the approaching deer comes close to the decoy. A feeding doe is the preferable form.

Hunters should place the decoys in open fields. This will lure deer from the thickets to get a closer look. Hunters should be positioned downwind and have a shooting alley or firing lane planned. The hunter would do well to have a doe-in-heat scent trail leading directly to the decoy, or decoys. Decoys are often placed at scrapes also.

Decoys may be illegal in your state. Check local regulations.

DEER DRIVES

When the success rate is low and deer sightings rare or nonexistent, when the temperature rises and your party becomes frustrated with the lack of deer movement, a deer drive may be in order.

On the long, wooded mountain ridges of the East, two men can conduct a drive. Both men follow a ridge with one man moving along the side of the hill and the other above and behind the first. Deer lying along the benches or flats on the side of the ridge are jumped by the lowest man. The deer usually circle up and back along the ridge where the high man gets a shot.

A noisy hunter can be used by others successfully. If through experience you know that one or more of your hunting companions is the type who will not be still for long but will yield to the temptation to go look for deer, then you can profit by hunting probable escape routes if you are plotting a hunt that takes advantage of hunter movement.

The normal drive incorporates six or seven people. A large thicket which is otherwise scarcely huntable is the choice location to drive. The hunters plan and organize the drive with care. The group is divided into standers and drivers. The standers will be placed at selected vantage points to cover likely escape routes and take advantage of good shots. The standers are aware of one another's locations. The standers should be elevated so that their line of fire will direct bullets toward the ground. Both the standers and the drivers are on the lookout for deer moved by the drivers. The drivers need to know the locations of the standers. The standers and drivers should avoid all shots toward one another.

In selecting hunters for each job, choose those with the proper equipment. Physical capabilities will need to be considered. A hunter with a long-range scoped rifle would be best suited for a stand. A hunter with a brush rifle makes a good driver. A rabbit hunter who has hunted without dogs makes an appropriate driver since he has learned to take jump shots. Another consideration might be who needs to shoot a deer most. A hunter who is after his first deer, or one who has not experienced success for awhile, might be given the advantageous position of stander.

The drivers should walk within sight of each other. In dense vegetation where visibility is hindered, the drivers need to coordinate and rehearse a system of mouth signals. These can be whistles or other vocal calls which do not sound like deer calls and are basically non-alertive. The whistles are given at regular intervals to let each driver know the location of the others. This will also help them to stay in an even line and not get ahead of one another. The ground hunters should move at a slow pace, as this will be more successful and safer as well. It will also increase their chances of getting a shot themselves.

Drivers need not be too careful about making noise when they feel certain that standers will suitably cover escape routes. Too much sound, however, may not flush deer which are wary of predation by sneaky hunters. Stalkers often walk right past deer. These deer will get up and move in the opposite direction soon after the drivers have passed. For this reason, drivers should keep an eye to the rear for escaping deer. It is a good idea for one driver to remain at the starting point of the drive when he can be spared for this purpose. Sometimes the quiet approach will be most effective. Deer are less apt to circle back when it is difficult to locate sounds.

If large numbers of hunters are positioned in stands that cover all the possibilities for escape and there are an adequate amount of drivers to thoroughly cover an area, then the drivers can leave their rifles behind and reduce the danger. One hunter I am familiar with uses his wife and three children to flush deer from a funneling thicket while they are clad vividly in orange.

Some drives, mostly used for census taking, consist of 20 to 60 men divided into one-third watchers and the rest drivers.

Do not take your cues from movies set in Africa showing noisy drives with native beaters. The wary whitetail is less frightened when he can keep good tabs on hunters' whereabouts by the sound they are making. In some states, noisemakers are illegal anyway. Noisy drives put deer on the run, making shots difficult.

Drivers should head downwind toward standers. This hides the stander's scent but doesn't panic the deer, which are keenly aware of where the drivers are and retreating unhurriedly to avoid them.

A "staggered drive" is used to keep deer from circling where the terrain lends itself to such a reaction. Here drivers hunt un-armed and in a V-shape to keep the deer from going around the sides.

Another type of drive might be to push deer toward a water barrier, a cliff, a canyon, a peninsula, or some other natural bar-rier.

Remember that deer can jump over 8-foot barriers effortlessly, can run in excess of 30 MPH through obstacle courses, and can jump in bounds of 25 to 31 feet from a running start.

The joint effort of those participating in a drive which has proven successful is fellowship with lasting reward. It usually works out harmoniously with little disagreement. Leaders get a chance to lead. Some might plot the drive with the capability of an elite military strategist upon the advice of a scout. The ones that really like to get out there and move around get their chance. There is something for everyone in the group plan. Just always remember that the chance of shooting a fellow hunter is to be the constant, conscious, thought preoccupation throughout the drive.

STILL DEER

A motionless deer has an uncanny ability to camouflage itself. By taking full advantage of protective coloration and cover, a mo-tionless deer may be very hard to spot. This is the first survival tool taught to the fawn. To spot such a deer, the hunter is advised to visualize the deer in advance. This might be termed "setting the mind's eye." For example, if a friend should ask you to help him find a pocket knife he has dropped, you would probably first ask him "What does it look like?" Visualizing the knife will make the knife easier to spot wherever it may be. The same principle applies to deer.

Hunters all know what a deer looks like. The whole deer is not always seen, though. The hunter needs to be familiar with the look of every part of a deer. He may see no more than a portion of a hoof sticking out from behind a tree trunk. The black nose of the whitetail surrounded by a white ring is a telltale giveaway. If the deer is looking at you, its eyes can betray its whereabouts although the remainder of its body is hidden from view. Deer lick their noses to keep them continuously moistened. This makes them gleam. The shine of an antler, or a section of an antler, will stand out dramatically in sunlight. The silhouette of a deer against the skyline might betray its presence. The horizontal line of a deer back contrasting with the vertical lines of forest growth can draw your attention. Look for a patch of white in the woods. Check out all patches of white. (But don't shoot at white until you have thoroughly investigated the source.) A deer coat is a distinct brown unlike other browns found in the woods, though usually difficult to differentiate.

Adult deer teach their fawns evasive survival skills just as Buddhist monks teach their initiates to become "invisible." Deer have a lot going for them that we do not.

A perfectly still deer can hide almost at your feet, can be only a step or two away and go unnoticed if it has chosen the right camouflage. Hidden deer often spook under the pressure of a hunter pausing nearby. They remain motionless, however, if the hunter continues at a normal pace. For this reason, still hunters should stop every few yards and pause to survey the situation. Deer can't handle the pause and will panic invariably.

The older bucks are especially adept at becoming "invisible." I myself am convinced that they often do it for amusement. Deer take great pride in outsmarting hunters. A bedded deer, especially a bedded buck, is very tricky to locate. Binoculars will give you an edge over the eyesight of a deer in situations where they are practical.

TRACKS

Prints are interesting but not edible. A hunting area may have lots of tracks but no deer. They tell you where the deer have been but not necessarily where they are. Studying hoofprints can be entertaining and exciting. Analyzing tracks is most useful in scouting to gain understanding of behavioral patterns for particular hunting sites. At times the hunter can "stalk" the deer by following its tracks.

Most hunters hunt large tracks. Although a large hoofprint is not a definite indication of a large deer, it is a good sign. When hunters spot abnormally large hoofprints and attempt to relate the size to others, the story is generally believed to be exaggerated as fish stories popularly are. Finding outstandingly large tracks is memorable for years. It is on the basis of such discoveries that many hunters stick to a particular area for hunting in hopes of sighting the monster deer. A small plaster of paris cast of such tracks is proof positive of the encounter and makes a great conversation piece. Simply carry a small bag of powder in your hunting vehicle and a small bottle of water for making the mold. Some very tiny and quite attractive prints are worthy of molding also for contrast and intrigue. Almost any veteran deer hunter will tell you that he wishes he had a cast of the biggest track he ever saw. Such a cast makes a great ashtray.

A buck and a doe have quite similar hoofprints. Controversy surrounds the hunter's ability to differentiate between the two on the basis of tracks alone. The educated view is that this cannot be positively done without fail. Yet many hunters continue to do so with considerable success. The ability to tell a buck track from a doe track is largely intuitive. Other signs are observed in conjunction with the hoofprints to aid in determining the sex of the deer. For example, the tracks may lead to a fresh rub with urine stains in the snow which are obviously produced by a squatting female or a leg-raising buck. (Standing bucks move one leg forward or backward to urinate.) Only bucks make rubs, but a doe might visit it. On the basis of a track alone, only an expert, a person with significant experience in tracking successfully, can truly see gender differences, and then if only under ideal conditions such as half an inch of sand or snow.

A common fallacy is that dew prints in the deer track show it is that of a buck. The two small holes in the earth behind the two main toe prints are the dew prints. All cloven-footed whitetails have dewclaws on all four feet, bucks and does. Young and old of both genders have them and use them. The dew claws give the deer added traction when needed and help to stabilize their balance. Very large deer use them more often on flat and dry terrain to support their massive weight than do smaller deer. On softer terrain all deer may use them as mud grips to prevent crippling falls. Wounded deer nearly always use the dewclaws for stabilization. If you are following a deer which may have been wounded and notice that the animal has switched to using the dewclaws, it is good sign the deer has been hit.

Hooves are as different among deer as fingerprints are among humans.

When several sets of prints occur together giving evidence of a group movement and only one of the print sets has continuous dewclaw marks, it may well be that a heavier buck is traveling with a group of does. The buck, with his larger physique and heavy antlers, needs the added support. This assumption is most likely to be proven correct in the fall. In the spring, does carrying fawns in later stages of pregnancy need the additional support also.

Big does have big hooves too. That big buck that you trailed all day based on the size of the hooves alone may turn out to be a skinhead at trail's end. The same applies to tracking on the basis of dew prints alone. All deer except the springy, light youthful ones use their dew grips when going up embankments or traversing terrain where the additional toes will help them maintain balance.

Fresh tracks have sharp edges. Older tracks have more rounded edges. Also, the sides of fresh tracks will be damp and not crusty. In a swamp or lowland, look for water trickling into the prints. If such trickles are just starting, you will know the track is freshly made. Track freshness can be determined through common sense. Examine the track and consider the medium in which it is deposited, the humidity level, the sunlight, the wind exposure, and any other relevant factor. Some tracks are easy to explain. If there is fresh mud dropping from the foliage all around, you can bet that you just aroused some deer!

The distance between tracks indicates the pace of the animal. If they are more than 21 inches apart, it is picking up speed. The normal distance between sets is 17 to 19 inches. If prints are more than 2 feet apart, the deer is trotting. If they are 6 feet apart or more, the deer is running.

Mating tracks can be distinguished easily where deer have actually gone through the act. The same is true of fighting tracks. Browsing tracks wander and follow no set course. You will find tracks that indicate young animals were playing. They like to play "Billy goat on the mountain" on small mounds. In the search for fall bucks, look for tracks which are large, dragging, slightly pointed outward, and forward-moving with little meandering. A tired buck in rut who has been chasing women and fighting his fellows day in and day out will drag his heels. He's got a one-track mind and displays very little interest in feeding.

Some deer have such large hooves that you may think that the tracks are those of a cow. The hunter who has been conditioned to average deer prints may actually overlook a very large deer track. It is very seldom that a heavy weight deer will have small feet. A marvelously antlered deer may have small feet.

It is commonly said that the rounded edges of the deer toes are more pronounced in the male of the species. This is attributed to the buck using them more than the does in making scrapes and gallivanting about looking for mates. There may be some truth to this in some locates where the terrain is coarse. In soft soils worn-down hooves only indicate age at best, that the deer is older than young.

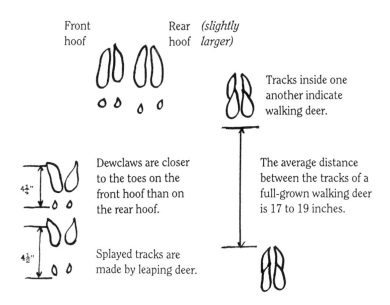

Front hoof

Rear hoof *(slightly larger)*

Tracks inside one another indicate walking deer.

Dewclaws are closer to the toes on the front hoof than on the rear hoof.

The average distance between the tracks of a full-grown walking deer is 17 to 19 inches.

4¼"

Splayed tracks are made by leaping deer.

4½"

Tracks of galloping deer show hind hooves ahead of front hooves and tracks 5 to 7 feet apart.

The regeneration of the hoof is a continual variant in making any assumptions about the sex of a whitetail. Their hooves regrow just as human nails do. The only time that I would put any store into the buck prognosis based on rounded toes is very late in the rut when a particular track is separable as distinctly different than the others nearby.

STALKING

Stalking deer means following deer tracks, usually fresh ones, to the animal itself. Another term for stalking is "trailing." Trailing is most commonly used to describe the action of following a wounded deer for collection and stalking generally declares the following of an unharmed animal.

A fresh snow is the best time for stalking in the North. Stalking is a useful method for hunting deer in Western range habitats where hunters traditionally go after deer instead of letting the deer come to them. Whether the hunt is in the North, South, East, or West, the stalker needs to be in good physical condition if he intends to outwalk the animal. A hunter who comes upon a set of fresh tracks might follow them only a short distance before he discovers the deer he is seeking. Or he may travel miles. The seasonal range of an individual deer does not greatly exceed one mile. Deer which are not pushed will seldom venture farther than that and rarely even that far. A deer that is walking fast walks five times faster than a hunter who is walking fast. To walk one down is unlikely. The idea is to follow the deer to a destination where he can be taken after he has stopped to bed or feed.

Deer which have been live trapped and fitted with telemetric collars then released within 20 miles of their home range return invariably to their home. Deer released over 20 miles from home head out in any direction. These controlled situations for research are subject to change somewhat with habitat variations in differing locations elsewhere but serve as a good average for understanding whitetail behavior. The deer prefer familiar surroundings. When pushed, a deer will usually attempt to circle back to its home range. If need be, the deer could venture as far as 20 miles and still be back the next day. Like stories of dogs finding their way home over seemingly impossible distances, there are a couple about tagged or collared deer doing the same. In one documented case a deer traveled 350 aerial miles to return home. Such are exceptions. What a stalk that would be for some diehard.

When stalking a deer, always move from cover to cover. Take advantage of tree trunks, rocks, or other possibilities for concealment. Deer check their rear path often for predators. Man is usually a predator during only one season of the year, whereas the wolf, wild dog, coyote, bobcat, lynx, and panther are predators all year long. Examine the area well ahead of you before moving and exposing your torso to any deer which may be watching. Look far ahead for the deer, but also look nearby. Binoculars are useful and recommended, but don't rely on them alone and overlook closer deer. If you can, stalk crosswind instead of upwind since deer check their backtrail. If the deer have scented a tracker, they will cross wide-open areas to make him expose himself. Here the hunter must stop and look carefully into the cover on the opposite side, or perhaps even go around the clearing.

Knowledge of the terrain helps immensely in a stalk. With a handy topographic map, a stalking hunter can predict the route the deer will follow and possibly circle ahead of them for an ambush.

A group of does with a buck will sometimes split up right before entering a bedding area. Deer are very aware of the fact that they have left a trail and tracks. They don't know that humans do not have the ability to smell as well as they do. Does like to be bred when nature endows them with receptivity so they like to have a buck on hand when the time comes. When a proven breeder buck with the right things going for him encounters a group of does in or near the rut, the does look out for him. The deer know that the bucks are the most sought after members of their family. The largest number of does will go in one direction a short distance, leaving an obvious trail, while the buck and possibly one or two does will sneak off on another trail, leaving fewer imprints in the soil. They do this instinctively to protect the buck. In the fall season, when they are in groups with a dominant and virile buck, they will do it nearly every time they are going to bed down. They will use the split maneuver when they are not planning to bed down if they see, smell, or otherwise sense you following. Sometimes the buck will hop trail in thick cover and actually plan to attack the predator following the trail with his lethal antlers. Look very nearby for such bucks, even when you can see deer in the distance. The bucks are unlikely to try to ambush a human. But if they thought they were being followed by some other predator, hid by the wayside to attack it, and suddenly discovered the enemy to be a human hunter, they still might act defensively. Get ready when you see a track split on a hot trail, a good chance for victory may be imminent.

When you are stalking, your shot will often be rapid. When you judge that you are fairly close to the deer you are following, change over to a still-hunt. Stop often and remain stopped for awhile thoroughly scanning the area and using available cover for concealment. It is often under the pressure of one of these stops that the big buck blows it and exposes himself.

Stalking should only be seriously considered during snowy weather or when the ground is very damp. Stalking is most successful where there is a good "tracking snow."

STILL-HUNTING

Most beginning hunters are a little confused when the term "still-hunting" is mentioned. As the name insinuates, the hunter undergoes periods of stillness. The hunter does not remain stationary but undergoes a hunt by a slow search. It might be more appropriate to call a still-hunt a "sneak hunt." Walk a few paces then stop while taking advantage of cover and examining every bit of the woods for the least telltale sign of deer. Look for horizontal lines in vertical thickets, for a leg protruding from behind a tree, for a cold, black nose patch surrounded by white, an eye, any patch of white or unusual brown. Always search for the slightest movement—a twitch of an ear, tail, or foot. If the deer flag you and you see nothing but a big white tail bouncing like an ostrich plume, you are going too fast. If you work up perspiration you are moving too quickly. The object is not to cover a maximum amount of territory but is to find a deer in a minimum amount of territory. The traditional still-hunter moves a few feet at a time then pauses until he is certain that he has observed the area ahead adequately to spot any deer before moving cautiously a few more feet. Every few feet in the woods your view will change.

Sometimes you can smell deer. Use your nose—it is better than you may realize. Though it is not nearly as keen as the nose of the whitetail, it is still a definite asset. If you smell deer, the chances are great that one or more are hidden and watching you from a well-camouflaged spot very nearby. The odor left by deer dung or bedding is insignificant in comparison with the strong body odor of a deer. If you are not familiar with this scent or need a refresher, then get close to a deer someone else has taken and record the smell deep within your olfactory memory bank.

In your search, above all follow instinct. Get into it. You have within you great intuition. First hunches are the most truthful. The first intuitions are usually quite fleeting. They do not linger. You must grasp them quickly before reasoning power overpowers them. We do not have to be E.S.P. experts to follow hunches.

Look behind you occasionally, as well as far to the sides. Concealed deer which did not flush and which you overlooked may be creeping off in the other direction to avoid you. If you are using fox scent or have scented your feet with deer droppings, they may actually be following you. It is seldom the case, but it does happen, that a deer will actually follow you at a distance to keep tabs on your whereabouts when it is aware that you are a human.

Deer often stay really tight. Does are most likely to display themselves. Trophy bucks are not into showing off for hunters during hunting season. Young bucks frighten easily and run for safety. Taking off at speeds that can reach 45 M.P.H., with the ability to jump over 10 feet high and as far as 30 feet on the ground, is their best choice. Big old bucks, however, choosing to use their heads instead of their legs and to outwit you, will remain still and hidden in brush so thick you couldn't imagine them making it through until you almost step on them. When they do suddenly get up, their size and sound will inevitably give the hunter such a start that he won't shoot or will miss. I think big bucks get a kick out of doing this. Another reason they do it is that they are not nearly as afraid of what they can see as of what they cannot see. They know that to run off into other territory will make them vulnerable. Most big bucks choose to play it cool. They blend their antlers with staghorn sumac or other vegetation like chameleons.

Still-hunting is most useful in wilderness. In areas with large hunter populations, it is not a good choice. Where there may be 40 hunters per square mile, for instance, still-hunting just moves deer toward other hunters. The still-hunter finds himself serving as driver and never gets his deer.

Still-hunting is particularly effective when you see the cattle lying down in the fields. This is a fairly good way to tell whether deer are moving at that time of day. As mentioned earlier, cattle tend to follow the same solar/lunar feeding cycles and weather cycles. So check the behavior of cattle in the fields you pass as you drive to your hunt site.

You may not want to sit in a stand all day. Some hunters are reluctant to do this and some are incapable. Still-hunting offers some relieving exercise, scenery changes, and circulation of blood.

For obvious reasons, it is not wise to stalk or still-hunt in hunter-filled woods. Look *up* for other hunters as you go so you won't disturb their hunt or risk an accident. Many have been the times that novice still-hunters have walked directly underneath my tree stands without noticing me above. It is embarrassing to have a hunter in the tree above you make his presence known.

Avoid running into sapling limbs. This is something deer do not do when they are traveling. A whipping limb, especially hitting against clothing, is a sure sign of human encroachment to deer.

Don't break big sticks underfoot. Breaking twigs is acceptable and usually unavoidable. Deer step on twigs too. Walk point-toed like deer. This is important. On a still-hunt, clod-hopping will be fruitless, and at best you may get a rear shot. Walk on your fore-foot and toes. Take sharp steps. Vary the speed of your steps. Running at a trot on your toes may even be in order at times. Deer will never expect you to come running; they expect man to be a sneaky predator. Surprise at a hunter running in might dumbfound the deer so that it is too confused to act.

Attempting to imitate the footsteps of another deer by toe-walking is a good idea when noiseless walking is impossible, as on dry leaves, noisy gravel, or ice. This hunter action will hold deer instead of pushing them away from range or sight. During the rut, bucks will holdup in cover to wait for the coming deer, un-suspecting of hunter misrepresentation.

You can stalk faster in open woods, but you should slow down to a snails pace near the edges of thickets or other dense cover. These transition zones, where the forest changes into something else, are the most likely places to find deer. These areas require more detailed attention.

In your still-hunt, carefully examine all logs and fallen or logged tree-tops for deer. There may be time in your hunt when the sight of a few deer back hairs popping up behind a log puts you on target.

Putting the sun at your back forces deer to look into the sun. This dulls their sighting ability and gives you a needed advantage. Keep cover behind you so that the sun does not create a halo behind your silhouette which might alert the deer.

SOUNDS OF APPROACH

 Squirrels can really get your adrenaline flowing. Squirrels have never been considered dangerously threatening to man, but I am certain that in some deer stands, hunters have died of heart attacks from hearing them.

After a few squirrels have alarmed you, you will become more conditioned and less sensitive to their sounds. Do not tune out such noises, however, for deer sometimes make similar sounds upon approach. The sounds of squirrels, woodpeckers, jays, crows, and so on (when these animals are not disturbed and alerting the deer) are useful to the hunter in that they make the deer less suspicious. A deer is much more apt to enter an area where a squirrel is hopping about the forest floor than it is likely to enter a silent area.

When the wind is still, deer move more because they can hear better. This is to the stand-hunter's advantage, for he can hear better too. On still days in leafy areas, a stand-hunter can shut his eyes and sit motionless, listening for deer instead of watching for them, twisting his neck, and making other detectable moves.

If you are in a stand before daylight, you may know where a deer has bedded down by listening when it ceases making noise in the leaves or brush. Then you will be ready for a shot when day breaks.

In dry, leafy areas where it is possible to move quietly yet still find cover, bucks do not like to announce their presence any more than people do. You may follow the deer's lead and try pine growths where the needles muffle the sounds. Deer walk here as if they were wearing sneakers.

TREE STANDS

Permanent stands should be built well in advance of deer season. A stand prepared a year in advance will certainly be scent free. Deer will have become accustomed to its presence also. The best time to place a permanent tree stand for future use is following the preceding deer season. When you have hunted an area successfully or have spotted a particular deer which you were unable to connect with during the season, your hunting experience is not over when the season is closed. Where appropriate, a stand built to your liking could be built now, when the deer behavioral patterns are discernable for the particular seasonal time period of the legal hunt and when the forest growth is at the stage it will be when you hunt the following year. A new permanent tree stand will alter deer activity nearby. Given a year of harmless interference with their lives, a tree stand becomes a natural part of the landscape which is unalertive.

If wood is the material you use be sure to consider color and scent as well as usability and durability. Pressure-treated wood lasts longest. This is the choice wood for stands you expect to use more than one year. When using treated wood, however, do not expect the deer to venture in close for a long time, due to the presence of chemicals in the wood which must air out and stabilize.

Barn wood is good to use nearer to hunt-time for a short-term stand. Some find the sturdy wood of discarded pallets, or the whole pallet, to their liking. Wood should be inconspicuously weathered to avoid stark contrasts in the woods. When you are certain of your stand position, I suggest that you build it to last. Good stands do produce year after year. Climbing into an old, decaying stand is dangerous and a temptation to others who may encounter it after your abandonment.

The tree you use for the stand should afford a good view of the area you want to hunt while hiding you as well as possible from the deer's view. A stand built to overlook a field or clearing should be into the woods somewhat and not placed right on the edge, where it is very noticeable. Examine your particular hunting situation well before setting a stand. With proper scouting, you can avoid continually moving your stand to locate the best placement. Are you increasing your visibility or the deer's visibility? After the leaves have fallen in the fall, will you still have a desirable stand?

Stands should rise above the deer's line of sight and keep scent of the hunter away from the zone near the ground. They are especially useful to those who must smoke. Stands in flatter areas do put hunters above the line of fire from other hunters and thus contribute to hunter safety. During heavy hunter pressure, your stand should be higher in the tree (or your ground blind higher on the terrain). Those uncomfortable with high stands should settle for lower stands. There are times when a high stand is not the best idea—for instance, when the hunter is using archery equipment, and a short-range shot would mean having to make a spine shot with the arrow due to the acute angle. Don't build on a hillside where even a high stand will put you in the deer's line of sight or scent. And don't build on a ridge where you will be skylighted from below. Although deer usually keep their line of sight at head height, they do look up, especially when there is movement. Deer familiar with stand hunters look up often. Once they have spotted a hunter in a stand or been shot at from one and seen the hunter move, be assured they will be alert to hunters in tree stands all their lives. Be as still as you can in your stand. Even after taking a shot, be still.

A stand may not be the best possibility for a good shot. This is often true on hillsides. To sit on a stump, log, or rock, under a fallen tree, or in front of a tree trunk or bush may be the idea. Just scrape a few noisy leaves out from under you, sit tight, and blend in. There is no point in putting your torso up on a platform so that the deer can see or smell you more easily.

When you build, select a sturdy tree which does not sway in the wind. Only put a nail to a tree unlikely to be used for lumber at any time. A nailed stand in a good log will make a friendly farmer irate. If using nails for permanent stands, choose galvanized nails size 16 or larger. Galvanized are hard to impossible to pull out but they do not rust out as readily as common nails. If you are planning to dismantle your stand avoid galvanized nails. Limit the number of steps you need to build by using green limbs to full advantage. The most common permanent deer stand is built 12 to 25 feet above the ground in a fork of a tree. The average tree stand height is 16 feet up the tree. For steps, 2 × 2 or 2 × 4 lumber is cut into short lengths and nailed onto the tree trunk securely. Two longer 2 × 4's, 6's, or whatever is available are used to support a platform. Some place old chair seats, backs, or other comfortable accessories in the stands to prepare for long waits. I've seen them with recliners. Larger platforms will allow for more stability and surefootedness when making standing and turning shots and are usually necessary for bow hunters.

Step types are many and varied. Holes drilled by brace and bit with one-foot lengths of half-inch rebar steel hammered into them make excellent permanent steps for stands. The ridges on the steel give good footing. Place the steel in the tree from a ladder. A folding aluminum ladder is a lot easier to handle in the woods and a handy addition to the house. The rechargeable drills take a lot of work out of the chore if they are sharp and heavy duty. You can buy screw-in steps.

Wedges cut from 2 × 4's also make good steps. Cut blocks eight inches long and cut 45-degree angles on the bottoms. Drill a hole in the angle to facilitate driving a nail without splitting the step open. Place an additional nail on each side of the step by toe-nailing. Take care to select wood which does not have long grain and splits easily. Most steps are easily placed from a ladder. Some people just leave the ladder and forget the steps. Remember to check each step or limb out well before putting your weight on it.

Make sure you are not on national or state forest land or in some other restricted area before building them in many locations. If hunting on private property by permission of a land-owner, be certain to confer with him about this matter.

A safety belt is a good idea in case of awkward shots, anxiety, or stand breakdown. People have been known to just walk off their tree stands in the excitement of shooting a deer. Dozing off can lead to a fall. If your stand is large, consider adding handrails made from tree limbs. Fifty percent of all hunting accidents during deer season are attributable to tree stands for one reason or the other. The most common tree stand accident is due to falling asleep, preventable by the addition of a safety belt. Other accidents occur when ascending or descending the stand, stand breakage or slip-page, falls from intoxication, carrying loaded firearms while climbing, or pulling loaded rifles into the stand with rope. All tree stand accidents are preventable.

Some hunt clubs, individuals, and commercial hunting reservations have deer stands so elaborate that they look like house trailers in trees. I actually saw one that was just that—a fully equipped vacation trailer up in the trees. Some are covered and heated houses on stilts with gun ports to conceal the hunter and overlook deer food plots. Some provide protection from wind and rain as well as other comforts. You can take stand design to any length.

Often your best bet will be to shimmy up a tree and perch on a good, wide limb. If your plan is to locate such a tree, a portable pillow will be a tremendous asset when hunting from uncomfortable tree crotches.

When climbing to a tree stand, be absolutely sure to unload and sling your weapon. You can use rope secured to the firearm or bow to improvise a sling. You may also use rope to pull it up to you after climbing. Tie one end of the rope to your weapon and the other to your belt for climbing. Be sure not to get any dirt in the bore of your gun because this can blow up your barrel. Loaded firearms can have safeties moved, hammers cocked, and triggers pulled from drops or contact with limbs.

Portable stands are increasingly popular. Smart old bucks do avoid tree stands and often check the permanent ones from a safe distance. A surprise stand, a portable, is best for hunting them. Portable stands are usually homemade, welded metal devices with a grate platform and a seat. They are designed to secure to the tree firmly with the addition of hunter weight, the weight pushing metal points in the platform into the tree. The top of the stand is secured to the tree by a chain and lock. These stands do no permanent damage to trees and are removable. The hunter enters them by means of a rope ladder or by using climbers attached to hunting boots, if not by utilizing limbs. Quiet and convenient detachable boot-climbers are available. With some practice, these will allow you to scale trees like telephone poles.

A good temporary stand is simply a piece of wood notched out on the ends and secured in a limb fork.

"Climbing" tree stands are commercially available for hunting where tree trunks are limbless. These are just the thing in pine forests or straight-trunked hardwood stands. Each year, new patents for such devices are applied for in great numbers. These stands are lightweight and comfortable. So called "self-climbing," portables do not climb by themselves. If they did, you would be on the ground watching them go up and still have to scale the tree to get to them. If you desire one of these I suggest shopping around. Practice with the climber adequately prior to the hunt. Such tree stands are great to own but can be noisy to erect. To get those squeaks minimized use vegetable oil.

I am a serious hunter with a great diversity of hunting sites available. I have permanent stands in numerous locales, temporaries out many spots, and portables which I move around. This gives me many options in deer hunting, with flexibility to compensate for various changing circumstances. In addition to stands in different places on the map, i have more than one stand in most individual locations which I hunt. This allows the hunter to take advantage of wind directions and changes in the deer's travel patterns due to other hunter's activities. It will also allow a welcome change of scenery when needed.

Deer, especially mature bucks, usually travel into the wind with their nostrils wide open. Stands should be positioned to the side of such avenues. Some stands just may be too cold at times too. You may need one out of the wind chill to go to at especially brisk times.

If the area you are planning to hunt has deer (in the present age most everywhere does) then you might find a deer just about anywhere. The deer really get around. At some time or another they will walk over every foot of the ground in their home range. The accomplishment of properly placing a stand and being successful in hunting deer from it is a great reward. Just exactly where that spot is is something you will have to work out according to your individual hunt situation. I just hope that you don't get into one of those games where deer hunting is like bass fishing when you move your boat from an unproductive spot to another place and, when you do, you see a lunker jump right where your boat was. The most popular and most productive location for a stand is halfway between bedding areas and feeding areas. First, this gives you time to track a hit animal in daylight. Second, deer are less alerted here because they are browsing along the way, which distracts them.

Be sure to check on stand height laws. In Minnesota it is 10 feet. Some areas allow no tree stand hunting at all, considering it unfair advantage, and taking no risks with forest products destruction. This restriction is usually just for permanents.

If you can't see carrying a whole lot of wood into the woods to make a permanent stand, can't see spending any more money on deer hunting by acquiring a factory climber or portable, and wish to have a very natural looking stand with a couple of year's use, then you can fashion a stand and steps to it from tree limbs or stout saplings cut on the spot. A compact, folding pruner's saw and a handful of nails is all you need.

In some areas virtually everyone hunts from an elevated stand. In such places the stand hunters shun still-hunters as invaders from the next state or as "city folk." In other areas stand hunters are considered lazy and unskilled. The ground blind hunter and the stump-sitter must be remembered as taking their share of deer also. Although tree stands are currently the most productive method of taking deer, you must do what you consider the most enjoyable, employable, and harmonious method in your individual circumstance. If you are uneasy with heights, vertigo will not disable you as a whitetail deer hunter.

IN-STAND MOVEMENT

Once you are in a tree stand or in position on the ground using some natural feature of the landscape for cover or using a blind, being still is critical. Being alert is critical also, but being still is far more important. The hunter's movement can be detected by a deer long before he can detect the deer by being alert. The hunter who tries to control his movements through meditation and discipline will enjoy more success. Remember that eye movement may be very noticeable to deer. Roving eyeballs can be a major disadvantage for the hunter.

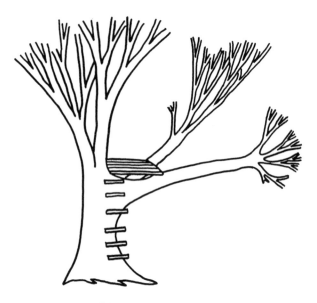

SUSAN ASKED: "DADDY, I UNDERSTAND WHAT A
DEER STAND IS, BUT HOW ARE YOU GOING TO GET
THE DEER TO GET INTO THE STAND SO YOU CAN
SHOOT IT?"

Deer have true peripheral vision. This allows the deer to see everywhere but out of the back of its head. The only time that deer are incapable of noticing a movement is when they are facing away. The eyes of the whitetail are located on the sides of the skull and toward the front. When these large eyes are focused on an object or a travel route directly ahead, they are still capable of detecting slight movements far back to the sides.

If early morning chills, buck fever, or weather such as a brisk wind has you shivering, attempt to hold your quiverings down to an undetectable level.

A good rule to remember in moving in a stand is to move only when you cannot see the eyes or the eye area of the deer. This will assure you that the deer will not see you.

Make slow, deliberate, and calculated moves like a stalking cat.

Focus your rifle or draw your bow when the deer is quartering away as this will allow your shot to find the vital area. If the deer should notice your shot preparation movement to the side and slightly to the rear of its view, then it will turn its head and neck in your direction thereby increasing your vital organ target area.

If you are a new hunter, as an exercise, sit down on the ground by a tree in your yard and see how long you can remain completely motionless. Few persons are capable of this, without *full concentration* for any extended period. It is not possible if you are tense. Quite the opposite, it requires *relaxation*. As you practice, let the muscles of your body relax.

Try the trick of concentrating on keeping your tongue from touching your teeth and letting it wholly *relax*. Keep eyes alert and looking, but let the lid muscles relax and concentrate on this also. Curiously, the emphasis on tongue and eyelids will affect the whole body. All movement must be very slow and steady.

Leaving or adding some leafy branches around your stand will further guard you against movement detection. A couple of yards of camo cloth and some thumb tacks are handy to pack along.

PREDATOR VIBES

Do not look deer in the eyes if you can help it. Eye contact should be consciously avoided. If you are approached by a deer which you plan to shoot, focus away from the eyes. Eye contact will excite the deer, get its adrenaline shooting through its system, and give it enormous power to run. Deer which are wounded after having eye contact tend to run farther and are harder to find. If approached by a deer which you do not intend to shoot, avoid contact with it as well. It can and usually will warn other deer and put them on the alert. You can be certain that deer communicate with one another by means of their own complex system. If your shot with a rifle has to be head-on, then look between the eyes for the shot, not into them. It is important to avoid eye contact with whitetail bucks when scouting also. The trophy that you wish to hunt later will be more difficult to locate once that it has registered your specific psychic vibrations. He will know it when you are in the woods. I am serious.

When in the stand, try not to emit predator vibes by thinking of things other than killing. In-tune deer sense predators as do in-tune humans. Deer have psychic abilities as do most other animals, and wary old bucks have learned to rely upon them. The aggressive vibrations hunters throw out have a definite repellent effect. Sometimes you need to get your mind off deer hunting completely. You can put out a deer repellent by just thinking. Often hunters tell of hunting hard for days on end and not seeing deer then having one come up while they are absorbed in something else. This is why! They are actually putting out a negative force field with their thought waves which alerted deer.

Whitetail deer seldom look each other in the eyes. This is aggressive behavior for the species. Fighting bucks, however, open their eyes widely and fiercely.

WIND CURRENTS

Of the many superb survival gifts given deer, the best is its nose. You can count on the deer to use it. The hunter should never underestimate the ability of that long, multi-chambered snout. Wind is the single most important environmental factor in a hunt. The hunter can work the wind for or against himself. The deer use the wind to their advantage, and the hunter must learn to use it in order to equal the odds. Disregarding air currents will significantly reduce success. If you want to go to the woods for reasons other than seeing or obtaining deer then pay the wind no attention. To hunt without considering the nose of the deer is inconsiderate of oneself,. inflicting failure even though major effort in other hunting rules have been followed to perfection.

Traveling deer move into the wind. This is invariably true with older bucks and does. A mistake most beginning stand-hunters make is to position themselves downwind from a likely deer approach thinking the deer will be less likely to smell them that way. This is seldom true in a stand situation since moving deer try to head into the wind, even more so in times of hunter pressure. Still-hunters and stalkers, those who wish to go *to* an animal, are the only hunters who should head into the wind.

If you are positioned in a stand, notice the prevailing wind direction by observing the leaves. There is always some wind, even if it is not readily detectable. Air currents swirl continuously. There is always some movement in the air. Check less obvious wind by holding a thin garment thread on your gun barrel and noting the direction of faint wind flow. Another method may be to pitch some dried grass or dust into the air. The direction to which the wind is blowing will usually be the direction your deer will come from. Once a very small goose-down feather was protruding from my vest. When I pulled it out and discarded it, it gently drifted to the ground a distance from my elevated tree stand. Where it landed was almost exactly where I noticed several does becoming alert to possible danger. The feather became a valuable tool to me in deciding when to shoot a buck before it might detect my scent.

Wind currents called "thermals" control the air near the ground where deer walk. Thermals move vertically and are largely governed by the sun and ensuing warmth. Other factors which control thermals are the prevailing wind and barometric pressure. The sun makes thermals rise as it, the sun, rises. Likewise, as the sun sets, thermals move nearer to the ground. How near to the ground and at what heights is controlled by terrain, humidity, and any available wind. This understanding is used by the hunter who knows that as a rule, his scent will be going uphill in the morning and downhill in the evening. Although smoking is a bad idea on the hunt because of its smells, tobacco smoke will enable the hunter to visualize these minute air currents as they dissipate. If your deer camp has a fire, you might gain some insight by watching the behavior of the smoke.

So, if the hunter is positioned in a stand or blind, he might best expect his quarry to enter his view from the downwind direction, and he should focus most of his attention that way. The hunter should look in all directions for deer but can position himself for a shot which will require minimal movement when he is aware of the most likely appearance point.

A still-hunter in search of deer should always hunt into the wind or crosswind from the area he is hunting. Deer nose out the scents from upwind but have to rely on the weaker senses of sight and hearing to detect predation from downwind. Although a deer's sight is poorer than its sense of smell, the deer does have a keen eye for movement and can distinguish the smallest move at a great distance. There is a tendency of most outdoor writers to downplay the eyesight of the whitetail. It is true that their eyes are not nearly as good as that of an antelope, with telescopic eyesight, but it has been my experience that the eyesight of the whitetail is every bit as good as that of a human if not better. It is my advice to never discount whitetail vision as inferior. It is quite adequate for most of their range. It is not necessary for them to see like plains creatures for they are designed for dense cover. One look at the length of those ears should convince us of their hearing ability also.

A stalk, actually moving within range of a spotted animal after a glassing or a still-hunt sighting, requires the hunter to always hunt into the wind or crosswind.

Hunters should try to have alternate stands to visit when wind changes occur. On those days when wind direction constantly shifts, the hunter may have to disregard the wind and hope for the best. The hunter might try to find a hunting position that shelters or blocks the wind somewhat for an ambush instead of playing "musical stands."

Windage must be considered when making longer rifle shots or bow shots. It is a good idea to practice at the range on a windy day as well as on still days to increase your knowledge of your projectiles. The effects of wind on high-powered rifle bullets will not throw you off target dramatically as will it affect the arrow. The light arrow, with its mass and slow speed, is strongly controlled by the wind. Windage adjustments on rifle sights are very valuable for field, powerline, or other longer-range shots during windy conditions. Practice using your scope as you would use windage controls on iron sights. The longer the shot, the more crucial windage adjustments become, regardless of the weapon employed.

In establishing a stand in a tree, remember that a high stand in more limber trees of smaller diameter can sway more than is desirable in winds. A moving tree stand works in favor of the deer as it may notice a large overhead movement readily. If the wind makes your stand noisy it can be a detriment. Wind must also be considered in deciding on the height of a tree stand. A lower stand will keep scent lower to the ground, and a higher stand will spread it over a larger area when the relative humidity is high. When humidity is low, a higher stand will send your scent away from your hunting area better than a lower stand.

The deer can detect the presence of the unprepared hunter who is in a valley of considerable size by checking out the air currents funneling out through the mouth of the valley. The deer have specific territories, and learn the best scenting locations in their home range, which they use when under hunter pressure, and to detect does in heat or rivals. Consider this when placing mating scents or other deer lures as well as in eliminating your own wastes.

Ground currents are another type of air movement. The wind blowing in the tree-tops may not signal the wind direction that is most important. It is the area from ground level to eight feet that should be your primary concern. The deer will put its nose to the ground like a beagle hound, or it will reach high with its nostrils. Does have been observed standing on their hind legs to reach an air current for scenting. Remember that the ground level is the level of the deer. Due to features of the terrain, the wind direction on the ground may be completely different from what the leaves on the trees are telling you.

Bedded deer will face downwind. When a group bedding down positions itself for rest, at least one of the older deer will be assigned the function of sighting in the direction from which they are less likely to smell intruders. The deer that are asleep still keep their noses and ears working at reduced power. They do not just zonk out unaware.

Deer have a tendency to bed down or otherwise restrict movement as they carefully browse a small area when the wind is making the woods noisy. They know that their senses of hearing and scenting are limited. Many hunters don't even bother to hunt on windy days. The hunter can use the wind sounds in the leaves and trees to his advantage, however, on such days by taking the offensive and searching for deer instead of waiting for them to come to him. This is a good time to stalk standing corn fields. The deer are there, wind or no wind.

Hunters who never see deer moving on windy days always attribute their poor success to the fact that the wind kept the animals from moving. However, it is often the case that the hunter is forced to hunt with the oppressive wind and does, after all, find deer moving. One overlooked factor which inhibits deer sightings under windy conditions is barrel whistle. The bore of a rifle, shotgun, or even a pistol can produce a high-pitched sound which is detected as foreign by deer but is inaudible to the hunter. High-pitched sounds are used to repel deer from crops. Most of us have at some time made noise by blowing over the top of a cola bottle. This sound can repel deer effectively, leaving the hunter blaming the windy conditions for failure to make contact with deer while all along he was shooing them away with a foreign sound undetectable to him. To remedy high-frequency barrel whistle, place a thin plastic membrane over the barrel tip and secure it with a rubber band. Be sure to use *thin* plastic to avoid possible danger. A small balloon will do nicely for this purpose. This will not need to be removed when the weapon is fired as it will have no marked effect upon bullet velocity. After all, the hunter need not sit in his stand with a deer repellent beside him. An empty, uncapped drink bottle sitting near you may be serving the same function. If you drink a bottled beverage replace the cap.

BIRDS

Having watched the movie *Bambi*, most hunters wonder what role the feathered creatures of the woodlands play in the deer hunt.

In observing the relationships of birds and deer, I have concluded that in the shared habitat, all things work together. Deer
are quite accustomed to birds. This animal, the deer, is doing its
best to avoid the hunter. It is only natural that the deer use the
birds to its advantage.

Bluejays do warn deer of human intrusion. The hunter should
try not to alarm them because they can be really loud and put a
damper on success for the moment or the entire day. Movement
scares birds away, and whether the birds are the noisy type or not,
the deer may exit if it senses abnormality. The still-hunting or
stalking hunter should take the presence of birds into consideration with each move. If he encounters birds, he should restrict his
movement until they have moved on.

Crows can spread the word of hunter presence all over the
woods.

The pecking of woodpeckers spells peace and safety to deer. A
deer that hears the pecking of a woodpecker cease will halt and
search the air for signs of invasion. When the pecking resumes,
the deer continues on. When stand-hunting, a busy woodpecker
can be a hunter's ally if he is careful not to frighten it. Jays and
crows are also allies if their noise is that of play instead of escape.
A flurry of birds coming out of a thicket might signal the approach of a deer, but do not come to full draw or aim because it
will more often be another hunter.

SLEEPING IN THE WOODS

If you should find yourself starting to
doze off in the tranquility of the forest,
then leave your elevated stand and unload
your firearm or quiver your arrow. Lay
your unloaded firearm or bow a safe
distance away and flat on the ground.

If you start to "nod out" in a tree stand, you cannot rely on waking up as you start to slump over. It is like driving a car. Pull over in a car, get down in a stand. When hunting from an elevated stand, a safety belt is a necessary safety device to catch you if you should fall asleep. But this is obviously a situation to avoid. Dangling from a tree by a safety belt is awkward to say the least.

If you choose to sleep at the base of your tree or elsewhere in the woods, be certain to expose some clearly visible material of hunter orange.

When it is not your choice to yield to sleepiness, deep breathing exercises seem to be the best method of stimulating the brain.

WISDOM

Wisdom is acquired. No one is born with it. It is especially useful in making quick decisions. It must be sought after to be found, and experience brings it. Listening to others who have had experience also brings it. It takes some of it to outsmart wise old bucks.

GREED

Hunters who are willing to share are by far the most successful lot. Share your deer with any hunters you are with who were not privileged to bring one home. Split the gas and share other costs. Share with the landowner. Hope that your fellow hunters do as well or better than you do. Leave things unspoiled for the next person. If you see someone already hunting in the area you plan to enter, be respectful and find another place to hunt.

In short, greed is associated with darkness and failure, whereas generosity leads to light and the glow of success.

FEAR

Fear and doubt are great enemies in the hunting experience. The hunter should do all that is required to stay within the law, and he should feel at ease with nature and with his firearm. Practice with your bow or firearm until you have no fear of the weapon recoil and explosive power and no doubts about your own performance. If you are fearful of your bow and arrow, remember that statistics show there are fewer accidents in bowhunting than in any other major sports.

Caution and wisdom are not to be confused with fear. Fear is a negative force that deer are able to pick up with their sixth sense. If you are uncomfortable with the height of the tree stand you are in, then head for the ground to hunt. Those fear vibrations will ruin your hunt. There is little to fear yet definite reason to be cautious when using weaponry capable of taking big game. Man is the most dangerous creature in the woods. Contrary to legend, the lion was never king of the jungle. You should be at the head, not the tail, of the woodland. You are dominant in the food chain. You have the power to subdue any lesser creature. A healthy respect for the creatures of the woods with various defense mechanisms for their protection coupled with the understanding that we humans are capable of making mistakes, should be enough to keep us at the head.

LUCK / SKILL

There is a great amount of luck involved in deer hunting, just as in any sport. Luck is the single largest factor in whitetail deer hunting. Without the aid of Lady Luck, the best hunter in American won't get a deer.

Hunters who have been at it awhile prefer to rely on skill and knowledge, along with hard work, more than fickle luck. Rarely do you hear a seasoned hunter admit, "I got lucky."

If you get really lucky, a world-record buck may hop up into the bed of your truck on the opening morning of your first hunt and pose for a shot with a pie-pan on its chest.

This luck phenomenon is something that keeps veteran deer hunters scratching their heads. "Beginner's luck" is common, while some hunters seem to stay in bad-luck ruts all the time. Remember that at any time your luck can change. Change is the most changeless thing in our world.

For some reason which I have not pinpointed, wives who decide to go hunting with their husbands score highly on luck.

One acquaintance had hunted deer for nine years unsuccessfully, never spotting a legal buck. He hunted hard and seemed to do everything right but just had no luck. He was discouraged to say the least, but he went out opening day on the tenth year. On the way to his stand site, he shot a trophy at close range. As he lay down his rifle to field-dress the buck, another even larger buck skidded up a few yards in front of him. Startled, he grabbed his rifle and shot the second trophy at seven yards. He was home by noon with two bucks of a lifetime. His luck had finally changed.

In hunting whitetails, the important accomplishment is building and following a workable plan. If your hunt has been thoughtfully and skillfully executed, if you have employed study and discipline, you will have a great feeling of accomplishment whether or not you got lucky.

Some people have good-luck formulas, like the half-joking "Hold your mouth right." If you think that finding a four-leafed clover might help you to enjoy success at hunting, by all means find one.

Positive superstition won't hurt you and may set your mind on a better-luck plane. It is when you were unable to find the clover and are convinced that you will fail as a result, that you should begin a superstition cleansing.

I wish you all the luck in the world, beginner or pro.

WIVES / HUSBANDS

Some people are fortunate enough to have a spouse who shares their interest in deer hunting and makes a good hunting companion. Some wives, or in the case of ever-increasing women hunters, some husbands, prefer not shooting deer but still like the woods and other recreational aspects of the deer season.

Some wives who wish to see more of their husbands in the fall of the year adopt the philosophy of "If you can't beat them, join them." A spouse may elect to keep camp as a non-hunter and still enjoy the hunt. Still other husbands and wives enjoy and benefit from the time apart when one or the other goes hunting. More and more often today, as deer hunting becomes less of a macho sport reserved for men alone, women take to hunting. In the 1990s, due to increased divorce rates and youth problems, we can expect still more emphasis on participating in sports as a family unit.

This chapter is written in hopes that deer hunting will become a growth factor in your relationship with your marital partner instead of a hindrance.

Too often, a hunter goes into the woods with dampened spirits because he has left behind a spouse irate over the cost of the hunt, opposed to the killing of deer, jealous over the hunter's zeal, overly concerned about danger, or paranoid that the hunter is going to be surrounded by playboy bunnies and influential rogues. So take care to get your wife's blessing before you leave for the woods. This is all-important to a successful outcome. You don't need negative feelings hanging over your head in the quest for whitetails.

First, no matter how absurd it seems, ask your spouse to join you. Everyone likes to be invited and not excluded. Let your spouse participate. Don't make the mistake of leaving him or her out. Your spouse might surprise you and actually want to go, so be prepared for that too!

Sometimes a careful introduction to the value of venison as a food is in order. Most people are unfamiliar with deer meat and need to learn how to use it in ways the whole family will love and enjoy. Once your spouse truly appreciates venison, he or she will see more value in deer hunting and less financial loss.

Show good fruit from your hunt, and your efforts will be rewarded. If you neglect your wife, family, job, and home to hunt deer, then you can expect trouble.

I asked that part of our wedding vows include that my spouse would not interfere with my hunting. She has lived up to these vows which she made with clear understanding that she was marrying a hunting fanatic. I try to be reasonable.

Chapter
7

After the Shot

LEASH DOG RETRIEVAL

If you are certain that you have wounded a deer but you are unable to locate it after a thorough search, you may choose to use a dog for help with retrieval.

A dog of almost any sort can follow a good blood trail. Probably the best dog for such trailing is the bloodhound. A bloodhound may be a sound investment for a conscientious sportsman who might also make a little income from finding lost deer for others. Deer retrieval services are much desired. A hunter who has shot an outstanding deer and met only frustration in searching for it himself will go a long way to seek such services. The dog handler who offers this service can expect to be up all night during gun season as well as spend many nights at work during the bow seasons.

The labrador retriever is a good choice for this purpose. A barking hound is not necessary. Individuals can use almost any available dog they can communicate with. If it boils right down to it, a chihuahua might even fill the need. Losing a wounded deer is a bad memory that lodges permanently in the hunter's mind.

Only a few hunters are unconcerned with knowing they have left a suffering deer in the woods to be wasted. It is the responsibility of every sportsman to find deer which they have shot. Hunters who give up on a search without reasonable effort and those who make no effort at all, should be admonished to change by their fellow hunters. Almost every hunter has had the experience of having to spend more time than desired to trail a wounded animal. Hunters who have hunted a good many times just about all have a story about one that they never found. It is common to walk through a hunting area a couple of weeks after deer season and be drawn to the decaying carcass of a lost deer in the underbrush. Such animals are easy for humans to locate after their smell obtains knock-down power. The dog is the answer for earlier retrieval. Enthusiasm and persistence on the hunter's part, coupled with blood trail and tracking knowledge, will usually enable him to produce the fallen deer, but these qualities do not always complete the job.

It would be best to leash your dog when tracking a wounded deer. This will allow you better control of the canine and keep the dog from harm. Leashing the dog might be the only acceptable method of using dogs in your state.

Some states allow dogs for retrieval and others do not. Other legal stipulations may limit the number of dogs used, require that they be used by day or night only, or specify whether or not the dog handlers may carry weapons. It is sad that those hunters with the honest intention of putting natural resources to wise use are hampered by the dishonest actions of the few who use retrievers for poaching and robbing the environment. Check with a game warden.

Professional deer retrieval services charge a minimal fee for their services. They are generally services provided within certain distances. Additional fees are paid upon location of the animal. The dog handlers ask that you be able to place them at the beginning of a blood trail.

BLOOD TRAILS

After a deer is shot, more often than not, the animal will run for some distance before dying. This distance is rarely over 500 yards if the deer is not pushed. It is much more often within 100 yards when there has been good shot placement. You will hear stories of particular specimens going for miles after having their hearts shot out. A mile in the deer woods is a considerable distance.

I have found that the yardage at which a deer was distanced and the distance which the hunter tracked the deer before finding it for tagging are the two most commonly exaggerated stories of deer hunters. These stretched truths are not voluntary reactions by hunters but are miscalculations. The truth is that just about anything can happen in hunting whitetails and I am in no position to discount that possibility.

The situation of a wounded deer vacating the area can be very frustrating to the hunter. Each year thousands of hunters shoot deer and, after having searched briefly, give up on finding them. It can be exhausting to locate them. The hunter should make every effort to locate downed deer. Having a system for hunting wounded deer will help. Most important is understanding the "blood trail." This is helpful to the firearm hunter and is absolutely necessary for the bow hunter. Blood is about the only way to track an arrow-shot deer, indeed the most common way.

First, wait for 10 to 30 minutes before you leave your stand or blind when you feel certain you have hit the deer. There are exceptions to this, as you might expect, such as when the deer dropped in its tracks. Among the times you should leave your stand immediately is when you can clearly see the deer is going nowhere as a result of a spinal shot or a head shot. A solid kidney or rectum shot might do the same. These deer might struggle somewhat but give up the ghost quite readily. There will likely be a few involuntary reactions such as writhing or kicking followed by collapse and complete immobility. A shot to the vital area of a deer, which is considered the heart or lungs (a six-inch circle behind the front shoulder) will drop at once or might allow the deer to run 200 yards or more.

Take after the deer immediately but quietly when it is snowing or raining. Snow filling tracks and rain washing blood sign will hide your animals trail. If you have made your shot in the last moments of sunlight you may wish to immediately pursue your deer to attempt recovery before darkness sets in. A lantern does show fresh blood better than a flashlight but either will do if darkness has set in. There will be a time to wait for darkness for better tracking instead of making the choice of avoiding the night-time bloodtrail. These choices, as well as many proclaimed in this book, are to be made by the individual hunter under the individual circumstances.

A good reason to wait for a while after having shot an animal is to get *yourself* together.

The hunter cannot ascribe to the waiting philosophy or the pursuing philosophy without exceptions which are made to adapt to the conditions.

One common statement made by the confirmed "wait" deer hunters is that the venison will not taste as "wild." It is claimed that the deer will be "stressed" and this will alter the taste of the meat. If this is true then those who make such proclamations have superior taste buds to mine. I find no variation in taste confirmable. The taste is relevant to the diet of the deer, the gender, the time of year, and the method of cleaning, but not to stress. Sampling a deer identical to another shot on the same day, in the same location; one stressed by dogs and the other taken by ambush, with nearly identical shots to vital areas, and so on, showed no distinguishable difference. "Stressed" is out.

A running deer has three times the heart rate of one bedded. If you push a wounded deer it will bleed faster. Pushing the animal will frighten it more which will produce more adrenaline (speed) but will also slow clotting. Push the deer if you expect it to collapse from blood loss, as in cases where you expect to have hit an artery. A whitetail has an average of 8 pints of blood (150 lb. deer). A wounded deer must lose at least a third of the blood in its body to collapse (3 pints).

Waiting will tend to keep the deer from going too far away and will allow it more time to lose strength and bleed. Deer in a state of shock can run for some distance with lethal injury. The hunter should wait for the deer to settle down. Deer not pushed or panicked are easier to locate.

Usually, when shot, either deer are knocked down, or they stumble as they run off. There should be some noticeable difference in their movement. The sound that a bullet makes upon impact with flesh is audible and unmistakable in most situations. If an arrow was used, this sound is distinguishable also, but to a lesser degree. You might see the arrow in the fleeing deer, though most often the arrow runs cleanly through.

After having waited long enough before pursuit, mentally mark the exact spot in the landscape where you shot your deer and also the last place where you saw it. When you reach the spot, mark it well for future reference. You may have to come back and start all over, so mark the spot while it is clearly in mind. Look for blood or hair. Blood sign is about the only way to track an arrow-shot deer since such animals die by hemorrhaging; however, hair or bone chips may be used in the case of a bullet, which kills by impact.

Short, white hair and no blood usually means that you have shot too low and grazed the underside of the deer. Very long white hair is only found on the tail. Hopefully you will find a large blood spot on the forest floor. This is a clear indication of a lethal shot. It is a good idea to put your fingers in the tracks of the wounded animal you are attempting to stalk and make note of the hoof size of that particular deer. Note any markings peculiar to the individual, such as a chipped hoof at a certain spot. You may need to separate the tracks of your animal from other prints found along the blood trail. Blood trails can be clearly marked on the ground with noticeable puddles at regular intervals and with steady drops. They might be as easy to follow as painted marks on pavement. Commonly they are more difficult to follow than you might expect and require considerable thoroughness. Look on weeds and other vegetation or brush up to deer height (three to five feet) for smears and splatters. You may need to search on hands and knees.

As you are following the trail, drop pieces of toilet tissue to mark your trail. Toilet tissue is highly biodegradable and will not litter the forest for long. Remember when using the tissue that white is a dangerous color to display to trigger-happy hunters. If you should have to backtrack or to seek the assistance of a more experienced tracker, then these markers will be appreciated. Your blood trail may not last long enough to finish a difficult tracking. Blood dries up and becomes difficult to find the next day, so if you have begun a stalk and darkness sets in, continue with a good artificial light instead of waiting for daylight.

Try not to give up easily. It is a shame to shoot a deer and never find it. If you cannot find it the first day and absolutely must give up your search, then do come back the next day and continue your search. If you have to work the next day, catch a plane, or whatever, then tell someone else about the situation who will hunt for and find the deer. Once you find blood do not give up.

Downed deer camouflage easily. They usually head for the thickest cover available rather than out in the open to die. Wounded deer tend to head downhill and toward water. There may be exceptions when deer are shot in valleys and the only escape route is uphill, or they head away from water if the projectile and noise came from between the deer and water.

It helps to preserve a blood trail if you do not walk on it. Track the deer slowly and try not to overlook anything. If you can't find blood, then get down on your hands and knees and look for the slightest disturbances in the leaves. If the tracks have a severe drag mark, indicating a limp or broken leg, the deer will normally stay on low ground. If at any time you can't find any trail, then go to the area surrounding the nearest water and look. Hurt deer head for water to cool fever and help hide scent. When trailing wounded deer look to the sides of the trail for thickets where the deer may have quartered back to watch its backtrail.

As a rule, heavy hemorrhaging stops in the first half-hour, and the only sign will be a yellowish stain washed from the hair, with an occasional pinpoint of red blood.

A badly wounded animal will leave the marks of its dewclaws in the rear of its prints as its legs weaken.

When blood trails give out, start making semicircles in search of the deer, gradually fanning out ahead. Continually make larger semicircles or spirals while making note of the area searched. If this does not produce your fallen deer, then at least you have eliminated a lot of land, and you can use the exclusion method to judge the possible whereabouts of the deer. You may need to make an impromptu map of the area and plot searches to recover your deer by the process of elimination.

When you find the deer, approach it cautiously. The hooves of any deer can render a dangerous blow. Many hunter fatalities throughout history have been inflicted by wounded deer. It may be necessary to fire a mercy shot to finish the animal. Never mind trying to conk the deer on the forehead. You don't want to knock the deer unconscious, you want to kill it. Deers have hard heads. If the eyes of a downed deer are closed, the deer is almost always alive.

Dead deer have still, open eyes. Watch for the rise and fall of the chest and observe the nostrils for dilation. A dead deer will usually be on one side with legs outstretched. Presuming that a deer is dead as a result of making the observation that the eyes of the deer are glossy is fallible. It is, under normal conditions, a very good clue that the deer is dead but deer get cataracts.

FIELD DRESSING

As soon as possible, your downed deer should be field-dressed. This means that the entrails should be removed and the animal bled and aired out. Entrails and excess blood left in a carcass for extended time after death putrefy the flesh. Field-dressing is not difficult to do. Most people take to the task readily with little or no instruction.

In warm weather, field-dressing should be done immediately to begin cooling the animal, and the carcass should be refrigerated as soon as possible. If a cold-storage facility such as a meat locker is not available, then fill the chest cavity with a bag of ice before the carcass sets up and becomes rigid. The deer begins to decay the moment of death. Cooler weather will allow you more time as the process of deterioration is considerably slower. In very warm weather, two hours may be enough to spoil the deer meat or at least give it an undesirable taste. In cold weather, a field-dressed deer may be just fine after several days in the open air.

BE CERTAIN THAT YOUR DEER IS DEAD BEFORE YOU ATTEMPT TO FIELD-DRESS IT. BIG BUCKS ESPECIALLY DON'T LIKE IT!

After you harvest your deer, decide whether it is a good idea to leave a pile of entrails at the spot where you field-dress it. You may want to hunt there again, or perhaps someone else will. It is a very frightening experience for a deer, a dedicated vegetarian, to encounter a big pile of deer guts. You may want to take the deer elsewhere for gutting. Most hunters leave the guts in a pile where they shot the animal. Entrails left in the woods do make good food for scavengers, but they also lure scavengers. Scavengers of the larger varieties repel and disperse deer. Hunters often say of the entrails, "They won't be there long before a coyote or some other animal disposes of them." This is true, but the remaining live deer may not be there long either. It is preferable to bury your field-dressed deer wastes deeply or collect them in a five-gallon bucket or a doubled trash bag to be disposed of elsewhere. The extra effort is commendable.

To field-dress a deer, turn the deer with belly toward the lowest point in the terrain. This will help you remove the mass of internal organs more easily. As you work with a sharp knife, gravity will allow the bulk to spill. Some hunters make the first incision at the anus and work upward to the chest. Others begin at the chest and work down to the anal opening. Those that start at the anus ream the anal opening and pull it out. They then tie it off tightly with a stout rubber band or other handy material. They then clean their knife and finish their incision upward to the chest. Having made the opening cut, the rear-to-front advocates pull the anal opening through the pelvic bone and thus keep fecal material contained so that it won't spread bacteria on the meat. Those who start at the chest and finish at the anus can tie the opening off also. Some proponents of the chest-to-rear method feel they avoid contamination of the knife from the anus by starting at the chest. Unless they wipe off their knife very well, they will have to use it inside the chest cavity anyway. So start wherever you prefer. One way is as good as the other. Take care to cut the skin only and not to puncture the entrails. If you want to save the skin for tanning, center the belly cut precisely.

While wearing rubber gloves, rake out the guts. It is good to have a cavity dug next to the animal to catch and contain the blood and guts. Do not allow the urinary bladder to discharge its contents inside the deer as this may taint the meat and render it inedible. This is true for both buck and doe. The urinary bladder will be easy to spot. It is a creme-colored ball about the size of a tennis ball and shaped like a hot-air balloon. A few raking cuts with your knife will free any organs clinging to the walls of the upper abdomen.

You have probably heard it said that you must be very careful to remove the gall bladder from the deer and not allow any gall to touch the deer meat. There are books which put forth this theory, describing the gall bladder in detail and pinpointing its location as right next to the live. Don't worry too much about the gall bladder. Deer don't have them. That's right. Cattle have them, sheep and most other animals have them, but deer do not. Deer belong to a particular variety of ruminants that forage on a high cellulose, low-fat diet. They don't need those bitter secretions for food digestion. The bile won't ruin the meat because there is no bile. Urinary bladder, yes, gall bladder, no.

Save the liver if it looks good. A healthy animal will have a clean, unblemished liver. A diseased liver will be obviously discolored. The liver will be delicious and nutritious sliced thin and cooked like beef liver. The heart is also good to save. Simmer it slowly in soy sauce, slice it, and serve it with crackers. Wash the heart thoroughly while pumping out clots from the ventricles. Some hunters even save the small intestine for making sausage links. When cleaned thoroughly and soaked in salt brine, the delicate intestine toughens to become the best casing you could use. The stomach is another organ which is normally discarded during the field-dressing process. It can be salt-preserved to make a wineskin or a musical drum. The impossible-looking stomach liner removes easily after a little soaking.

Boiled tongue is a delicacy to many. The healthy brain is sa-
vored by some for food. The tongue and brain are removed later in
the butchering process instead of in field-dressing. Use plastic
bags to collect the organs you want to retain. A one-gallon zip-
lock baggie is great for each organ. You will need several.

*THE WILD TASTE IN VENISON IS
USUALLY DUE TO IMPROPER DRESSING.*

It is generally claimed that the field-dressed cavity should not
be hosed down or washed but merely wiped out with a damp cloth
because water breaks the meat down. If water is allowed to stand
on the meat and is not drained properly, this may be the case. I
certainly agree that deer which are going to be hung for aging of
the meat should be kept dry. The dry, skin-like crust that forms
on the outer portion of muscle tissues which are exposed by field-
dressing protects against decay and helps to seal in flavor. But
deer which are going to be skinned and processed immediately

can be hosed down with no problem. Be sure to wash the deer thoroughly if the urinary bladder or the intestines have been ruptured. I have immersed deer in creeks and lakes to thoroughly clean them after field dressing with no harm done to the meat.

If the weather is warm enough for flies to be present, the carcass should be wrapped in a deer cloth. Cheesecloth works well. Commercially available deer bags are great. Any porous material which will allow the meat to air out will do. A bed sheet will fill the bill. Black pepper should be sprinkled liberally into the chest cavity to repel flies.

Field-dressing significantly reduces the weight of your deer for portage. The weight of deer entrails is roughly one-fifth of the live weight of the animal. Gutted deer, on the average, weigh 70% of the live weight. The average deer of 150 pounds on the hoof weighs 120 field-dressed.

Traditional bleeding is unnecessary. Many hunters cut the deer's throats for this purpose. This will ruin a trophy. If your animal is dead, bleeding it will serve no purpose because the heart has stopped and will not pump any blood. Sufficient bleeding usually takes place when the animal is shot, creating a blood-letting wound. If you have a particular aversion to blood, then you can soak individual servings of venison in water before cooking to remove it. "Bleeding" animals refers to the practice of killing them by slitting their throats, which is hardly the case with deer.

When cleaning the animal, avoid the smelly tarsal glands and the metatarsal glands located on the front and rear legs. These smelly glands are tufts on the lower and inner sides of the legs. These scent-producing glands will musk up your venison, and the odor will not wash off. The taste will be wild, indeed. Some hunters cut them off before field-dressing. This is not a bad idea, but if you foul your knife while removing them and use the knife to finish dressing the animal, you just spread the musk. It is not necessary to do anything at all with these glands. In fact, it is best to leave them alone since the legs are cut off above these glands in butchering. Some hunters cut them off to use them for cover scent. If you are taking them for this reason, then keep them blood-free and frozen until you are ready to use them. I have been unsuccessful using these smelly glands in the hunting craft.

If you do not plan to save the cape of the deer (the skin from the mid-chest upward) for a chest mount, then open the ribs all the way up for improved air circulation. This will require a larger knife. Splitting the pelvic bone helps in airing also. You may need to pound a large knife with a tree limb to break these bones.

Take care of your own animal if you can, and do not expect others to help in field-dressing unless you are prepared to give them a share of the meat.

Most often, a bad or "gamey" taste in venison is the result of poor field-dressing and care of the animal, such as improper airing, standing blood, tallow, gland contact, heat deterioration, water deterioration, or bursting bladder, stomach or intestines. Deer, like livestock, are better to eat when they are gaining fat. Thus the venison will be less tasty whenever the animal has been losing fat —late in the rut season in the case of bucks, or just after weaning fawns in the case of does. Animals eating woodland forage have a more pungent flavor than those which frequent agricultural crops.

TOTING DEER

Retrieving your fallen deer can be quite a dilemma if you have not given adequate thought to how you will get the deer out. Many a hunter has ventured far from his auto over rugged terrain to bag his deer and after finally managing to get it out has sworn to "never do that again."

Don't just think "I'll worry about that later." Though you may later laugh at your difficulties, the hardships involved could be disastrous. Heart attacks often occur when hunters subject their bodies to such unusual strain.

A deer carcass is dead weight. Field-dressing reduces the load considerably. Still, except for some yearlings and smaller whitetail varieties, most deer are very hard for one man to pack out. Some larger deer can barely be budged. Dragging a deer downhill over forest leaves is a snap, but dragging one uphill for even a short distance is a challenge. Attempt to avoid having to tote deer uphill or over great distances.

A small deer can be swung over the shoulder. The deer will be slick and will slide off easily if the feet are not tied together. For a more stable cargo, use a short length of rope to tie all four feet together.

If you plan to drag a doe, tie her hind legs together and pull by the tie. Drag a buck by the antlers head-first. Dragging will mar the hide of the animal and may bruise the meat. If you intend to salvage the deer skin, take no chances with dragging.

If you want to save the hide, consider dragging the animal on a tarpaulin or on a skid made from saplings lashed together and pulled by you in mule fashion. Some guide services and other individuals offer the service of deer toting, using a single drag wheel to great advantage over specific types of terrain.

A motorized three-wheeler, four-wheeler, or other all-terrain vehicle is obviously quite handy for deer retrieval. Such vehicles are already dangerous enough, so be careful in riding one with the added weight of the deer.

Accessories for transporting deer are available for these ATV's. You can wrap your deer in a tarp and drag it with ease with these vehicles.

Two people can handle the carcass without a problem, and three make the job even easier since the third person can carry the weaponry, knapsacks, and other gear, freeing the other two to handle the deer only. The third party can also clear the path before the carriers.

Two people can use a deer pole. Use whatever is available and sturdy to make it. A cedar three inches in diameter and about eight feet in length works well. A carrying pole with a good fork in it can be very useful. The rear carrier can span both shoulders with the fork and thus distribute the deer's weight while improving overall balance. The fork should be large enough to eliminate a choking hazard.

The rope which you thoughtfully brought along will really be handy in these situations.

Quartering the animal to allow for portage is sometimes necessary. Local laws should be considered in this case. Some areas require the intact deer to be checked in (field-dressed only). This is apt to be the law where does are illegal game. This law also discourages the mere taking of trophy heads without utilization of the meat. Quartering is a measure generally taken in mountainous areas, where the difficulty is overwhelming.

If you require the help of hunting companions or others to retrieve a deer, then be courteous. Give the other hunters every opportunity to get a deer themselves before you break up their hunt by asking them to help you. If because of the weather or for some other reason it is necessary to get immediate help from them, then help them to get back to their hunt when you have complete the retrieve. You might not be invited to hunt with someone again who has had his hunt interrupted to assist in the dragging of an inferior deer when he has turned down many such animals himself.

Never drape a deer over the car hood for transport. The heat from the engine will harm the meat by causing deterioration and subsequent poor taste. If you use the trunk of the vehicle to transport a deer, you should leave the trunk open a foot and should not wrap the deer in plastic. Good ventilation is a must.

To make a dragline for toting deer, tie the forelegs together and lash the head to the legs with the muzzle pointing forward. The dragline can be attached to the forefeet. This makes a streamlined bundle that slips easily over most smooth surfaces.

You might consider using two poles to keep the deer from flopping from side to side and to distribute the weight on the shoulders of the two carriers. Tying the deer legs to the tote pole above the knees, leaving the forelegs sticking up above the pole, will further steady the animal for longer hauls and also keep it from dragging. Commercial deer drags work very well. They have been designed for one-man use, and some of the flaws have already been worked out of them. The commercial variety that doubles as a safety belt is handy.

If you pack your deer out over your shoulders, be sure to have plenty of hunter orange showing. You may want to place your vest on the deer instead of wearing it yourself. Some orange surveyor's ribbon tied around the deer is not anything but sensible in the deer woods. For many hunters the first sight of a deer is enough cause for immediate action.

HANGING MEAT AND SKINNING

When you get your deer back to camp or to your home, hang it up by the hind legs from a tree limb, a rafter in the garage, or some other stout structure with the hind legs spread by a spacer. You may want to use your vehicle to hoist the animal to such a position.

If you are hanging the deer from the rafters or ceiling joists of your garage and are using your vehicle to hoist the heavy deer, then be careful to not pull down your garage. A snag in the rope can do just that.

In cooler weather, let your field-dressed deer air out in this manner with the body cavity well-ventilated long enough for the meat to cool down and bleed out before you remove the hide. Deer skin more cleanly after hanging a couple of days. A bucket beneath the deer will catch blood droppings for easy disposal or for use in fertilizing a nearby plant, bush, or tree. Slits made through the skin of the lower hind legs between the bone and tendons will hold a very heavy deer quite well. The idealistic gambrel pictured above can be inserted through these slits, as well as wire or rope.

In skinning, begin by making a circling cut with a sharp knife where the meaty sections of the legs pan out to become bony. Then make cuts in the skin down the inside of the rear legs to the underneath of the tail at the anal opening. The deer skin may now be peeled down one leg at a time. Occasionally you will need to use a duller kitchen knife to keep the flesh and skin separated, since some flesh does hold the skin of the animal onto the body.

Next, you must take care to skin the tail if it will be left on the hide. If you wish, simply cut off the tail flesh and bone from the underside and leave the bone in the hide to be removed later under more comfortable conditions. It is tedious to remove the tailbone without damaging the tail itself. If you are going to send your deer hide to a tannery for conversion to clothing, the tail will be excluded.

Continue to peel the skin downward, fleshing the skin as you pull, until the skin is completely free. When the skin is removed, the deer is ready to age a little in a cool outdoors, in your garage, or in a meat locker. Two or three days of aging greatly improves the flavor of venison. Some people prefer to hang their meat in cold storage for up to two weeks. The only part of the meat harvest that is best very fresh is meat ground for venison "burgers."

Caping your animal for mounting requires considerable skill when you are removing the skin from the head of the animal. The average hunter should leave the head and neck intact until the taxidermist removes them. In field-caping, the hunter should cut the skin in a circle around the body behind the deer's forelegs. This will allow the taxidermist ample skin for a good shoulder mount.

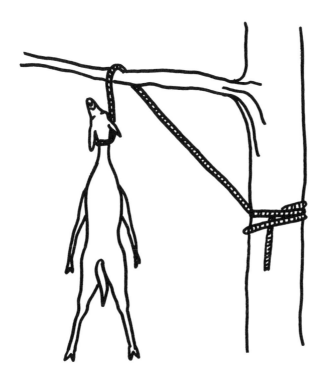

TO CLARIFY ONE FOR THE ANIMAL RIGHTS ACTIVISTS, DEER ARE HUNG AFTER THEY ARE KILLED, NOT KILLED BY HANGING.

A quick method of skinning a field-dressed deer is first to hang the deer securely by the neck and/or antlers. Next, free the neck-skin all the way around with your knife. Free the four feet by cutting them completely off with the hacksaw. A sawsall can simplify a lot of the cutting processes if you should have such a construction tool available. Pull the tough skin at the back of the neck down sufficiently to roll a roundish rock or a golf ball up in the skin and tie it off securely with a rope or a cable. Fasten the rope to your vehicle and pull the skin off the animal quickly. You will leave some meat on the hide by this method, but you will save some time.

Unless the rope is very strong and the object the deer is hung from very sturdy, this is futile. In the right circumstances, though, this produces a very clean deer carcass in minimal time with minimal effort. The hide will require extra fleshing, which can be done at a later time.

In the fall, a well-nourished deer has fat inside the body cavity as well as around the kidneys and on the heart. There are also fat layers over the saddle and the hips, outside the ribs, on the brisket, and elsewhere.

A good way to tell whether a deer is in good condition is by examining the bone marrow. Use the upper portion of the lower leg to examine the marrow since this bone is exposed and accessible, having been removed in the cleaning process. In a well-nourished deer, the marrow is solid in consistency and is a rich, creamy white. A starving deer, in its last stages, has bone marrow that is reddish or yellowish, gelatinous, wet to the touch, and without fatty quality.

Yellowish fat means that the deer is best for deerburger because the meat will be tough. White fat means that the deer will be tender and suitable for butchering into cuts.

Anyone who has cleaned small game such as rabbit or squirrel will have little trouble learning how to clean a deer. Deer are just big, tough rabbits to these hunters.

JUDGING DEER AGE

You can determine deer age by examining the teeth. Of course, the outward appearance of a deer will give you an idea of whether it is young or old. Antler growth is seldom a reliable sign of age. If whitetails did not shed their antlers annually, it might be possible to tell their age by examining antlers like tree rings, but this is not the case. The only true way to determine age is to study tooth wear and replacement.

Determining the exact age of a harvested deer is amusing and surprising. Usually the animal is much younger than expected. Most bucks taken are 1½ to 3½ years old. Bucks over 6 years of age are much rarer. Some old bucks seem to defy the laws of longevity and keep hanging in there year after year. Deer have been reported to live as long as 20 years. The oldest specimen I have been able to locate lived for 16½ years. Biologists inform me that deer could live to 23 years, but old age for most deer is 8 to 12 years. The normal lifespan is seldom over 10 years. Death from old age may be due to dental failure if the deer does not succumb to hunters or other predators, disease, or critical periods of food shortage or drought. Does, as a whole, live longer than do bucks. Bucks are traditionally sought after by hunters, which takes the majority of the prime male deer out of the woods before they can reach old age. In captivity does live longer than do bucks too. This is attributed to the fact that bucks waste a lot of energy and nutrition in the development of antlers and use of excessive energy in the rut. Neither the length of the antlers nor the number of points gives a reliable indication of age, since these attributes depend on winter nutrition, soil fertility, genetic inheritance, and other factors unrelated to years of life.

Any hunter who downs a deer is interested in knowing how long the animal has survived. Personnel at game-check stations, game wardens, and biologists are commonly well versed in the technique for telling age. But the everyday hunter generally knows little or nothing about it. With practice, the hunter can become adept at judging deer age. If you are interested in learning the skill, the following pages will get you started. If you compare a good number of deer teeth you will be able to tell age at a glimpse.

A GUIDE TO THE AGE OF THE WHITETAIL DEER COLLECTED IN THE FALL

Fawns (5—6 Months Old): Either all of the temporary milk incisors or possibly just the center ones have been replaced by permanent teeth. The first molar is present but the second molar is rarely erupted.

Yearlings (1½ Years Old): The temporary premolars are present, or the permanent premolars are replacing the temporary ones. The fourth premolar is three-parted. There is no wear on the permanent premolars. The rear cusp of the third molar is not usually erupted. There is little or no wear on the crests of the third molar.

Yearlings (1½ Years Old or Older): All of the permanent incisors are present. The third molar is erupted. All of the permanent premolars are in position and fully erupted. The fourth premolar is two-parted.

2½ Year Olds: There will be slight wear on the last cusp of the third molar. The lingual crests of all the molars will be sharp. The wear will be slight on the third premolar or nonexistent and slight on the fourth. If the last crest of the third molar is erupted and there is greater wear, you might expect the deer to be older.

3½ Year Olds: The lingual crests of all the molars except the first are sharp. The first molar is blunt. The last cusp of the third molar is flat, indented, or both.

4½ Year Olds: More wear is observed. It is hard to accurately tell the age above 3½ years old due to the variations in the forage of the individual deer and subsequent tooth wear. Deer which browse near the earth will exhibit increased tooth wear due to sand and grit presence. Those deer which have browse habitat which is higher have less tooth wear as a result. The individual habitat is a consideration to be made when possible.

4½ to 5½ Years Old: The lingual crests of the first molar are erupted and are flat. The crests of the second molar are rounded like the 3½ year olds. The rear cusp of the third molar could be worn into a downward and toward the rear slope. The third and fourth premolars are worn to a greater degree. The second premolar may show wear.

6½ to 8½ Years Old: The third molar keeps the lingual crests during all stages. In the upper age limits especially, the lingual crests of the second molar are absent, and the first molar and fourth premolar are flat.

9½ to 12½ Years Old: The wear on the cheek teeth is greater than any of the previous age classes exhibit. None of the deer in this age class have all teeth flattened. There is normally a lingual crest on the third molar, although it may be worn. Incisors may or may not be missing. There is great variation in wear in this age group.

Elderly Deer: There are no lingual crests. All the molars are rubbed flat and are most likely to be hollowed. Teeth may be lost. Gums and bone around the teeth bases will be receding.

Tooth Eruption in Whitetail Deer Fawns

KEY {
D   Milk or dediduous tooth

P   Permanent tooth

Parentheses indicate that the tooth is in the process of erupting at that particular time.

	Incisors			Canine	Premolars			Molars		
	1	2	3	1	2	3	4	1	2	3
1 − 3 Weeks	(D)	(D)	(D)	(D)	(D)	(D)	(D)			
2 − 3 Months	D	D	D	D	D	D	D	(P)		
6 Months	P	D	D	D	D	D	D	(P)		
12 Months	P	P	P	P	D	D	P	P	(P)	
18 Months	P	P	P	P	P	(P)	(P)	P	P	P
24 Months	P	P	P	P	P	P	P	P	P	P

Sequence of Eruption and Wear in Whitetail Deer
(Front teeth, lower jaw)

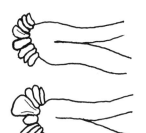

5 Months — All incisors are milk teeth

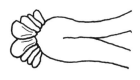

5 to 6 Months — Milk pincers (the two middle teeth) are lost during the fifth month and are replaced by permanent pincers.

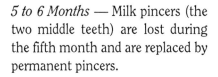

6 Months — Permanent pincers are fully erupted. Lateral and corner incisors are still milk teeth and are replaced during the tenth and eleventh months.

mm Scale

0
5
10

YEARLINGS: 1 year, 4 — 5 months

Milk premolars are moderately to heavily worn

Fourth milk premolar is three-cusped

Third molar is
not fully erupted

Permanent premolars

*Premolars are numbered 2 — 3 — 4
because of evolutionary loss of number 1*

YEARLINGS: 1 year, 6 months

Loss of milk premolars and partially erupted premolars

Molars are sharp   *Fourth permanent premolar is two-cusped*

Third molar is not fully erupted

YEARLINGS: 1 year, 7 months

Permanent premolars usually fully erupted with light wear occasionally showing on grinding surfaces. Slight wear but no dentine line showing on crests of last (third) molar.

Check upper third molar to verify class (third molar partially erupted)

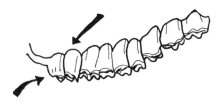

(Top jaw)

Upper third molar is fully erupted
at 1 year, 10 months to 2 years.

The *lower third molar* is fully erupted at one year, 8 to 10 months.

(Bottom jaw)

2½ YEARS

Permanent premolars and molars

Upper third molar is fully erupted, slight wear

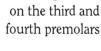

(Top jaw)   There is very little
                                                 wear on the second molar

Slight wear on posterior cusp of the *third molar,* slight wear
                                             on the third and
                                             fourth premolars

(Bottom jaw)

The lingual crests of the first and second molars are sharp,
the enamel is well above the narrow dentine of the crest

3½ YEARS: Molars

The dentine lines in the crests of the first
and second molar are wider than the enamel.

The lingual crests of the first molar
are blunt, the *secondary crests*
are prominent and blunt.

The first molar is worn to within 6 — 7 mm of the gum
on the buccal side

4½ YEARS: Molars

The first molar is worn to within 5 — 6 mm of
the gum on the buccal side.

*The lingual crests on the first molar
are almost worn away,* the secondary
crests are visible.

Second molar 6 — 7 mm

First molar is worn to
within 4 — 5 mm of
gum on the buccal side

5½ YEARS: Molars

The original lingual crests of the first molar are worn away and
simulated lingual crests appear, secondary crests are worn away,
and the first molar is worn to within 4 — 5 mm of the gum on
the buccal side.

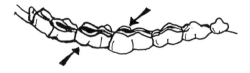

Second molar 5 — 6 mm

The dentine crests on all molars are much broader
than the enamel

6½ YEARS: Molars

No lingual crests on the first molar and worn to within
3 — 4 mm of the gum on the buccal side

Second molar 4 — 5 mm

7½ YEARS: Molars

The first molar is worn to within 2 — 3 mm on the buccal side

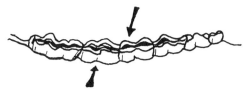

Second molar 3 — 4 mm

8½ — 9½ YEARS: Molars

All molars are worn to within 2 — 3 mm of the gum
on the buccal side

10½ YEARS AND OLDER: Molars

The *first molar* is at or below the gum line

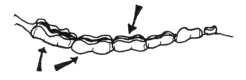

The second and third molars are within 1 — 2 mm of the
gum line on the buccal side

Chapter

8

After the Hunt

TROPHIES

Boone and Crocket and Pope and Young

If your deer is outstanding, it might be in the record class. To be considered a fine *typical* example, a whitetail buck should have:

1. Antlers that are both long and massive.
2. A good spread that is not due to freak points or freakish conformation.
3. Antler points that are long and of the normal type.
4. As far as possible, the kind of symmetrical beauty found in the typical antler pattern of the whitetail deer.

The official scoring system for a typical deer is designed to reflect how well a trophy combines all these desirable features. The scoring system for non-typical deer is separate and based largely upon the amount and the size of the antlers.

The official scoring methods were established to provide a way

286

of arriving at a sound comparison of trophies, so that our record lists could really mean something. Another purpose was to preserve our whitetail deer by encouraging sportsmen to hunt for fine specimens instead of shooting the first deer they encounter. Some may ask, "How can deer be preserved by killing them?"

Some feel that hunting should not be a competitive sport and that record-book entry makes it such. Some believe that shooting the finest heads deprives a species of its best breeding stock and results in an inferior race of animals. Wherever any species is scarce, trophy hunting must be considered in terms of its effects on conservation.

In the case of whitetail deer, the outstanding trophy specimen is an old male in the prime of his life; he has already sired descendants to carry on his genetic heritage. He has only a few seasons left. Since his species is polygamous, shooting him will not affect the numbers of his kind that survive.

Furthermore, we have learned about heredity. We now know that descendants of a young male inherit the same general characteristics as offspring sired by the same animal later in life. This means that if we shoot a younger animal instead of a grand old trophy specimen—in the belief that we are thereby preserving the finest breeding stock—we may be unwittingly destroying a son of the older one, or of an even better sire, when the young animal had many more years of service to give to his race.

The final argument in favor of trophy hunting concerns the sportsman himself. When a hunter passes up the small heads and waits for a real trophy, he will see more game, learn a lot more about hunting, and have the satisfaction of meeting a much more formidable challenge to his skill.

In certain areas of North America today, whitetail deer are so plentiful that they are destroying all the winter forage on which their survival depends. Trophy hunting in these regions is out of place.

Here the best possible conservation measure would be to shoot deer of both sexes and of all sizes until the herd is brought into balance with its food supply.

In order to qualify for the Boone and Crocket record books, a hunter must provide a notarized certification of "fair chase."

Fair chase is established by the following guidelines.[1] It is considered unfair advantage to take deer by:

1. Spotting or herding game from the air; followed by landing in its vicinity for pursuit;
2. Herding or pursuing game with motorpowered vehicles;
3. Use of electronic communications for attracting, locating, or observing game, or guiding the hunter to such game;
4. Hunting game confined by artificial barriers, including escape-proof fencing; or hunt game transplanted solely for the purpose of commercial shooting.

The sportsman must also state that he did not take a deer under conditions that do not fully comply with local game laws or regulations of the state, province, or territory.

In Alaska, the hunter must additionally state that the hide or meat was salvaged for human use.

Animals that are picked up or found or not eligible for these record books wherever they are taken in North America.

To qualify for the Pope and Young record books, for bow hunters only, the deer must not be taken under similar guidelines. Their current address is:

Pope and Young Club
P. O. Box 548
Chatfield, Minnesota 55923

---

[1]Revised Fair Chase Statement printed with the express written permission of the Boone and Crockett Club.

The sportsman who wishes to measure a trophy for record can get the necessary scoring chart by writing to:

North American Big Game Awards Program
c/o Hunting and Conservation
1600 Rhode Island Ave., N.W.
Washington, D.C. 20036

If you should kill an exceptionally fine deer that may qualify, write to this address and request the name of the nearest official scorer and measurer. He will help you fill out the necessary forms and provide the data necessary for possibly entering your specimen in the *Records of North American Big Game*. This record book can be purchased for interesting reading. Your public library might have an up-to-date copy.

It is suggested that you pre-score your own deer before attempting to locate an official scorer. Write the Boone and Crockett Club, 241 South Fraley Boulevard, Dumfries, Virginia 22026, for a measuring chart which will help you determine whether or not your buck merits official scoring. There is a nominal charge for the charts of $ .50 each or four charts for $1.00 (1990). If you believe that you have a buck worthy of scoring after you have followed the charts, you can write the same address to find a scorer near your area. The official scorers are volunteers who simply cannot afford the time to score every deer that hunters take.

All trophies shrink to some extent in drying out, so regulations provide that a head cannot be measured for official record until at least 60 days after the animal was killed.

Many a taxidermist has taken a fine pair of loose antlers or pieced antlers and made an exaggerated trophy from them by mounting them on a head for sale. These heads are common in hunting lodges. Another common practice is to split the skull of the deer to increase spread. Official scorers use a lot of judgment and caution in examining heads and racks for deceptions or unnatural deviations.

Quality deer are added to the official records each year.

Hunters have taken record-breaking deer that have not reached the record books because they were unaware of the existence of such a standard and the method of applying. Occasionally collectors encounter old deer heads at auctions or the tool sheds of rural dwellings which are significant.

RITUALS

Some circles of hunters in different areas practice ritualistic behavior. Some of these practices are based upon Native American beliefs, and some are designed to initiate new or young hunters or new hunting club members, often by means of the sort of ridicule used by campus fraternities. For example, the first-time hunter and club initiate could be required to wear the testicles of a buck around his neck. Other rites may involve drinking some blood or eating some of a particular raw organ, such as a piece of the heart or liver. Such rites are superstitiously believed to insure further good hunts or are considered to add appeal to membership.

It is not recommended that anyone eat or drink any raw component of a deer. If you fry a liver with onions at camp (another ritual) or boil a heart for a tasty treat, it will surely accomplish the same task.

If you are a beginning hunter, be forewarned that social interactions on organized deer hunts may involve such practices, which are a little more than one might expect in days so far removed from those of the cave men.

A more sensible ritual might involve the ritualistic cleansing of scent from the body of the hunter in a sweat hut and asking blessing for the hunt with thanksgiving as the Native American did.

LITTER

Take everything you carry into the woods back out with you. Litter is appalling in the natural environment. It is a real downer to chance upon a chewing gum wrapper or cigarette filter when you are appreciating the unspoiled beauty of nature. It doesn't take much effort to keep our trash to ourselves. In fact, it is easier to pack it out empty than it was to pack it in full. You'll feel better about it if you do no littering. If you want to be really on target, then carry out a sack of litter which others have thoughtlessly discarded.

FENCE RESPECT

When going under, through, over, or around fencing, the hunter should show consideration for the fence owner as well as for personal ease and safety. Whenever crossing a fence, a hunter should unload and place his firearm on the opposite side or hand the firearm to another hunter to hold until the fence is crossed. The best way for two men to cross barbed wire is with one man holding the strands apart for the other. If climbing over the fence causes the wire to break loose from the post, then get a rock and fix it. Help the landowner to maintain his property, which helps to insure future privileges.

If it appears necessary to remove a section of fence to allow vehicle passage to retrieve a large deer, then check with the fence owner first. Remove logs and limbs that have fallen on your host's fencing as you encounter them in the hunt. If you spot a section of fence that is down, notify the landowner and offer to help with the repair.

TREE RESPECT

Never put a nail in a tree which will someday be harvested. One small nail can ruin an entire tree when the tree goes to market. Permanent tree stands should only be built in oddly formed trees which will obviously never be used for lumber. Check with the landowner before erecting a stand to determine where one can be placed. You may have to use a stand that is not nailed to a tree, such as a climber or other portable. Be careful not to damage tree bark and avoid puncture wounds to the tree with these stands as well.

Be selective when cutting firewood. Any deer hunter worth his oats has familiarized himself with tree species. Selective cutting is the right approach regardless of where you are hunting. If you are unable to differentiate tree species, familiarization is merely a matter of asking someone to point them out.

GRATITUDE

Remember the owner of the land you like to hunt with a simple card during the holidays or with a thank-you note anytime throughout the year. Offer him some of your deer meat. A simple gift such as a bottle of his favorite drink or a box of candy or fruit might be in order. Offer to help him work on his land to fill chuck holes, chop firewood, improve wildlife habitat, or whatever seems appropriate.

Actions speak louder than words, but sincere words can be recognized. Such gestures will improve your chances of being allowed to hunt there the next year too. Offering your labor for the produce of his land is an attitude that most any farmer or landowner will honor with permission to hunt.

UTILIZING THE ENTIRE DEER

Virtually all parts of a deer can be put to some use. Those parts you can think of no other possible use for make fertilizer.

Simply bury them next to a tree or bush deeply enough to conceal their odor and make them less accessible to cats, dogs, and wild scavengers. You might put a rock over them to avoid a mess from digging animals.

The following are some of the many uses for deer parts. Using your creative faculties of imagination and improvisation, you can make artistic and functional items from the deer.

Skin: You may tan the hide yourself or send it to a taxidermist or a tannery. A tanning factory can tan the hide and convert it into any number of articles for you. It takes a surprising number of deer skins to make larger garments. Only the choice parts of the hide are used symmetrically. Some articles made from deer skins are gun cases, gloves, moccasins, carpenter's aprons, hunting chaps, rifle slings, seat covers, baby shoes, vests, wallets, pocket books, and any and all manner of clothing. For subzero use, Eskimo "mukluks" are the very best footwear and will keep the feet from freezing during long hours of outside exposure. Mukluks are hair boots of nearly knee height, worn over an inner boot made with the hair turned inside.

Ribs: In addition to being a choice dinner item, the ribs make good, old-fashioned baskets. The rib bones are woven together to create the basket frame. Ribs may also be used to make cages for small animals. Perhaps this is why the mid-section of the anatomy is referred to as the "ribcage." Ribs can also be made into leaf rakes.

Hooves: The legs of the deer can serve as the legs for an attractive coffee table, end table, plant stand, or stool. These make well-received gifts and work quite well when given time to stiffen uniformly. The hooves make interesting bottom tips for walking canes. An attractive ashtray can be made by extending the dewclaws for support and placing a small bowl on the ankle top. American Indian youth made cup toys from the hooves by hollowing them out; they used the cups to catch and throw balls. The gummy substance between the hooves was used by the Native American for cover scent in hunting deer. A hoof can be used in making mock scrapes.

Antlers: Antlers are sold to Oriental buyers for use in potions, medicines, and cosmetics used across the world. Ground antler makes an uncommonly good flowering houseplant fertilizer. A magnificent chandelier can be made from four or more antler sets. Antlers are used for knife handles, gun racks, hatracks, racking antlers (rattling antlers), and trophy mounts. Antler pipes can be fashioned from the section of antler that includes the brow point and the crown. The crown is cut from the skull and hollowed out for the bowl, and points are drilled from the brow tine tip and the bowl to fashion the pipe. You can put just about any kitchen utensil into an antler with a drill and some super-glue.

Small intestine: When cured in brine, the small intestine can be used in making deer sausage or link venison. You might make a bow string from one for the fun of it.

Fat: Deer fat makes a high-quality tallow soap.

Brain: The brain is high in food value. You can use it to soften hides just as pioneers and Indians did.

Liver: Liver too has high food value. It can be used alone or in sausage.

Testicles: These also can go into a tasty sausage.

Kidneys: With the fat layer removed, these organs go into sausage.

Tongue: The tongue makes a good cold cut and can be used in your deer sausage.

Glands: All glands can be harvested for scenting purposes.

Urine: Urine for scenting purposes can be collected from the bladder. This is easily extracted with a syringe.

Larynx: The larynx (wind pipe) can be used to make a grunt call by adding a splatter of reed in the end.

Tail: The deer tail makes a very good, buoyant fishing lure. Lure manufacturers buy the tails from hunters through the mail. If you put a big hook on a deer tail and beat the water with it long enough, you might just fool a very large bass into thinking it is a muskrat and attacking it.

Leg bones: Leg bones can be used to make awls, needles, and bodkins for sewing deer hides together to make rugs, clothing, and teepees. The delicious marrow was prized by the Indians as food.

Shoulder blades: The shoulder blades of deer can be attached to wooden handles and used as hoes.

Skull: The skull of an antlered deer can be boiled and cleansed of flesh. The lower jaws can be glued back on where muscles held them onto the skull. The mouth is positioned open. The front two teeth are pulled from the upper jaw, and tine tips about four inches long from another set of antlers are fitted into the tooth sockets and glued. Put a smaller tine tip in the

middle of the lower jaw just behind the clipping teeth. You
have a sabre-toothed deer, which makes a unique conversation piece which you can have a lot of fun with.

Stomach: Soak the emptied stomach in salt for a few days. The
stomach lining will peel easily from the wall. Drape the skin
over a lard can, nail keg, milk can, or other tubular object,
stretch it, and secure it with a nylon lock strap from the electrical store. The resulting drum will be surprisingly resonant.
The tanned stomach can be used to make a wineskin in the
manner of the nomadic tribes of Africa and Asia.

There are distinct differences among deer hides. The best
hides for fur are harvested in late August and early September by
bow hunters. The summer coat is the shortest-haired coat; the
hair grows longer and thicker, and subsequently coarser, as winter
approaches. The hairless hide is always a quality leather which is
thin, soft, tough, clean, and workable.

Decide what you are going to do with the deer hide as soon as
possible. If you plan to send it off to a tannery, then roll it in non-
iodized salt after fleshing the hide. Scrape off all the meat you can
while being careful not to cut the leather. Salting the hide heavily
and allowing it to dry some will make the task easier. To send the
hide off, wrap it in newspapers but do not freeze it. Most tanneries
send a brochure explaining their processes with instructions as to
how they prefer their hides to be shipped.

If you should decide to tan the hide yourself, your local library
should have how-to information. You can do it with hair on or
hair off. Hair-on kits from leather companies cost about $15.00
for two deer as of 1990. The tanning ingredients are premixed and
blend well with the salted hide. The skin is allowed to dry with the
paste rubbed in. Excess tanning paste is scraped off, and the hide
is worked by hand over the back of a wooden chair, table edge, or
other appropriate rounded surface to break the fibers and make

the skin limp.

Removing the hair requires the use of lye, or lime and wood ash. Making your own tannin from the oak bark, softening with brains, and smoking the hide over a fire is authentic and fun if you have the time. For most of us the mail-order course of action is the best choice.

Be sure to cut the metatarsals from the legs of the hides before any processing to avoid their strong, enduring odor.

It takes one hide to make a cap, three to make a vest, three to four for trousers, four to six for a coat, and one for moccasins. Two pairs of moccasins can be made from a big skin.

Deerskin was very popular for clothing at one time. Tons of deer skins were exported from all areas of North America to Europe. In 1756, the Province of Georgia alone shipped about 6,000,000 deerskins to England.

The deer were mainly killed by guns, but many were captured in concealed pits dug deep along deer paths and other frequented byways.

PROCESSING MEAT

Once upon a time, most butchers would process your venison for you. If you had field-dressed the deer and removed the skin, about any grocery store would be willing to do the chore for a modest fee. Today, regulations forbid butchers from bringing anything other than government-inspected meats into their establishments. Consequently it is rare to find a supermarket that provides this service for customers.

Meat-packing houses or slaughter houses with large meat lockers are found throughout rural America and Canada. These establishments try to have most of their livestock taken care of before deer season arrives so that they can serve the seasonal customers. They usually charge a flat rate in the range of $30.00 to $50.00 for a deer of any size. You need not skin the deer before taking the carcass to be butchered. They will ask if you plan to have the head mounted so that they can leave sufficient cape should that be your wish. If you have a very special head that you intend to mount, it is best to take your deer directly to a taxidermist for professional caping and not trust anyone else with the job. The packing house will ask you if you want the skin. Most people say they don't. Usually the price is the same either way. The packing houses make good money by shipping the raw hides collected through a season to a tannery.

The butcher will ask you how many people you expect to feed at a time so that he can package the meat in handy freezer parcels containing the right quantity of venison per meal in relation to family size. Although butchers do a fine job of wrapping the meat, you should wrap it with a second covering of freezer paper to make it last longer in your freezer. The majority of successful hunters only occasionally dine on venison so your venison needs extra care for longer freezer life. The process takes three to five days on the average, depending on the work load at the packing house. It is better to let the deer hang in the locker for a week or so for aging if that is allowed. It does improve the already wonderful flavor of venison steak. Ground meat is better fresh, however. The butcher might ask you if you would like the smaller portions of meat, the neck and everything else that does not make a traditional cut, put into deerburger. Beef suet is added to the meat. Surprisingly, most hunters say no. They are throwing away a large amount of good deer meat which someone else would gladly use if given the opportunity. There is generally no extra charge for grinding deerburger, a very tough task at home which butchers can do with comparative ease. To those who have experienced good deerburgers there is no better flavored hamburger material. The ground meat is the principal reason for visiting the packing house to those who have undertaken the chore on their own. The butcher will also ask you how thick you want your steaks to be. You will probably like them the same thickness as your choice in beef steaks. One-inch venison steaks are great. Many people have their steaks sliced thin. The thinner cuts are faster cooking and easier to consume for them. Venison cooks well, thick or thin.

TRADITIONAL CUTS OF VENISON

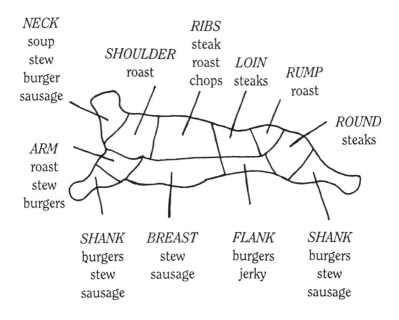

NECK
soup
stew
burger
sausage

SHOULDER
roast

RIBS
steak
roast
chops

LOIN
steaks

RUMP
roast

ROUND
steaks

ARM
roast
stew
burgers

SHANK
burgers
stew
sausage

BREAST
stew
sausage

FLANK
burgers
jerky

SHANK
burgers
stew
sausage

At the end of the hunt, the hunter is usually worn out. Taking the deer to a packing house is a great relief. You may not have adequate space to do the job yourself. A garage, a washtub, a bathtub, or a few five-gallon buckets and a big sink are all that is really needed, but it is quite a chore. It is also an unlovely sight. The rest of your family might eat deer meat more readily if they do not witness the process. Packing houses are interesting to visit during gun season to see all the harvested deer and get in on all the conversation. During a good season, some packing houses refuse to take any more deer because their lockers are full. It is a good idea to phone them beforehand to see if this is the case.

If you process the meat yourself, you will need a good hacksaw, a sharp butcher knife and paring knife, and containers for the meat. Many people prefer to do their own butchering. People who have the legs barbecued and those who like the tenderloin left in a long strip rank among the do-it-yourselfers.

There are five in my family. We all like venison and consume it regularly. As a matter of choice, I take two deer a year. I have one custom-packaged and home-butcher the other. This way we enjoy a greater variety of cuts. The only problem I have at home is finding an adequate meat grinder. Deer gristle is tough. Hand-cranked meat grinders are simply inadequate for deer. The muscle sinews will drive you batty if you try to grind the meat manually. It takes a hardy electric grinder to do the job, which is too expensive for the average hunter. A friend of mind has a good grinding apparatus attached to his ½-inch electric drill that serves him well. Since deer have very little fat, you will want to add beef suet, beef sausage, or pork sausage to your deerburger meat. I save the whole neck for making a big pot of soup, having plenty of parts for grinding without it. When I do the work at home, I also let the meat soak in salt water to drain out the blood, simply a personal preference.

An average adult deer sliced and packaged in flat, regular shapes will require six cubic feet of freezer space. Home economists state that freezer life for deer meat is six months. When extra care is taken to double-wrap the meat and eliminate all air pockets, the meat can easily be kept for a year. Vacuum sealing machines are a practical luxury for those who freeze wild game and garden produce. When the next deer season comes around and it is time to put a new deer or two in the freezer, then give away any deer meat remaining from the previous year.

Canning deer meat is an option when freezer space is unavailable. Canning deer requires temperatures of 240 degrees Fahrenheit. You will need a good pressure canner that can function over an extended period of time. It takes 40 quart canning jars for one whole deer.

Deboned meat yields 40% of the dressed weight of the meat. For example, a 150-pound deer yields 60 pounds of processed meat. The hunter who spends $240.00 on his deer hunt from beginning to end has invested $4.00 a pound in venison.

In my home area of Western Kentucky we like to have barbecue suppers. It is a tradition in these parts which involves church groups, companies, family groups, and clubs. We have a stew called "burgoo" that is a favorite. This mulligan is made by blending various vegetables with meats in a large pot over a fire and stirring with a canoe paddle. Deer makes a great additive.

DRYING MEAT

The time spent shredding thin layers of the striated muscles of deer meat for making jerky is worthwhile. These shreds of venison are then salted and very slowly smoked until well done and dry. Traditionally this is done over a smoking pit or campfire. Today the popular method is to use a dehydrator. These devices do an excellent job of drying the meat while preserving and enhancing the natural flavor. The investment is a good one. When using an electric evaporator, you can slice the meat thinly for drying instead of leaving it stringy, since it does not need to be hung to dry. This also leaves the jerky easier to chew since you are cutting across the grain. If you want to add the smokehouse flavor, dip and drain the meat in a hickory-smoke sauce dilution. Slow-drying in an oven works well also. Just allow for moisture to escape by leaving the door open slightly. It takes a long time by the oven method and you will have a shorter shelf-life since all the moisture will not evaporate. If you do a thorough job in drying these morsels of meat, they make great gifts.

SMOKING DEER IS INCREASINGLY POPULAR,
BUT IT'S HARD TO KEEP IT LIT.

SHARING MEAT

Many people would greatly appreciate a gift of some of your deer. It is a rewarding experience to share the meat with others. If you hunt for the sport only, then you have a magnificent opportunity to help someone less fortunate by providing them with meat. You will not have to look far to find someone in need. You may want to keep only the choice cuts of the deer and give away the ribs or some other parts. These too will be relished. Your local welfare office could always help you find a specific family who could benefit from a nutritious gift of venison.

SALVAGING URINE AND MUSK GLANDS

You can make your own concoctions for scenting purposes by salvaging glandular excretions from your harvested deer. These scents can be collected by means of a syringe, by squeezing, or by soaking the glands in grain alcohol and then evaporating the alcohol to collect the extracted scent. It is impractical to most hunters to collect their own scents due to the ease of visiting the sporting-goods store. You will know what you have got, for sure, if you do your own collecting. Store the scents in sterile glass bottles and refrigerate them. Be sure to seal them well. Refrigerated scents will last from one season to the next if not contaminated with bacteria or blood. Scents that have developed an ammonia smell should be discarded. Frozen scents must be utilized immediately after thawing due to rapid breakdown into gases. These glands are:

1. *Interdigital.* Located under the skin between the two hoof lobes. They produce a sweat and an odor that lingers on deer tracks. This is the scent that dogs follow.
2. *Pre-orbital.* Small, trench-like slits of nearly bare skin in front of each eye by the nose. They are dark blue or black. They produce pheromones which act as sex stimulants.

3. *Tarsal glands*. Large, hairy areas of the hind legs at the hocks that are about three inches across. They are pheromone-producing but are mainly urine depositories. Deer check each other out by smelling them. When a deer is alarmed, the hair of this gland stands out. The dominant buck has bigger tarsal glands than other bucks.

4. *Metatarsal glands*. Located between the hock and the hoof. These are not true glands because they have no openings or ducts. When deer lie down, the metatarsals deposit scent to mark their beds. These glands are larger on dominant bucks.

5. *Sudophorus*. Located between the antlers and the forehead. This gland distinguishes individual animals and acts as a sexual attractant.

6. *Urinary bladder*. Urine taken from does during the rut contains the scents of sexual readiness. This is the easiest scent to collect, can be kept purely natural, and is the most useful for the hunter intent upon luring a buck. Keep the air out of the refrigerated bottle and you should be able to keep this one without any trouble. Have some rubber gloves and a container ready when field-dressing for collecting this scent.

ROAD KILLS

Hundreds of thousands of deer are hit by cars and trucks on our highways annually in North America. It is common to spot deer lying on the shoulder of the road or on the median.

The kills reported to the Department of Motor Vehicles represent only a small part of the total, since many road kills go unreported. Most reports are made only when insurance recovery is an issue. Since deer populations have become so large, it is no longer important for game wardens and state policemen to report each deer kill.

Road kills are a fair indication of good deer-hunting locations. The frequency of road kills is one of the factors which are considered by officials in selecting the best time for conducting the hunting season. The period when deer are most active is the choice time. Most of those black skid marks on interstates near heavily wooded areas were put there by motorists colliding with or braking for deer. If you see no scraps of tire tread from a blowout near the end of the skid mark and you are in a double lane headed in one direction and divided by a median from traffic going in the opposite direction, then you can presume a motorist encountered a deer. Sometimes you can stop to investigate and find a deer that was not recovered by the driver who hit it. The people who mow and maintain the roadsides frequently come upon dead deer which made it to the fence line but did not make it across after having been struck. Deer crossing paved highways may slip in fear and excitement before an oncoming vehicle. The headlights of an automobile daze deer and sometimes actually attract them. Mostly such deer are crossing the road in travel, but sometimes they have come to the roadside to forage the well-kept greenery.

Wintertime road kills are usually taken for meat before it is too late. Sometimes passing motorists hop out to cut off a ham or two or salvage the antlers. Keeping a road kill is nearly impossible during warm weather, when most road kills go to waste. If the deer is not stiff, the hair does not pull out easily, and the animal is still bleeding, then you have a fresh kill. If you pick one up, it is a good idea to call the game warden just for the record. The warden will almost always allow you to keep the animal, although officially it is the property of the state or province. You will need consent from a warden to take the deer to a processing plant or taxidermist.

A road kill salvage does not require the purchase of a license and does not count against a harvest quota for hunters. Taking road kills will free you to hunt for a trophy deer, having your venison supplied without firing a shot.

On the average, hitting a deer will cause $1,000 worth of damage to a car. Sometimes only a headlight is broken, but other times cars are totally destroyed and the driver killed or hospitalized. Drivers should be aware of this danger and drive defensively. Be especially alert at night, and in areas where unclipped vegetation grows beside the roadway.

Look for eyes on the roadside at night. The headlights will reflect in them and make them stand out. The deer will almost invariably peer into the light. They may appear just as a flash or may stand out as white, yellow, orange, red, or blue. They will usually resemble a pair of muffled flashlight beams. Look for deer while driving to your hunt. The hours just before daylight and right after sunset are a time of noticeably increased deer activity. Hunters do push deer into increased mobility when they enter and depart the woods.

This is a particularly good time to wear seat belts.

Ultrasonic whistle devices which attach to the front bumper or grill of your car, truck, or mobile home are effective safety precautions. When speeds that exceed 30 miles per hour are reached, the resulting wind passing through the devices produces a high-frequency sound that alerts animals up to a quarter of a mile away and discourages them from entering the highway. They are claimed to be inaudible to humans and 80% effective.

I believe in their effectiveness, as do insurance companies. They can be purchased for a nominal fee from your insurance office. While they are inaudible to passengers in the vehicle, I can hear them on vehicles which are traveling the roads while I am hunting nearby. These deer alerts are also effective to warn dogs and cats.

The law usually stipulates that the hunter must be 500 yards or more from a road when hunting, so don't jump out of your vehicle and shoot.

Take advantage of road kills. You need not feel like you are an opossum if you utilize deer from the road.

VENISON RECIPES

There is nothing mysterious about venison, which can be treated like any other meat. It will taste different from beef, but so does lamb, veal, or pork. Someone accustomed to a diet of deer flesh who was introduced to the flesh of the cow might think the taste of beef strange! In this case, the beef would probably be considered inferior in taste. Venison may take a little getting used to, but it won't take long to learn to appreciate its distinctive taste.

Deer meat can be quite dry since it is not saturated with fat. The flesh of deer is lean with what little fat there is located next to the skin. The fat that does adhere to the meat is of a disagreeable flavor and quality, making it necessary to use as soap and not for cooking. For this reason, some cooks soak or marinate venison in vegetable or nut oil before cooking. Bacon is used while cooking to keep the meat moistened, as is basting with pan juices. Attempts to disguise the flavor of venison can ruin its taste. Most objections to properly-dressed venison are actually due to the potent seasonings, sauces, and gravies often used. Recipes are almost always very fancy and involve the use of too many spices. Simple cooking methods are best.

Venison is good braised, broiled, cooked over a campfire, over charcoal, in a crockpot, fried, dried, roasted, in a soup, stew, burgoo, corned, smoked, canned, frozen, made into sausage, burgers, meatballs, meatloaf, used in spaghetti sauce, or used in any other way in which meat is traditionally used.

Remove all the slime encountered on the surface of deer flesh, and all the sinew possible. Cut away all fat. The resulting flesh may be used in countless numbers of recipes including these:

Deer Brains and Eggs

Brains should be pre-cooked in a pan of water. Bring the water to a boil, then add the brains and a teaspoon of lemon juice. Cover and simmer for 15 minutes. Plunge the brains into cold water and peel off the outer membrane. Mix the crumbled brains and some creamed cheese into a frying pan with whole eggs. Add salt and pepper while scrambling. The delicious result is served atop toast. I add garlic powder and cayenne.

Deer Neck Soup

This is an easy recipe for even the most inept of cooks. All you need is a deer neck, a large pot with a lid, some vegetables and seasoning, water, and a heat source. I recommend that you stick with the usual vegetable soup type vegetables of carrots, celery, peas, beans, corn, potatoes, tomatoes, onions, beets and turnips. Go lightly on more pungent vegetables such as broccoli, cauliflower, and cabbage. A dash of cayenne pepper will enhance flavor. Use a little salt and a little garlic powder. Just cook the mixture over low to medium heat for several hours. You can remove the neck to flake off the meat and replace the meat into the soup without the bone.

Hunting Camp Stew

A good and hearty venison stew is just the thing for lunch or dinner in the woods. This recipe requires a cast-iron pot with a secure lid. Cut venison into one-inch cubes. Peel and cut up some potatoes, carrots and onions. Place the meat and vegetables into a buttered pot with a little salt and pepper. Top it off with some more butter and some parsley flakes. Secure the lid. Dig a hole in the earth a few inches deeper and wider than your pot. Take the coals from the previous night's campfire and place a pile of them in the bottom of the hole. Put your cooking pot into the center of the hole and add more coals to the sides and over the top of the lid. Shovel the dirt from the hole back onto the top of the coals. If you do this early in the morning, by the end of the day you will unearth a very nice stew. There will have been no need to tend the cooking and no chance of fire. This also works well with beans.

Deer Heart and Tongue

Soak the heart and tongue in salt water overnight in the refrigerator. When ready to cook, drain the soaking solution. Place the heart and tongue in a small cooking pot with a lid. Add a couple of inches of water and some soy sauce. Simmer the heart and tongue for two or three hours, rolling them occasionally. Let the slowly cooked organs cool well before slicing and serving with crackers.

Deer Liver and Onions

Slice thinly your well-drained deer liver, and dip in milk. Roll the milky liver in flour. Cook slowly in a covered frying pan to which some cooking oil and some sliced onions have been added.

Deer Sausage

Using the heart, tongue, brain, liver, and scraps of deer meat which have been boiled and ground together, you can make some of the tastiest sausage ever encountered. Premixed sausage seasoning can be obtained from most grocery shelves. You will want to be sure to use some sage and some red pepper, black pepper, and salt. The small intestine from your deer which has been soaked in a salt brine for toughening and preserving is used for casing. Pickle juice is good to add to the refrigerated salt brine. If your deer intestine was very brittle, as most are, you might add some alum to tighten it up. Using a small spoon and your index finger, shove the ground mixture into three inches of the intestine and twist to make links. If you wish to avoid using the deer intestine casing then purchase a sausage casing from your grocer. After your sausage has been cased, cook it in a 400 degree oven until browned well. Refrigerate for use in the near future or freeze it for the special occasions later.

Tenderloin

Just about everybody agrees that the tenderloin is the most palatable part of the deer. It is the right choice for introducing people to venison. You can cook it in a crock pot, fry, bake or broil, even boil it, and wind up with a tasty food. I even like it cooked over the fire on a stick like a hotdog. About the only way that you can go wrong with tenderloin is choosing the wrong stick—like the poisonous oleander of the South.

Chapter

9

Safety and the Law

BUCK FEVER

Buck fever is the extreme excitement a hunter feels just prior to the shot, at the moment of the shot, or just after the shot. It has various demonic symptoms.

Some refer to "buck fever" as the pre-hunt intensity of the hunter preparing for an expedition. The individual with this mild form of the ailment pores over magazines, frequents sporting-goods stores, and seems to speak of nothing else. This type of buck fever can hamper productivity and promote daydreaming. But it is of far less concern than the type of fever that can strike a hunter in the field with live ammunition.

Buck fever in the field can get you hurt. Hunters feeling rushes of adrenaline have been known to jump up and walk right off their tree stands. A safety belt can prevent a dangerous fall, but what can prevent buck fever?

Mental preparation is the only preventive medicine, and mental relaxation is the cure. In the hunt situation, if you should suddenly start shaking violently and you sense that you are losing control, gently lower your weapon to a safe position, close your eyes, and try to return to a state of peace and calm. Many times the deer is still there when you regain your composure, or perhaps it will come back. There's no point in taking a shot when you're hit with buck fever.

What is actually happening? Medical men refer to the phenomenon as "nervous shock," a subject of much study during World War II. In response to the strong emotional stimulus of the sight of a big deer, the hunter's mind and body cease to function as a unit. The heart speeds up. Blood pressure rises. Hormones pour into the bloodstream with reckless abandon. Blood sugar rises then drops. The whole voluntary and autonomic nervous system goes haywire.

Some hunters suffer a lack of muscular coordination so pronounced that the simple act of aiming a firearm becomes impossible. Some hunters are simply paralyzed. Others may perform complicated muscular maneuvers, but their actions have no logical relation to their immediate objective. Buck fever can cause you to fire unintentionally. This is especially true with single-phase triggers. Also it can cause you to fire too quickly and run your deer off when you should have waited for a better shot. Under its spell, hunters have been known to rack their lever-action rifles until every cartridge in the magazine lies unexploded on the earth beneath them. They have also been known to shoot livestock or other hunters in a moment of pure frenzy.

The last flick of a white tail disappearing in the distance is likely to break the spell. The poor hunter revives with electric suddenness. He is left cursing the vanished deer and questioning his own sanity.

Beginning hunters usually experience a mild form of buck fever in their first hunting experience. The affliction becomes more pronounced when a hunter has waited a long time for his deer. Experienced hunters learn to detect the fever creeping up on them and take the necessary measures to halt its advance. Even the most experienced deer hunters are not immune. The hunter who has seen a lot of deer is less prone to overreact to the approach of deer, but he may suddenly go bananas over an outstanding trophy specimen. Most veteran hunters have a story or two about buck fever, but they may find them too fantastic or too embarrassing to relate to others.

The state of excitement is so extreme that people with heart trouble in particular should seriously prepare for it. After waiting ever so patiently for the deer, the afflicted hunter nearly explodes when it comes. A squirrel can activate deer fever as it rustles in the leaves on the hunter's blind side.

Hunters who have never experienced buck fever are few and far between. Buck fever is the subject of many a jest around the campfire. But in choosing to make light of the matter, hunters are merely laughing at their own mistakes. The beginning hunter should not be misled into believing that buck fever is a joke. I have yet to hear of any hunter laughing in the midst of an attack!

POACHING

People see the illegal harvesting of deer from different viewpoints. Some think of poachers as modern-day Robin Hoods and see taking the "King's deer" as exciting but dangerous. In many locations, the prevailing local attitude is "We take deer when we feel like it." Farmers concerned about crop predation sometimes condone the practice of spotlighting deer and seek poachers to hunt near their crops. A common justification for hunting illegally is, "My family needed meat, so I took a deer." Poachers are everywhere and are not confined to any particular economic or social group.

It is fact that a particular breed of humans who possess firearms and enjoy shooting find it more exciting to hunt illegally and consider it somehow "sporting" to break the law. These people are considered "slob" hunters by true sportsmen. Legally, poachers are guilty of criminal behavior.

The majority of the North American population, both hunter and non-hunter, have no respect for poachers. Poachers are considered cheaters and cruel, unsportsmanlike, undisciplined violators of the law. Toll-free numbers are used commonly to report violations of game law, and offenders who are caught are given stiff penalties. Those with an aversion to being a "snitch" may prefer to confront poachers directly. But it may be very dangerous to approach a lawbreaker carrying lethal weapons, so calling the toll-free number is recommended. Most poachers are found to be using alcohol when apprehended, a condition that does not favor a cooperative mentality.

Everyone agrees that a family with a legitimate need for food should be entitled to take a deer. This can, however, be done within the confines of the law. The game laws of North America are structured for the common good. It is a simple matter to purchase a license and hunt during given seasons. In addition, road-kill deer can be located year-round through contact with the local game warden or state police. Wardens and police no longer donate these deer to schools, orphanages, and penal institutions as they once did as a practice. Instead, with the current high deer population and accompanying high volume of highway kills, law officials seek out people who are willing to dispose of the carcass. Toll-booth operators can help you to locate a road-kill deer by taking your name. Wrecker operators can be given a call and asked for help finding a deer. Needing a deer is no excuse for breaking the law any more than stealing from the supermarket is.

There are three types of poachers:

1.   The accidental
2.   The opportunist
3.   The premeditated or criminal

The accidental poacher has faltered in judgement or marksmanship. An example of this type poaching situation is where a buck which was shot turns out to be an illegal doe. The opportunist is the get-ahead type of person who sees the relative ease of night hunting as a best bet for hunting, or perhaps one who sees hunting out of season as more suitable to him because the deer are not pressured and the hunting is less dangerous. The premeditated or criminal does it for the fun of it, or for the market value of the venison or antlers. Big antlers are big money.

Poachers usually "jacklight" by using a bright light to locate deer at night and then shooting the stationary animal. Spotlighting is the single most effective method of killing deer. No fair chase is involved. The light might be the headlights of an auto, a truck, or an ATV.

IF YOU'RE HUNGRY ENOUGH TO POACH DEER,
THEN YOU'LL LIKE FRIED BALONEY SANDWICHES.

Lights powered by the automobile battery and hand-held lights which plug into the cigarette lighter are the most popular. Poachers also use lights to hunt without their vehicles, making their locations more difficult to determine and reducing the risk that their means of transportation will be confiscated.

The light draws the deer's attention, making them vulnerable to an easy shot as they stand entranced. The poachers usually know to hold their lights toward the ground and not let the high-intensity light beams shoot up into the air, where they can be seen from a distance. Red lens covers help to make the lights less noticeable and are a little less alarming to deer. Poachers generally use a .22 magnum or other small-caliber rifle or pistol because the sound is not too loud. The noise produced by a .22 is similar to the naturally occurring sound of a tree limb cracking at a distance.

The .22 is deadly if the shot is well placed, which is rarely the case. Often such shots leave a lame and suffering animal to run off and die from internal hemorrhaging because the wound does not open enough for adequate external bleeding and because the caliber has such low knock-down power on animals that size. Shots taken with a .22 to the head, which is the only spot visible in most jacklighting situations where the poacher sees only a pair of eyes shining and attempts to shoot between them, often result in deer being shot in the mouth and doomed to prolonged suffering with eventual starvation and death. Since most poachers hunt in this manner because they are too lazy to hunt legally, they are also too lazy to track down wounded animals. After placing a shot, they do not take the risk of roving the area with lights to search for the deer in the night. Poachers are reluctant to return to the scene in daylight for further search. As a result, the majority of the deer shot by poachers are not used but merely wasted.

Many poachers convert to anti-poachers when their conscience begins to bother them. Such converts make excellent sportsmen.

A suspicious warden can search your automobile for a weapon or illegal game without a warrant. He can also search your freezer. He has very broad legal privileges to enter your land.

During archery-only seasons, game protectors and law enforcement officers use tests that enable them to detect traces of tin, lead, and copper metals to confirm that the death of a deer resulted from a bullet, not an arrow. These tests will reveal that a suspected poacher used a firearm to take the animal and jabbed an arrow into the wound afterwards. Wardens carry vest-pocket forensic kits for aid in detecting weapons violations. Since poachers sometimes come in the night before opening day and ruin the hunt for legal hunters or take shots before or after hunting hours, law officers are also equipped with a kit that can determine within 15 minutes the exact time when an animal was killed. Wardens are also able to chemically test a portion of frozen deer meat in your freezer and determine the sex of the animal it came from. Where doe hunting is forbidden, this test is often employed for prosecuting those who hinder the growth of the deer herd.

The most common reason for poaching is the so-called "sport." The second most common reason is the desire to obtain food. Other reasons are to take a personal trophy one was not able to collect legally, to sell all or part of the deer for financial gain, to keep dogs from running deer when coon or fox hunters go out, to keep deer out of crops, to enjoy the camaraderie of being a part of "the gang," to obtain dog food, and to show spite for governmental authority. A hunter may become a poacher when the deer he is seeking goes nocturnal on him, or when he has to work during daylight hours so decides to hunt after the legal hours at night.

The profit motive is a strong one. It is relatively easy to sell the carcass of a deer for upwards of $50 for its meat value. A quality trophy head begins in value at around $100.00 and climbs to prices in the thousands. Mail-order buyers pay $5.00 apiece for deer tails to make fishing lures. It costs a good deal, usually around $40.00 a month, to feed a large dog.

About the worst situations encountered are those where a group of deer are simply gunned down and left lying on the ground, killed for no apparent reason.

Poachers who were shooting does in the early spring for their unborn fetuses were apprehended eventually in a park located in the Northeastern United States. It was discovered that the violators had a lucrative business selling the soft skin of the unborn fawns to bookbinders in the city.

Poachers, stop poaching. Hunters, guard yourselves from temptation. Let us all do our share to protect wildlife and our hunting rights by conforming to the regulations that have been created for our benefit.

THE LAW

Game laws are created by panels of true experts with the public interest foremost in mind. The hunter should adhere without reluctance to all applicable rules set down by the state or provincial game management authorities.

Licensing requirements, for instance, should meet with joyful compliance. Our present deer herds were financed through licensing more than any other source of revenue. The small contributions which individuals make are pooled together responsibly to insure the abundance of wildlife for future generations of hunters as well. It is a privilege more than it is a right to hunt deer. For the privilege of purchasing a license, the hunter is entitled to the right to take his share of game.

Reading the information on or with the license is generally not enough to gain complete familiarity with existing regulations. Since laws concerning the harvest of deer may change astonishingly from season to season depending on the condition of the herd, it is important that the hunter keep up to date. It is best to obtain information from written material published by the wildlife authorities of the specific state or province in which you plan to hunt. These regulations vary considerably from one location to another. Just across the river, laws may be entirely different. What other hunters tell you may be misleading, for they may be ill-advised themselves. Ignorance of the law is no excuse. If you have any questions about game law regulations, feel free to telephone a game warden or write or call the wildlife commission.

Non-compliance with existing law can not only entail penalties, but it can cause you to lose the trophy of a lifetime through confiscation. Some game violations carry severe penalties, which can include fines, imprisonment, confiscation of automobile and firearm, loss of hunting privileges, or required hours of work.

THE GAME WARDEN IS YOUR FRIEND.

It is much more satisfying to know you are legal all the way around. When a hunter's conscience is clear, his confidence level is healthy and positive. To know that at any time a law enforcement officer could apprehend you is an unhealthy, negative state of mind. Obeying the laws and encouraging others to do so is the easiest path through the woods. Breaking laws is a rugged path to choose.

The game warden is not an enemy of sportsmen who do not cheat. He is a friend. If, when encountered, he appears a little rough, you must remember he has to be cautious in his dangerous job since nearly everyone he approaches has a loaded gun.

ALCOHOL, POT, DRUGS

In nature overall and with dangerous weapons anytime, all drugs that alter mind or body should be avoided. Alcohol slows reflexes, impairs judgment, and decreases ambition and stamina. If there is a proper time to use alcohol, then it should be after the hunt when the deer is on the meat pole.

If your intention in going to the woods during deer season is to enjoy intoxication, then leave your weapons in the trunk of the car and separate your ammunition from them. Put your keys up too.

In some social situations, as at some hunting lodges, drinking intoxicants is a ritual. Many a hunter has spent the night in one of these situations and left for his stand the next morning feeling rotten to the bone with a hangover. It is a good thing that a lot of the hunting lodges have sealed-in stands or handrails.

A hangover casts negative vibrations from the hunter which alert the deer's sixth sense that something is wrong. Check this for yourself. Even humans, who do not use this sixth sense as readily as other creatures of the earth, sense these negatives from hangovers in others.

Alcohol and marijuana have incredibly strong odors. Marijuana resin clings to materials, leaving scent deposits that last a long time. The smell of alcohol cuts through other scents like a solvent and overpowers them. These odors repel deer.

A warden can cite a drunken hunter for public intoxication. By so doing, the law officer may indeed prevent catastrophe. We all know the danger of mixing drinking and driving. Let us all understand that there is equal danger in mixing drinking and hunting.

Please, for your safety and the safety of others, and for the reputation of armed citizens in general, leave drugs and alcohol out of the grand experience of deer hunting, and enjoy the wholesome purity this experience has to offer.

Avoid hunting with those who use intoxicants with firearms. When they state that they take a shot or swig here and there to keep warm then inform them that the truth is that alcohol constricts blood vessels, actually making them colder.

DEAD LIMBS

Many deer hunting accidents occur when hunters attempt to climb trees for scouting purposes or to hunt from an elevated position. It seems that the excitement of the hunting possibilities often overshadow normal caution.

Remove all dead limbs when you are erecting a pre-season stand. You may step on one of these later when you enter your tree in darkness to hunt at sunrise. Check well before you put your weight on one of these limbs. When climbing, try not to place all your confidence in a particular limb, but distribute your weight by hanging onto other limbs or gripping the tree trunk at the same time. Always have both hands free to grasp with.

Large, dead limbs overhead are possible hazards as well. It is best to avoid trees with potentially dangerous overhead limbs. Ground-hunters as well as stand-hunters should be mindful of the trees above, especially under windy conditions.

Remember that your grounded automobile is the safest place for you during electrical storms. Get away from the trees while electrical storms are in progress.

EYE SAFETY

The poked, scratched, or otherwise irritated eye can be a calamity to the hunter. An eye swelling, reddening, watering, and twitching can ruin a hunt.

Watch out for your eyes, and prevent disaster. Make calculated moves. A lashing briar can cause the loss of an eye. When another hunter is behind you or you are following someone else, remember that limbs and other vegetation pushed forward by the body whip with backlash. For this reason, separate yourself from others by a couple of yards when traversing thickets and other densely vegetated areas.

Sunglasses, hunting glasses, safety glasses, or goggles are great to carry with you for eye protection. They are especially useful before sunrise and after dark.

Shooting glasses are a good investment. Choose those that filter sunshine and have no surface glare. Mirrored lenses are an obvious poor choice for deer hunting. A good-quality pair of hunting glasses will help you to distinguish deer from their surroundings. Some shooting lenses heighten color contrast and clarity.

Remember that the cosmetic value of a pair of hunting glasses is not relevant to the deer. It does not matter what they look like as long as they do not shine. If they are not flashy, they will help to break up the outline of the face and conceal the hunter's eyes from contact with the deer at close range.

Try to keep your hands away from your eyes when in the field. This will avoid possible contamination from irritant plants you may have encountered. The person who has walked through a patch of stinging nettles or a stand of poison ivy can transfer the irritants to the eyes by merely tightening boot laces then touching the eye area.

Those cursed little bugs that are attracted to the eyes and fly right into them, producing irritating excretions, should be flushed with water quickly to avoid greater discomfort. The more you rub your eyes, the more irritated they become.

Sometimes when doing early bowhunting, I think that the reason for these pests attacking me is to run me out of the woods; their purpose in creation. In this situation, the gnat can become the king of the jungle. Glasses stop them effectively.

Hunters firing muzzleloading weapons, whether percussion or flint-lock, should wear substantial eye protection.

HUNTER SAFETY COURSES

Some states require that hunters pass a course in safety before being issued a license to hunt. In almost every state, some places, such as military reservations, have this requirement. It is probable that in the 1990s, the merits of such programs will be so clear that the law will be instituted in all locations.

Veteran hunters might be offended by the requirement and reluctant to spend the time necessary to attend the seminar. But even veterans find the courses enlightening and interesting and are always happy that they attended. Everyone agrees that the other guy should take the course but feels less need for himself. It is an obvious truth that young or inexperienced hunters can greatly benefit from safety instruction.

Hunters should enter the programs without resentment and encourage others to do so. It is better to enroll now, at a convenient time, than to wait for attendance to become law and have to take the course at an inconvenient time in order to hunt.

Most hunter safety courses are given three hours a day for three days or over one full eight-to ten-hour day. The courses, offered for both gun and bow, feature films and other audio-visual aids. They focus on wildlife conservation ethics and ethical relationships with fellow hunters and landowners. Regulations are reviewed, and their value is explained. Most courses offer first-aid instruction. Usually there is a question-and-answer period at the end.

Safety courses are confidence-builders for everyone, and a well-designed class is a pleasure rather than a bore. It increases awareness and knowledge and makes the participants realize how much they did not know prior to the course. People who have obtained certificates are prepared to enter the woods with heightened and refreshed safety consciousness.

In the United States and Canada, we are freedom loving peoples who work to protect our rights and freedoms. None of us desire to have overly burdensome regulations imposed on our liberty in the hunt. We would all like to see each and every man, woman, and child that is in the deer woods with a loaded firearm or archery equipment knowledgeable in the functioning of the weaponry and equipped with the instructions necessary for safe and ethical hunting. Some people who go deer hunting do not even know where the safety is on their gun. There are novice bowhunters who have never used an arrow release mechanism prior to the actual hunt. It is the sad truth that there will come a time that all hunters will be required to pass a weapons test, similar to a driver's license examination, in order to insure their personal safety and the safety of others. We have advanced in our civilization to a space age. Our children are more familiar with *Star Trek* than they are with the wilderness traditions. Few of our youth are brought up with the understandings necessary for proper gun handling.

Hunter Safety Certificates are valid from one state or province to another. The United States and Canada have a joint effort. As of 1989, 40 states and provinces have certification requirements of some type. It is likely that all areas will adopt the policy eventually.

DISEASES YOU CAN GET FROM DEER

It is possible for humans to contract diseases from deer, though this is extremely rare.

As of 1989, according to the Southeast Cooperative Wildlife Disease unit in Athens, Georgia, there have been ten recorded cases of rabies in deer. Dr. Randy Davidson stated that no humans have ever contracted rabies from deer. It would be possible for humans to contract leptospirosis from deer, however there have been no reported cases of this either. Anthrax is possible in deer, and if an outbreak occurred in domestic livestock, deer might be involved. A person who handled the carcass of a deer dying from anthrax could contract the disease.

Dermatophilosis is a skin disease of whitetail deer found in and near New York State. There have been four cases in humans from contact with a single deer in that state. Two cases of tularemia in humans have been associated with contact with deer. Six cases of toxoplasmosis in humans have resulted from the eating of raw or poorly cooked venison. It is also possible to get salmonella from deer raised in captivity if the meat is not cooked properly.

You will note that the number of cases of all the diseases listed is very low as of 1989. In fact, deer have a very good record as far as human health is concerned, and there is no need for alarm.

Several guidelines may help to prevent disease due to contact with deer. First, all venison should be thoroughly cooked. Second, hunters should use rubber gloves when field-dressing deer, butchering deer, or tanning hides. Third, hunters should dispose of sickly deer rather than consuming them as food. Fourth, hunters should avoid contact of deer blood with open sores or cuts. If you should nick your hand while dressing your deer, cleanse the wound with a good antiseptic.

Parasites that might infest deer might possibly be transferred to humans through contact with droppings, consumption of under-cooked deer flesh, or contact of open sores with the disease organisms. Handling a cigarette can transfer contaminants to the mouth of a careless victim. Deer get cattle lungworms. The lungworms are picked up by the deer eating browse and ingesting snails on the vegetation. It is estimated that 36% of adult deer have this parasite. Nose bots are flies that incubate in deer nostrils and mucous membranes, particularly in high places. Nose bots affect 7% of adult deer. Liver flukes, called "blood suckers" by hunters, infest 11% of adult deer. Liver flukes cause the liver surface to look mottled and scarred. Lily pads and pond weeds are the most frequent source of deer infection since the larvae of the liver fluke are aquatic. In wetter regions, liver flukes are more common. Deer can have cattle stomach worms, footworms, whipworms in the intestines, and tapeworm larvae, which can be spotted in the liver. Deer contract screw worms from flies.

The liver of the deer will reveal the condition of the animal with regard to parasites. Evidence of disease should be fairly apparent in the removed liver. If the liver contains parasites, it should be discarded. If the remainder of the deer is handled and cooked properly, there should be no need to worry about parasite contamination from the whitetail deer.

Deer hides might contain external arthropod parasites. Some deer hides have thousands of small lice. These will die swiftly when a hide is placed in a strong salt solution or when the hide is frozen.

Brainworms, which are hairlike, are common in whitetails but not fatal to them. They are no problem to humans who cook brains thoroughly. Fleas are frequently hosted by deer. Deer which immerse themselves in water with regularity are less often infested, as are deer in cold weather. Fleas will leave a deer which has stiffened to seek a host which will provide warmth and flowing blood. They will probably all be gone by the time you get your deer on the road. Ticks are something to look for in early season hunting and in some of the southern areas of the U. S. Check the deer hide for ticks and remove any found. Fleas can carry a number of diseases, as can ticks. Lyme disease is a serious threat in the 1990s, as is Rocky Mountain Spotted Fever, both transmittable to humans by ticks. Check yourself well for ticks.

The Centers for Disease Control in Atlanta is constantly abreast of disease possibilities that are related to the deer herd. The center monitors the entire North American deer herd. Since the whitetail deer has such a wide range of habitat, it would be a likely mode of transmittal of disease if there should ever be an outbreak among livestock. Rest assured that any risks involved with the hunting and consumption of deer will be public knowledge if the situation occurs.

SNAKEBITE

Any deer hunter in the South or during early bow seasons or scouting pre-season in the North may well encounter poisonous snakes. Although most snakes are not aggressive, they will defend themselves. Bites usually occur when hunters step on the reptile or otherwise disturb it. A snake can strike only within a distance equal to two-thirds of the length of it's body. A snake does not need to coil to strike.

Most people react to a snakebite with panic. In the event of venomous snakebite, the hunter should program himself not to jump up and away from the snake or try to beat the snake to pieces but to grab the head of the attached snake the instant it bites and quickly throw the snake off his body. There is a brief moment between the biting of the snake with its teeth, which it uses for attaching to the victim, and the plunging of the fangs into the flesh. If you have ever witnessed the "milking" of a pit-viper, such as the copperhead, rattlesnake, or cottonmouth of this hemisphere, you will recall that the handler had to press the wide-open mouth of the snake flat in order to release the venom into the milking glass. This is because the fangs are recessed in the roof of the mouth and require a good second grasp by the snake to protrude, puncture, and eject. The actual teeth of the snake, which are designed for catching and holding prey, are first to attach to a victim, and only by making a second, muscular, stretching grasp is the snake able to fully project its sharp fangs and release the venom. By swiftly pulling the snake off, the hunter will reduce the amount of poison the snake injects, the depth at which it injects, or avoid poison altogether. The coral snake of the southernmost regions of the United States is a different story, since it has no fangs to project. The age-old story about someone dying from putting on boots that had fangs attached is fantasy, but do check your boots for the little coral snakes in the southern United States.

When a venomous snake bites and manages to inject its venom, the area of the skin will quickly swell and turn red. The hunter must administer first aid. "First" aid means just that. It is temporary remedial work done prior to and en route to competent medical help.

The old school taught that the victim should always make an "×" mark over each puncture wound, suck out the poison, and apply a tourniquet. Modern professionals disagree somewhat. Many are wary of "do-it-yourselfers," having encountered complications that resulted from people using this method and making matters worse. Since professional help is available almost every-where within a short time, doctors now suggest that the victim merely remain calm, exert himself or herself as little as possible, apply an appropriate tourniquet or none at all, and rush to a hospital for anti-venom.

Deer hunters do need to know the older method of treatment, since some hunt in remote wilderness areas and are dropped off for periods of several days at a time. So, a snakebite kit is among the necessities hunters should carry in warm weather, especially when it would be necessary to move quite a bit in order to get help. Canadians need not worry about poisonous snakes. There are only a few areas of Canada where poisonous reptiles exist.

A snakebite kit should have directions included. Read these before you hunt in an area known to be infested with snakes. The kit should include two rubber suction cups, a sterile razor, and a rubber tourniquet. The rubber cups are especially useful to the victim who is treating himself in awkward places. The cups also diminish the possibility that lesions in the gums or lips will come in contact with venom. Venom is not a stomach poison, so if you do swallow some, don't worry—just rinse your mouth. The venom can cause your teeth to fall out by destroying gum tissue in poor condition.

The razor kit is sharper than most pocket knives and capable of making clean cuts which will heal readily. Using the razor also prevents possible contamination from a hunting knife. The tourniquet is flexible enough that it should cause no problems by being too tight. The kit is compact, noiseless, and easy to pack along.

The most important thing to remember is to stay calm and move as little as possible. The more active the victim is, the quicker the poison will reach the heart and brain.

When a medical facility is nearby and your hunting partner can get you there soon, simply wipe the area of the bite with clean cloth. Cover the wound with a bandage, and apply a tourniquet between the bite and the heart. The bandage should be tight enough to firm the surface blood vessels and force some of the poison out. The tourniquet must be removed for a minute every 20 to 30 minutes. If you have ice, apply it to the area.

To use the kit, first tie a tourniquet (which may be your belt) three inches above the wound between the wound and the heart. Make an incision one-fourth inch deep. Do not make two cuts to form "×" marks. One cut through each fang mark is enough. And be careful not to hit larger veins or an artery. Next, apply suction, and keep it up for an hour. If it is not possible to apply suction, then follow the rest of the procedure but apply pressure to remove the venom. Common sense is crucial in any type of first aid. Not many people would foolishly place a tourniquet around someone's neck.

Being able to identify the snake accurately is important. We have only four poisonous snakes native to North America, so the task is not difficult. If you can kill the snake with minimal effort and little movement, then do so, and take it to the hospital for identification.

If you are tending a victim who shows signs of paralysis, prepare to administer artificial respiration, because he will soon stop breathing.

Alcohol is not recommended internally or for external application to the wound, since it has a thinning effect and speeds blood flow. In any case, a snake's mouth is nearly sterile and among the cleanest in nature.

If, while walking through the woods, you come upon a snake which has been beaten to death but not eaten, it is the work of either man or deer. Deer instinctively hate snakes, which can cripple them and make them easy prey. Deer have been observed leaping into the air and bounce-landing on snakes with all fours pointed to tear the snake to shreds. Does with fawns nearby are especially prone to destroying snakes and instructing their young as to their threat. In areas where deer are numerous, snake populations are greatly reduced and may even be endangered.

Scientists are currently studying a promising snakebite cure that uses electric shock. The practice has been used successfully in tropical areas where snakebite victims were treated by applying direct current from automobile batteries to the wound. The practice is said to neutralize the venom. Exactly how this happens is not understood, but the merit of the procedure has been proven. In the forthcoming decade, the scientific community will no doubt attain a clear understanding of this cure and publicly announce its findings. An electric-shock kit for use on animals such as hunting dogs is already commercially available in the United States. It is likely that electrical shock will be valuable primarily as first aid, but we shall see.

Remember that all snakes are not harmful. A great many species of snakes in America are beneficial. If you are not particularly fond of snakes, then you should leave king snakes, racers, and indigo snakes unharmed in the woods because they prey on other snakes. A king snake can actually eat a whole snake its own size. I have seen it. These creatures have developed an immunity to venom which merits scientific investigation. They kill other snakes by constricting.

Avoid poisonous snakebite by paying attention to what you are doing and avoiding unnecessary risks. If you are hunting Western brush country where rattlesnakes abound, wear protective leggings and boots.

Watch where you walk, sit, or put your hands. Hunters suffer relatively few venomous snakebites since they are generally more attentive to their environment.

HYPOTHERMIA

"Hypothermia" is the scientific term for "freezing to death" or "dying from exposure."

Hypothermia can kill you. Everywhere in North America, there is a winter season in which the wind, temperature, and moisture can take the life of a hunter by surprise. Victims are not only from the cold Northern regions.

"Hypothermia" means "low temperature." It describes the condition that exists when the body temperature, normally 98.6 degrees Fahrenheit, falls, and the body loses heat faster than it produces it.

The first symptoms are shivers. The victim begins to shake mildly and gets "goose bumps." When the shivering becomes rapid and uncontrollable, action must be taken. If the hunter does not do something to raise the body temperature, he will lose his coordination and become mentally confused. His condition becomes gradually worse until his body temperature reaches about 83 degrees and he passes out. When the temperature falls to 78 degrees, the victim is dead.

The "wind-chill factor" can make the temperature of the air at 50 degrees feel like it is freezing in 20 MPH winds. Wind blowing through wet hunting clothes made of cotton functions as an efficient evaporator and cools the body rapidly. Anyone, anywhere, who is not properly clothed or who is wet can be in a life-threatening situation under these conditions. These conditions can set in in a hurry and be totally unexpected.

How can you avoid hypothermia?

1. When using a boat to reach a deer hunting location, make sure that the boat is adequate for the conditions you might encounter.

2. When using a boat, always use a life-preserver.

3. Be sure to tell someone where you are going to hunt and when you will return.

4. Dress appropriately and be prepared for weather changes.

5. Stay informed about the weather and admit that certain conditions are too dangerous to hunt in.

Watch for symptoms of hypothermia in others. These include uncontrolled shivering, slurred speech, loss of coordination, stumbling, confusion, amnesia, or other mental lapses. Because hypothermia affects the mind, a victim may insist he is okay and resist your help. But if he exhibits these symptoms, he needs help desperately, so insist, overpowering him physically if necessary.

The treatment for hypothermia is to reverse the cooling process and warm the victim. Be careful not to do this too quickly. Too-rapid warming of the extremities can actually lower the internal temperature. Heat should be applied to the trunk of the body and to the head. If the symptoms have gone beyond shivering, call off the hunt and seek medical aid.

Hunters who are in poor physical condition or suffer from fatigue are more susceptible to this dangerous condition.

FROSTBITE

Frostbite is often a problem for Northern deer hunters. It can occur in any location where the temperature falls below 32 degrees Fahrenheit.

In the early stages there is feeling loss. When this symptom first appears, the hunter should take protective measures. The body parts affected most commonly are the feet, hands, and ears. In the early stages, the skin has a waxen appearance or develops whitish-yellow spots. The change in appearance can usually be seen before it is felt. If the signs go unnoticed, the flesh may freeze solid without the victim knowing it.

The three general rules of first aid for frostbite victims are:

1. Rewarm.

2. Protect.

3. Get help.

Rewarm rapidly but do not use excessive heat. Use water that is warm but not hot. The whitened area should be covered with something warm. A handkerchief soaked in hot coffee from your thermos will do nicely. The victim should drink hot liquids and pump blood to the affected area by exercising it in front of a heat source such as a car heater. Alcohol hinders internal blood flow and should not be administered. Do not rewarm the frostbitten part if there is a chance of refreezing, as this causes more damage than a longer period in a frozen state.

Protect the frozen part from any mechanical injury, both before and after rewarming. Never, never massage or rub with snow or any other substance. Circulation should be restored by exercising the affected part, not by massage. The victim should not walk on frozen feet or move frozen hands.

Make every effort to get medical help immediately, as the extent of permanent tissue injury is not at all apparent in the early stages.

To prevent frostbite, be adequately clothed at all times. Remember that the symptom of feeling loss might mean you could be in for a real nightmare if you do not do something about it immediately. Keep tabs on your hands, feet, and ears in cold weather to be sure they are not freezing.

BUDDY SYSTEM

The "buddy system," a term borrowed from the Boy Scout handbook, (and I do recommend the Boy Scouts) refers to hunting with or near someone else. It is generally safer and saner to have a companion in the woods. No one expects to encounter disaster, but accidents do happen. There are additional benefits to hunting with others. They can enliven your hunt. They can assist you with deer retrieval. They can offer help in countless ways—for instance, by honking the automobile horn to signal the way for a hunting partner that is lost. Two hunters can hunt effectively together, combining skills and increasing the chance of success. They can also part company in the woods after being very clear about the directions they plan to take. Hunting partners who choose to separate can communicate with prearranged distress signals, such as a particular sequence of shots.

Most locations have laws that require juveniles to hunt deer only when directly supervised by an adult. As of this year, 1989, in my resident state of Kentucky, the law has been updated to state that the adult must be able to seize control of the firearm of a juvenile. About one in ten thousand juveniles who deer hunt are involved in firearms accidents. This high rate seems to reflect inexperience and lack of knowledge about proper gun habits, although a less-developed sense of responsibility may also be a factor. Deer hunters make rather quick life-or-death decisions, which juveniles are not equipped to make. In some instances, it might be best for an adult to actually hand the juvenile the pointed and loaded rifle for accomplishing the shot. It is great to start hunting deer at an early age, but a young person needs the guidance of a mature hunter. There is an old saying, "If you take a kid hunting, you won't have to hunt the kid."

Statistics show that juvenile hunters are the most common hunting casualties, especially when two juveniles are hunting together. The hunting buddy of a youth should always be an adult. Last year in the nearby area, two teenagers were hunting together. A buck jumped up between them and one of the youths killed the other.

Many well-meaning, responsible parents keep firearms entirely away from youngsters in the belief that this will prevent accidents. This is comparable to denying children the right to enter water and learn to swim. Eventually the child is likely to fall in the water, and eventually he is apt to come upon a firearm. It is far better to let a child practice with a gun under competent and responsible direction when good habits are easily formed and before an accident occurs.

In communities where deer hunting is popular, school children get a lot of peer pressure to kill a deer. This burning desire should be understood and guided in the right direction.

POISON IVY, POISON OAK, POISON SUMAC

Every outdoorsman should be able to identify irritant plants and distinguish them from other native flora.

Many hunters are fortunate enough not to suffer allergic reactions to poison ivy, poison oak, and poison sumac. Some hunters seem to develop immunities. Others might require hospitalization when overexposed to plant toxins. Those who know they are allergic to these plants must take great care to avoid them.

After the foliage dies down in the fall, hunters can still suffer from the rash and itch-producing active chemicals of the species by rubbing against the woody parts of the vines. Vines that climb trees present a particular obstacle to the tree-climbing deer hunter, who can hardly avoid scraping against the vine. For this reason, susceptible hunters should be aware of what dormant and high-climbing vines look like. Hunters who sit on the ground or use ground blinds should be able to spot ground-level dormant vines and stems.

Plant poisons can be inhaled along with smoke when hunters burn wood with vines attached. Hunters who have walked through an unavoidable patch should realize they can be infected by retying their boot laces or otherwise handling their contaminated clothing. Hunters should work their way through poison ivy patches as lightly as possible, since the poison is released when vines or leaves are damaged or bruised.

A mistake which has produced disastrous results is that of the novice woodsman who uses the leaves of such plants in place of toilet paper.

During bow season or when the plants of the area are still green and healthy, jewelweed can serve as an effective preventative. This watery-stemmed plant grows in most low-lying areas where poison ivy is prevalent. a hunter can rub the crushed plant over areas of his body or clothing that he knows or suspects have come in contact with the plant. Fresh jewelweed neutralizes fresh poison ivy. A bath with fresh jewelweed added to the water will prevent ivy poisoning when taken immediately after the hunt. If you suffer allergic reactions to poison ivy, then you should make a trip to your public library to investigate jewelweed and learn to identify it in the wild. The only way to preserve jewelweed for winter use is to freeze the juice and apply it as ice. The plant does not work when dried, or mixed with alcohol or whatever for pharmacy shelves. The plant definitely works when fresh to prevent ivy poisoning.

Jewelweed reached a mature height of three to four feet tall.

The watercress-like stem is thick and watery with some transparency. The leaves are ovular with rounded serrations on the edges. The portions of the stem which produce the leaves are knotty in appearance. The flower is bright orange, and though small, quite attractive. The common name for jewelweed in some areas is "wild touch-me-not." This is because the flower casts its seeds when touched. A bath taken in jewelweed makes the water color a pleasant orange.

FIRES

Fires are a major safety concern for the hunter. The devastation caused by unnaturally occurring fires is disaster to wildlife. In autumn, when fallen leaves carpet the ground, fire can become a major hazard to the hunter as well.

A careless cigarette, untended campfire, or hot tailpipe dragging through dry weeds have dire consequences. It is no fun battling a forest fire. Your long-awaited deer hunting vacation could become a nightmare of savage firefighting.

Sometimes deer seasons are limited or delayed due to fire hazard conditions in the woodlands. Insufficient rainfall can lead to postponed hunting seasons and limited access to particularly dry regions of the forest. Often, seasonal law may stipulate that no fires can be built in hunter camps, or that fires may be built only after a certain hour, perhaps 4:00 in the afternoon, when the winds have a tendency to die down. Check the regulations for the immediate area if you intend to have a campfire, and be certain you are abiding by the law. In some cases, you might be fined for having a small campfire, and you might receive rather stiff penalties if you build a fire that causes damage.

If you do build a fire, be sure to design a safe one by containing it and isolating it from other flammable materials. Rake the perimeter of the fire to clear it of leaves or other combustible materials which might catch popping sparks. Encircle the fire with stones, dirt dug from the fire pit, or large green firewood to keep breezes from spreading the fire. Watch flying sparks which could drift to other areas. Be sure that the overstory is not apt to catch fire.

Never leave a fire unattended. Coals should be doused before you retire for the night. Keep a fire extinguisher handy, or bring along milk jugs filled with water for dousing fires. In freezing weather, put some anti-freeze in the water jugs. Be certain to clearly mark these jugs, indicating the water inside is poisonous and not fit for human consumption.

Setting fires to run deer out of thickets, forests, or fields is illegal, unethical, and foolish. Smokey the Bear is on the offensive these days to catch criminals who deliberately set fires and is adept at bringing arsonists to justice.

It is true that burning helps some types of terrain to become better habitats for deer in the years following the fire. A burn-off eventually produces lower browse and more nutritious browse, but for the first year or two, the deer will have to either relocate or starve. Unfortunately, the depletion of the first winter's forage is enough to cause a die-off where deer are unable to move to another area and find adequate nutrition. Deer require a considerable amount of barks, twigs and just about everything else that a brush fire consumes as it rushes through a woods. Since deer do not hibernate, they require a high caloric intake to stay alive through cold winters. If the area you hunt appears to you to need a fire to improve the habitat, please leave it to mother nature to accomplish this through lightning fires. You local fire marshal and forestry agents will be happy to assist you in the rare event that a man-made fire is warranted.

Fires started by hunters intentionally or by accident can cause tremendous losses in timber. It is unlikely that a small timber owner with his future depending on the woodlot you hunt or a mammoth paper company which allows hunting on its lands will want hunters to come back after a financially devastating fire. Let us preserve our hunting rights by being responsible with our fires. Fires that sweep the ground through a young forest permanently injure trees that are brushed by the flames. Although these trees may continue to grow, their value as timber is diminished. They are cull trees.

In some areas of the West where the deer feed upon mature brush such as bitterbrush and sagebrush, it may take 15 years for the range to restore itself after a large fire. When significant rangeland is destroyed, deer suffer dramatically. Fawn production and antler growth decline, and hunting prospects take a downhill turn.

Forest fires can generate winds in excess of 100 MPH. Even a modest ground fire can move faster than you can walk. You probably cannot outrun a forest fire, but you might be able to outflank it by running to the side and away from its path.

GETTING LOST

Few hunters manage to venture into the woods without becoming lost at least once. It takes only once to learn the value of taking precautions.

Lack of familiarity with the land is the chief cause of becoming lost. The well-prepared hunter should familiarize himself with the general area of the proposed hunt in order to keep his bearings as well as to better understand deer behavior and travel routes. Topographic maps are the best source of information. Carry the relevant section of the map with you on the hunt and refer to it as you go along so that you always know where you are and where you are headed. Aerial photos are excellent also. For fine, up-to-date maps, write:

U. S. Geological Survey
MS 507-PB
14B National Center
Reston, Virginia 22092

Or you can call 1-800-USA MAPS. Maps can be fun too! Good maps do not cost much, are easily obtained, and offer the hunter great advantages.

Another significant aid is the compass. Compasses work—so trust them. You will have to spend just a little time learning how to use them. The compass is magnetic, so remember that underground mineral deposits, your gun barrel, a pipeline, or the interior of your car can throw them off. If you avoid these magnetic disturbances, you can rely on the compass to tell the truth.

Compasses can be quite complicated. Most hunters simply use them for basic directional readings and don't get into degree readings. Degree readings can help you locate a remote stand or hunting cabin but most of us do not need such instrumentation. The average hunter needs only to note his direction of travel before starting out then reverse it for his return. Stick to this route, and make a careful mental note of deviation.

Stop occasionally and survey the country behind you. It will look entirely different than it did when you approached it from the other direction. You may spot a buck doubling back as well. You seldom need to venture very far. Many are the times that the hunter heads into the distant wilderness and returns empty-handed only to find tracks by his parked car.

Getting lost can really wear you out and can become a serious problem. Realize that you can become lost, even in a small area. Sometimes the situation is similar to that of a person struggling in the water and drowning when all he had to do was stand up. Mark your path mentally, noting landmarks. Be very conscious of where you are before making future advances. Stop periodically to examine your position in relation to your starting point. Slow down and don't panic, which usually leads you to walk in circles.

The hunter who gets lost, strays to another camp, or finds his way home and stays there until the next morning is careless and inconsiderate. This can result in other hunters having to spend long hours searching for you. Searching for a "lost" companion in the dark takes a good deal of time and energy and subjects the searchers to possible danger.

Moss does not necessarily grow on only one side of a tree or only one side of a valley. The old saying that "moss only grows on the north side of a tree" is not always true, since growth patterns depend on exposure to sunlight and particular features of the terrain. Don't put your confidence in this or any other saying from popular woodslore. Geese don't just fly south in the fall hunting season. They fly in every direction on their way southward, often altering their course briefly to forage and rest. The north star will direct you northward at night only if the sky is clear. The sun rises in the east and sets in the west. The sun is east in the morning, south at noon, and west in the afternoon and evening. But cloud cover can obscure the sun and make it impossible to rely on it for telling direction. Likewise, you cannot rely on sounds made by highway traffic or oil pumps for judging directions, because the traffic may die down or the oil well may stop.

If you are hunting hazardous terrain in a remote location where becoming lost or injured could result in an extreme emergency, be prepared with signal flares, waterproof matches, and a shaving mirror you could use to identify your location in a rescue operation. Someone should always know where you are going and how long you intend to stay.

As a precaution, many hunters mark their path by marking trees along the route with a large hunting knife or periodically tying tape of a particular color to vegetation. This practice could help you find your way back from an excursion or designate a route for a search or rescue party.

HUNTER ORANGE

Deer do see color. The myth that they are color-blind has kept many an old buck out in the woods. Research in the 1980s has proven that the eyes of the whitetail deer have even more cones and cells than human eyes have for color perception. Deer can indeed distinguish colors, particularly in the green portion of the spectrum. Exactly how they perceive color is not clear. How their brain registers and interprets colors may differ from how we hunters do. As more research is done, we may someday have videos showing the actual view from the deer's eyes. Perhaps our technology will advance to this point in the 1990s!

It has been, and still is, stated by the experts that deer are color blind—that they see only black and white, shades of grey. I always had trouble with this since bullfighters use red capes in the Mexican arenas to aggravate bulls. The experts state that it is movement that betrays a hunter, not the color of his garments. True, deer do have an advanced ability to detect movement. If a hunter does not move at all when approached with a deer the chances of his being unnoticed are good. Deer have not needed to be able to detect color for any significant survival reason until now. Hunter orange has become the law, a good law that saves lives each year. The deer did not need to use their color cones in their retinas much until now. The deer could see movement better without the distraction of colors previously so they just did not develop their color distinguishing ability. After seeing hunters walking through the woods and shooting their fellow deer and perhaps even at the particular deer itself, you can bet that the deer is going to utilize those color cones to the best of his ability in the future. As each generation of deer inherits the makeup of its predecessors, the eventual deer herd will soon become acutely aware of hunter orange at birth.

The traditional hunting shirt or jacket was usually red and black plaid. In some areas where hunter orange is not required, this color combination is still in use. This color combination is dangerous in the autumn woods, since hunter orange is the nationally recognized safety color.

When hunter orange is used often in the woods, on survey markers, pipeline markers, aerial markers, trees elected for harvest, and so on, deer become less apprehensive about this normally foreign bright color. Some hunters place a dummy in their tree stand or leave an orange hunting vest year-round or for a long time prior to hunting the location in order to allow the deer to become accustomed to the color. In fall when the leaves of deciduous trees are changing color, the orange does not stand out as much. The orange blends particularly well in sugar maple groves.

It is mandatory in most areas that a gun hunter have at least one garment made entirely of hunter orange on his body at all times when hunting. During archery-only seasons, bow hunters are not generally required to wear hunter orange, due to the fact that they hunt at close ranges and have comparatively low success rates. Bow hunters in the woods during gun season must wear the orange like everyone else. It is a good idea for bow hunters to carry some orange anyway, such as a reversible cap that can be put on or off easily. Archers can shoot other archers as well.

Fluorescent orange stands out less on overcast days, in mornings and evenings.

Hunter orange is a great idea which has significantly reduced hunting accidents. One close call will convince you to wear it. A very close call might lead you to dress in orange from head to foot. Arrows and bullets hurt. The color should be worn when scouting as well. Most gun hunters scout during bow season and should be clearly distinguishable when roving about dense foliage and thickets.

Where allowed, the hunter may wish to wear a lot of orange while entering the woods to take a stand and then reduce the amount of the color to a minimum when settled down and presenting less of a target to other hunters. Hunter-orange ribbon is good to have for your ankles if you are hunting in an area with ground visibility, such as young pine plantations or low-hanging white oak thickets. This ribbon can also be wrapped around your harvested animal when it is packed from the woods.

Camo orange (orange garments with black splotches) helps break the outline and the glare of solid garments, though its use is not always legal. All orange garments should be made of non-glare fabric such as canvas. Plastic disposables are excellent for safety purposes but will not last the average hunter more than one season, if that. They tear easily, are noisy, and usually shine. It is a good idea to have them along, however, just in case you lose your regular garment or encounter another hunter who has no orange. Give the extra to him; it may save his life. Serious hunters should invest in a comfortable, durable, water-repellent orange vest and cap. Many hunters who bring home big bucks consistently dress in full-length bright orange coveralls. To most of us, no deer is worth dying for. A good cap is the usual minimum. A round cap with an encircling brim is good for misty or rainy weather when temperatures are not too cold. A reversible wool sock cap with camo on one side and orange on the other is good for colder weather.

Hunter orange is not foolproof in protecting hunters from being shot. "Self-hypnosis," a condition also called "early blur," leads some people who want to see deer badly enough to see one, antlers and all, no matter how orange, upright, and distinctly human the object presenting itself may be. One bow hunter who fatally wounded another hunter said he thought the victim was a squirrel.

DANGEROUS DEER

Although not famed for their viciousness, deer are not wimps. The survival equipment they were issued includes hooves, high body weight, and antlers to ward off attackers. Deer have killed many hunters and have injured scores of others.

Most injuries from deer goring and flailing take place when deer are in captivity and not shy concerning humans. Certainly there have also been hundreds of reports of bucks, particularly in the rut period, becoming highly aggressive toward hunters with minimal provocation in the wild. A startled deer, like most animals, is quick to defend itself. It is rare that a whitetail will take the offensive, but it does happen.

Does are very aggressive the first day after birthing fawns. At any time, they can inflict serious injury by flailing. Bucks in velvet will not use their sensitive and underdeveloped antlers but will flail also. The sharp hooves can be delivered with tremendous force as the animal rears up in a punching position or leaps upon a victim.

Antlered deer have gored many hunters. Gangrene is a common result of such nasty puncture wounds. Gored hunters are usually impaled by the brow tines of a directly charging animal. Once charged by a buck, all you can do is to grab hold of the antlers. Even then the deer will throw you around like a bullfighter's cape. If a buck is going to charge, he will lay his ears back and stare directly at you with his head and neck extended. The hair on his back will stand up stiff. He may stomp, snort, and curl his lips. He may hesitate a moment or lower his antlers and attack. If a deer doesn't run off but displays any of these signs of aggression, you should ease off backwards while facing the deer if you have no better means of self-defense.

"BAMBO"

Ground blinds can produce some real excitement from this big game—especially if you are using doe-in-heat scent or are rattling horns. Set your blind up near a tree that you can get behind in an instant in the rare event that a buck should attack you.

Deer do not have to be wounded to be a threat, but most recorded hunter injuries were inflicted by wounded deer. Always approach a downed deer from the rear or a side. Throw a rock or a stick at the deer before getting too close. If this produces no response, draw close enough to see if the eyes are glazed over. This is a nearly sure sign of death. Sunlight filtering through the eye or even cataracts can produce this glaze, however, so don't count on it 100%. Check for breathing by watching the chest and nostrils. Wait a little while and be absolutely certain that the animal is dead and not just in shock. Remember that a deer with shut eyelids is alive. When a deer dies it has open eyes. Those hooves can kill.

Campfire stories about hunters jumping down from trees onto deer and wrestling them down or riding on the deer for a distance are to be taken with a grain of salt unless the storyteller has wounds to display.

More people have been killed by deer in North America than have been killed by bear.

Deer are not animals to fear. Just respect their potential to be dangerous.

HUNTING ACCIDENTS

Any number of accidents might befall a hunter in the woods —during travel, at the campsite, and in the hunt itself. The hunter never knows just what to expect. His own life might be threatened. Or he might be called upon to save the life of another hunter by administering first aid.

Every outdoorsman should have a good general understanding of emergency first aid and rescue techniques.

More important than first-aid equipment and know-how is

good judgment. Prevention is the cure. Most accidents take place when hunters are not as alert as they should be due to fatigue, exhaustion, sleeplessness or sleepiness, intoxication, or some other circumstance that produces inattentiveness.

Mother Nature can come up with some dramatic surprises for the hunter. Drownings, ice breaks, ice slips, mud slips, tree falls, lightning strikes, encounters with wild animals, insects, poisonous plants and mushrooms, forest fires, flash floods, and tornados are some of the many calamities a trip into the peace and quiet of the woodlands can bring. In addition, many accidents are related to choking on food, using vehicles carelessly, and poor mental and physical condition.

Each hunter should be constantly mindful of safety. There is little excuse for the hunter who shoots first and thinks afterward. Legislation providing heavier penalties for accidentally wounding or killing a man is much needed.

Every hunter must be responsible for his actions and interactions. Every hunter should study a first-aid manual and attend a course in first aid. He should realize that he himself is his main enemy and attempt to battle this enemy with all the discipline he can muster. Learn all you can learn, be all you can be, do all you can do, and care. Saving someone's life is one of the greatest accomplishments a person can make and satisfying to the highest plane.

WOUNDS

Hunters often suffer bleeding wounds due to improper use or handling of broadheads and hunting knives. The following emergency first-aid procedures are recommended.

Many hunter accidents cause severe bleeding, which can take the life of the victim if not controlled. When such wounds occur, there are four important considerations to make:

1. Stop the bleeding.
2. Protect from infection.
3. Watch for, and protect from shock.
4. Gain medical attention.

Stop the Bleeding

When severe bleeding exists, the wounds should be covered with the cleanest cloth immediately available. Otherwise a bare hand may be used. Place direct pressure to the wound. This is enough to control most bleeding wounds.

Unless there is evidence of a broken bone, a severely bleeding open wound of the hand, neck, or leg should be elevated with the wound raised above the level of the victim's heart. If severe bleeding from an open wound of the arm or leg does not stop after direct pressure plus elevation, you may need to employ the pressure-point technique. Try direct pressure first, then elevation, and pressure-point last.

If the bleeding wound is in an arm, press the artery located in the upper arm against the arm bone. You may need to feel around a little bit to find the best spot for pressure while you are watching the blood flow for response.

The pressure point for the leg is found in the front, center section of the diagonally slanted crease of the groin. It is here that the artery crosses the bone to feed the leg. Use the heel of your hand for direct pressure here, watching the wound for the right placement and pressure.

The Tourniquet

Using a tourniquet is dangerous and should be the last choice of first-aid to be used only when the wound is life threatening and the blood cannot be stopped by any other method. The decision to apply a tourniquet is in reality a decision to risk the sacrifice of a limb in order to save a life.

BURNS

Hunters using various lanterns and grills or building camp-fires may suffer burns when far away from quick medical attention. All hunters should have a minimal amount of training for such emergencies.

Burns present particular problems with infection and shock. The emergency treatment for burns depends on the severity.

First-Degree Burns

Sunburn, contact with hot radiator caps or radiator steam, light contact with hot objects around the campfire, or touching the glass of a kerosene lamp are common hunting examples of these, the least serious burns. First-degree burns are treated by immersing the injured area in cold water to relieve the pain and covering with a sterile, dry bandage. There is usually just reddening and tenderness.

Second-Degree Burns

These burns are generally more painful than burns which are so deep that they destroy the nerve endings in the skin. Second-degree burns are more severe than first-degree burns.

Treat these burns by immersion in cold, not icy, water until the pain is relieved, then apply cloths that have been wrung out in ice water. Blot the skin dry and place a dry and sterile covering over the burn. Do not remove tissue or break blisters.

Never use home remedies such as butter, antiseptics, or ointments on severe burns. If the burns are located on the legs or arms of the victim elevate the limbs.

Third-Degree Burns

These are the worst burns. They can be caused by contact with electricity, scalding water, ignited hunting clothes, or combustion of a cook stove or lantern. The length of time that you stay in a burning sleeping bag will determine the severity of the burn. Most tents are flammable.

Do not remove bits of clothing that stick to these wounds when treating them with first aid. Cover these burns with thick, sterile dressings. Do not use water or ice on severe burns with tissue destruction. Treat third-degree burn victims for shock and rush them to a hospital.

It is important that we learn how to categorize burn severity in order to apply the proper first-aid.

Chemical Burns

Contact with battery acid resulting from battery explosion when jump-starting a vehicle, contact with lye while preparing a deer hide for hair removal, and aerosol can explosion are examples of hunting situations involving chemical burns.

Remove the clothing from the area affected by the chemical and flush with large quantities of water thoroughly. Apply a sterile dressing. Make note of the chemical involved and seek medical aid.

POISONING

Hunters should never eat any wild plant that they are not thoroughly familiar with. Mushroom identification is tricky. Even the experts make improper field identifications. Just a couple of the edible-looking *amanita phalloides* (the death cap or destroying angel) tossed into a camp stew, can wipe out the entire hunting party in a short time.

In the treatment of poisoning by mouth, the immediate objectives are to dilute the poison quickly, to maintain respiration and circulation, preserve vital functions, and get to an emergency room or poison control center. Identify or collect a specimen or sample of the poison.

If the Poison Victim Is Unconscious

If convulsions are not present, have the victim drink a glass of milk or water to dilute the poison. If the victim vomits, discontinue oral dilution. If unconscious, keep the airway of the victim open. Give artificial respiration, mouth-to-mouth resuscitation, or cardiac resuscitation (CPR) if necessary. At this stage it is imperative that you call for emergency help. Get to a phone and call "O" for operator or dial "911." You will need the advice of a doctor or a poison control center as to whether to induce vomiting or not.

First-aid kits should include a small bottle of syrup of ipecac for inducing vomit, activated charcoal for binding and deactivating, and epsom salts to serve as a laxative. Be prepared for encounters with others who need your help. None of us will go through life without experiencing the need to apply life-saving techniques to some victim.

ARTIFICIAL RESPIRATION

In some types of hunting injuries, such as near-drowning, strikes by lightening, heart failure, suffocation, and serious falls, the victim may stop breathing. Seconds count, so another hunter must start putting the breath of life back into the body at once. Don't waste time moving the hunter unless the location is unsafe.

If the victim is unconscious and will not respond, tilt his head with the chin pointing up. Place one hand under the neck and lift gently. Push with your other hand at the same time on the forehead. This will position the tongue to open the airway providing there are no obstructions to be removed. Look for air movement. If there is none, give four quick breaths mouth-to-mouth. Keep the head tilted backward, pinch the nose with the hand that is on the victim's forehead to prevent air leaking, open your mouth wide, take a deep breath, seal your mouth around the hunter's mouth, and blow four quick breaths as fast as you can. Watch for breathing to resume. If the hunter still does not breathe, change the rate to one breath every five seconds for an adult. You can also use the mouth-to-nose method by holding your hand over the mouth while forcing air into the nostrils.

CHOKING

Any number of situations in the deer-hunting experience can involve choking. An example may be while two hunters are meeting for lunch and one becomes desperate when a sliver of cold pork-chop bone lodges in his throat.

Choking victims should attempt to remain calm, to give the cough reflex a chance to expel whatever is caught in the throat. If the hunter victim evidences distress, prompt action is urgent.

Apply four back blows delivered with the butt of the hand over the spine and between the shoulder blades. Place yourself at the side of and a little behind the victim. Put one hand on his chest for support. Lean him forward so that his head is at chest level or lower. Continue the sharp blows until relief is obtained.

If this method fails to dislodge the caught material, you should deliver the abdominal thrust maneuver. First, stand behind the choking victim and wrap your arms around his waist. Place the thumb side of your fist against the victim's abdomen, slightly above the navel and below the tip of the breastbone. Grasp your fist with your other hand and press it into the victim's abdomen with a forceful upward and inward thrust. Do this four times in rapid succession.

BROKEN BONES

While not always easy to recognize, a broken bone might be expected if there is pain when the injured part is moved, swelling and tenderness in the injured area, or an apparent deformity of the bone.

Broken bones are divided into two types: Simple (closed) fractures and compound (open) fractures. Simple fractures have no open wound at the point of the break. In compound fractures the broken bone usually protrudes through the flesh. Open fractures are much more serious due to tissue damage, bleeding, and the danger of infection. Do not attempt to set a fracture or push a protruding bone back in. If splinting for transport is necessary, the bone may slip back when the limb is straightened for splinting.

Do not attempt to move a compound-fracture victim unless (which is often the case in hunting) help from medical professionals is not readily attainable or other dangers are present.

There are many ways to improvise a satisfactory emergency splint to hold the injured part in place. In the hunting environment, you may use a straight stick. The idea is to immobilize the fracture however you can. Use strips of cloth or limber vines to secure the splint to the broken limb. Hunters who have packed a small roll of duct tape into their "possibles" can really put it to use here.

Injuries to the skull, neck, or spine should only be treated by trained medical personnel. If you have a victim with one of these injuries, keep the hunter absolutely still and do the following:

For skull injuries, turn the hunter's head to one side so secretions may drain from his mouth after being certain that he has not swallowed his tongue and that there are no foreign objects in his mouth.

For neck injuries, keep the hunter in the position in which you found him. Keep his head well supported to prevent further movement. Do not lift or turn the head.

For spine injuries, keep the victim lying flat and do not move him.

If you should absolutely have to move such victims, you need assistance. You must be very careful to provide adequate support for the injured part and to handle the victim gently so as not to make the problems worse.

SHOCK

Shock is a condition resulting from a depressed state of many body functions, a depression that could threaten life even though the hunter's injuries would not otherwise be fatal.

The signs of shock are easily recognized: pale face; moist, clammy skin; nausea; faint, rapid (over 100) pulse rate.

The best position for a victim depends on his injuries. Generally, the most satisfactory position for the injured person will be lying down to improve the circulation of the blood. Cover the victim only enough to keep him from losing body heat.

If medical care is delayed for an hour or more, you may give the victim fluids by mouth. Give half-glass doses of water that is neither hot or cold every 15 minutes. Stop the liquids if the victim becomes nauseated or vomits. Get to a hospital in all cases of shock.

NOSEBLEEDS

Hunters sometimes injure their noses when firing high-powered rifles in quick-shot hunting situations. This results from not seating the rifle properly. A hunter with a nose bleed should sit quietly, leaning forward if possible. Apply pressure directly to the site of the bleeding by pressing the nostrils toward the midline. It also helps to apply cold compresses to the nose and face. If the bone has been broken (rarely the case with injuries caused by rifle recoil), head for the hospital.

MOVING INJURED HUNTERS

If you can avoid it, do not move the injured sportsman until first aid has been administered and trained medical personnel have arrived at the scene. If the victim must be moved to avoid further injury, transported to a rescue point, or taken to a medical facility, he should be pulled length-wise unless neck or back injury is suspected. Move him on a blanket or skid. An injured person should never be bent or twisted. Also, his head must be kept in the proper relationship with his body, according to the type of injury he has suffered. The injured or bleeding part should always be elevated or at least level.

If you are alone with an injured hunter, you might carry him out on your back, should his injuries allow. If another hunter is available to help, the two of you can form a seat for carrying with your interlocked hands and wrists. A blanket stretcher can be fashioned with a couple of saplings.

OTHER DANGERS

Carbon monoxide poisoning causes the death of some hunters each year in Northern hunting regions. Hunters who become too cold may let their engines idle while warming by the automobile heater. If carbon monoxide vapors collect in the stationary car, the hunters suffer poison inhalation. Some hunters sleep in their vehicles with the engine running. The hunter becomes sleepy in the early stages and eventually lapses into unconsciousness.

To carry these poisonous vapors away from the car, the tailpipe of the automobile should be in good shape and function properly. Hunters should leave a window cracked for ventilation at all times and should move the automobile so that the wind carries the fumes away from the hunter. CPR should be administered to victims.

Earlier in this century, with the advent of the automobile, an oil boom took place that sent enterprising people searching for oil just about everywhere on the globe. Most drillers would go no further than 100 feet into the earth in their search. If they did not hit a well that would produce over 10 barrels a day, they abandoned the well and went in search of greater wealth. There were no regulations for filling the holes. Many of these wells have caved in enough to create pitfalls which have proven hazardous to hunters.

The forest produces vegetation that disguises their surface while the earth beneath erodes into the shaft, creating cavities. These old wells are generally found in the remote areas that hunters frequent. Hunters should be aware of this possibility and avoid any stepping spot which appears to possibly have been once a well. Their presence is usually evidenced by a crater-like disruption in the terrain.

Old water wells located near one-time buildings are another source of hunter mishaps. Hunters should be very careful when walking near old homesites and barns. The only trace of the former dwelling might be a cornerstone.

Falls through ice are a common deer hunting mishap. The rope or nylon cord that every hunter should have in his "possibles" bag should be used when crossing iced-over streams. The hunter should take every precaution to check out the ice. In crossing an icy stream, tie the cord to a secure object on one side of the stream and carry it to the other bank. Secure the rope on the opposite bank and then return to untie the rope on the side from which you originated. A fall through the ice is miserable.

Lightning strikes take some lives in the woods. A hunter should always exit tree stands and stay away from trees altogether during electrical storms. Just being underneath and near the struck tree can get you fried. Groups of cattle have been killed when they sought shelter under the canopy of trees in their fields. If you should feel the need to seek shelter under a tree, choose the shelter of a beech. I have never seen a beech that had been host to lightning strikes.

Quicksand in swamps is not a joking matter in some areas. Hunters who are seeking the swamp-loving whitetail should always prod suspected sinkholes. There is silt so thick that you cannot get out of it by yourself in most all locations of North America.

The critter at the left deserves recognition. It is said that once contact has been made the best remedy is a bath in tomato juice. Its high-acid content provides minimal relief. These skunks can spray a breathtaking fluid ten feet with accuracy. They don't even need to hit you to make you gag. Eventually you will encounter one of these pretty animals. It is not a laughing matter to surprise one and become a victim. I think that if I were given the choice of what woods creature I could be other than what I am, it would be the skunk. Nothing in its proper mind would mess with me.

A Last Word

WHAT TO EXPECT IN THE 1990s

1. Longer doe seasons and hunter quotas to balance deer herds.
2. More interest in culling deer herds of inferior animals.
3. More hunters sparing nicely antlered younger deer to allow them to reach trophy status.
4. Effects of environmental pollution more evidently affecting the weather and seasons; subsequent changes in deer behavior.
5. Widespread personal interest and action in habitat restoration.
6. Increased use of deer decoys.
7. The introduction of the ancient spear for deer-hunting.
8. The use of hearing aids by hunters to detect approaching game.
9. Computerized deer-scouting.
10. Increase in number of game ranches and in pay-hunting.
11. Increase in hunting-club organization and land-leasing with quality management.
12. Increased legalization of hounding for deer.
13. Electronic deer-hunting devices gradually infiltrating the commercial market as their use is accepted by law, developing to a peak, then going back to basics.

14. Trail timers in wider use.
15. Deer skin's value rising and put to more use.
16. A very high price placed on the head of a trophy deer, making the illegal kill of superior animals seductive.
17. Authentic-looking artists' reproductions of deer trophies widely available.
18. Superior home videos, hunting video swap clubs.
19. Many rabbit hunters taking up deer-hunting as rabbit populations decline and deer populations increase.
20. The tick and the mosquito becoming greater problems than ever. Hopefully a vaccine will be available for disease prevention.
21. Fewer poachers due to hotline usage.
22. Fewer drunks in the woods as alcohol awareness increases.
23. Increased insurance costs for covering deer collisions.
24. Farmers soliciting hunters for help, instead of vice-versa.
25. Anti-hunting groups gaining support and increasing activity to the point of militancy.
26. Tighter gun control measures which particularly restrict those with criminal records.
27. Venison superiority acknowledged by the AMA.
28. Hunter orange required in full display in all states and provinces.
29. Mandatory hunter-safety courses for all license applications.
30. Deer retrieval services widespread.
31. Comfortable, reinforced fiberglass deer stands.
32. A massive return to the land, such as that which failed in the '60s.
33. More females hunting deer, more black participants.
34. The marketing of an odorless insect repellent.
35. Mock scrapes and rubs so popular that it is hard to tell real ones.
36. Deer becoming more nocturnal than ever.

37. The adoption of hunter safety requirements by some states and provinces, which include minimal rifle or archery range qualifications.
38. Organized efforts for the control of wild dogs.
39. Hunters becoming more vocal in legislative matters due to the loss of privileges as a result of personal effortlessness
40. The emergence of the genetically altered deer which has been hybridized by the scientific community.

HAPPY TRAILS!

If there was one thing I could say that would be a truth about whitetail deer you could count on absolutely all the time, it would be that you will not get a deer unless you go out and hunt one. I hesitate to make even this statement, however, for fear that one will jump through my picture window as I type.

I know that this book is filled with statements preceded by "most of the time," "usually," "often," "as a rule," "generally," and other qualifiers concerning most of the subjects relating to the deer. Deer are "largely" unpredictable. It is only after the hunter has experienced the whole spectrum of the hunt and met with successes and failures, truths and falsehoods, ups, downs, rights, lefts, insides, outsides, yings, and yangs and has become a master hunter that he completes the circle and returns to his original starting position, realizing that he knows less about deer than he thought he did. It is the master hunter, having come full circle, who wishes his hunting partner "good luck."

Hunters should follow the tradition of prayerfully asking for blessing of the hunt, safety and success.

Happy trails to you. May your hunting be happy and your problems be few.

About the Author . . .

THE AUTHOR, a 41-year-old Kentuckian and ex-Marine, started his woodsmanship training at the age of six, when his father introduced him to ginseng and small-game hunting. Studies of wildlife flora and fauna have taken the author through Mexico and Canada as well as the continental United States. By exposing himself to unnecessarily adverse conditions for the sake of obtaining understanding—by doing things most hunters would deem impractical—the author has proven his understanding of deer hunting again and again. Deer seasons found his family sacrificing so that he could spend every available moment in the woods interviewing hunters and studying deer. Regular jobs could only be taken with the understanding that during deer season, the author would not be available.

In his long field experience, the author has witnessed mistakes which take lives and create permanent disabilities. The need for public education and awareness of the functions of the deer herd and hunter population, safety, and courtesy is clear. Seeing a need for a low-cost and comprehensive guide for beginning deer hunters, the author set to work at the typewriter with the goal of creating a "how to" book for the average hunter. In addition, he has taken a number of deer both large and small; zeal for deer study has sometimes kept him in the woods year-round.

Many available books on the subject of deer hunting are out-dated. Modern research techniques have disproved some of the earlier theories about deer. Some of the books on the library shelf were written before the whitetail repopulated. The need to update information with modern research findings was clear. Humor was added for fun.

Wilderness Adventure Books
320 Garden Lane
P. O. Box 968
Fowlerville, Michigan 48836

Please send me: _____ copies of **BAMBO** at $13.95

—Shipping & Handling—

1 book	$1.50
2 books	2.00
3 books	2.50
4 or more books	3.00

TOTAL ORDER $ _____   Enclosed is my ☐ check

Charge my ☐ VISA   ☐ Master Card

Card No. _____   Expires _____

Mr./Mrs./Ms. _____

Street _____

City _____ State/Province _____ ZIP _____

Telephone (_____) _____